PRAISE FOR

My University of the World

In this remarkable book, Neill McKee takes us on an extraordinary journey with him around the world to some of the poorest and most underserved communities. We travel to remote parts of Latin America, Asia, and Africa to meet courageous people who struggle with endemic poverty and adversity, while finding new ways of overcoming seemingly insurmountable challenges. The book is a personal memoir of McKee's long and distinguished career in international development. Human progress in health and education has lifted millions of people out of extreme poverty and despair in a very short period of history. National and international development efforts since the end of World War II continue to be complex and require multidimensional factors to succeed. But one thing is clear: communication and social and behavioral outreach have helped underpin successes because they attempt to empower people to bring about change. It is in these areas that McKee excels. He is creative, innovative, and persistent. He grasped that rapidly evolving technology in film and animation could be utilized to help change entrenched attitudes and behaviors. Initiatives such as *Meena* in South Asia and *Sara* in Africa, which he and his teams developed, brought about important social change through skillful storytelling and entertainment. This book humanizes the lives and work of development workers and the environments they work in. With humor and sensitivity, McKee also allows us into his own life and family for some of the most endearing parts of his story.

–**MEHR KHAN WILLIAMS,** former Assistant Secretary General and Deputy High Commissioner for Human Rights at the United Nations

My University of the World is a wonderful memoir full of adventure, insight, humor, and feeling. Readers are treated to a balanced mix of technical challenges, "on the road" adventures, a love story, behavioral sciences, and proof that development-related communication makes a difference—all presented with remarkable details on the history, culture, and context of countries around the world, bringing the stories to life in ways that add richness, deeper understanding, and appreciation. While very much a personal story, anyone and everyone who has ever worked in the field of development will be able to relate to McKee's stories and experiences.

—**GARY SAFFITZ,** former Deputy Director/Faculty, Johns Hopkins University's Center for Communication Programs; and marketing executive

I don't even know where to start while talking about my feelings after reading *My University of the World*. I first need to explain that as a mother with six young children and as the owner of a small Wisconsin dairy farm, I don't get an opportunity to travel much. I've never even left the country. I don't share that information in hopes of your pity, I just want to explain how well Neill McKee's writing draws the reader in. I physically feel as though I've now been to South Africa, Uganda, India, Sri Lanka, and more! McKee's powerful writing pulled me into the environment and relationships he forged throughout his career as an international film and media producer. I am grateful that he was willing to share his experiences through photos and stories. This is a book I would recommend to those who have traveled extensively or those, like myself, who wish to travel—if only through the pages of the books we read!

—**CRYSTAL J. CASAVANT OTTO,** Avid Reader and Book Blogger, and more!

This is a memoir that will appeal to the first generation who lived the opportunities offered by the creation of the international volunteer movement—Peace Corps, CUSO, VSO, UNV. McKee's curriculum vita, which is the essence of autobiography, is also a history in miniature of an era in international development, a firsthand report of the past waning, a future waxing. McKee reaches back to the challenges of the 1960s and 70s efforts to work for a better world (the utopias we thought possible), and brings the story up to the 2000s. He has lived international development and encountered people, places, and prospects to document and film the wished-for changes. Readers familiar with Canada's International Development Research Centre (IDRC) will appreciate how well McKee narrates the story of its promoting local knowledge-making to foster and empower problem-solving where inadequacies of health, nutrition, and education had previously delayed development. *My University of the World* is a necessary read for anyone considering work in international development.

—**CHRISTOPHER SMART,** former CUSO volunteer and erstwhile Director, Special Initiatives, IDRC

Neill McKee's memoir revisits a four-decade career of crisscrossing the globe during different chapters of a highly successful and personally rewarding career in international media production and later in development communication. The lucky reader travels shotgun with McKee during his adventures in numerous countries: harrowing flights, back-breaking overland trips, frigid lodging, humorous cultural misunderstandings, and local foods consumed to be respectful. Interwoven in the narrative are engaging details of his multi-continent courtship with Elizabeth, who would become his life partner in this odyssey. Having won multiple awards for his films, McKee segues to UNICEF in Bangladesh. Here he creates an animated character "Meena," a South Asian girl who for years afterward would bring messages about girls' education and empowerment to countries across Asia, followed by a similarly successful "Sara" in Sub-Saharan Africa. He would finish his career working for behavior change communication programs at Johns Hopkins University, before directing a similar USAID-funded project that reached about 25 countries. Throughout this account of 40+ years in communication, McKee's memoir reflects the formula for his own success: commitment, integrity, compassion, and a sense of humor.

—**JANE BERTRAND,** Professor, Tulane School of Public Health and Tropical Medicine

It is important to note that Neill McKee has written much more than a memoir about filmmaking and media production. He has shared an avalanche of diverse, inspiring, informative stories of actions aimed at helping the world become a better place. These stories highlight the extraordinary activities undertaken by an ordinary Canadian, whose dreams began in a small town in Southwestern Ontario. His significant accomplishments are presented in a relaxed, highly personal manner, enlivened both by the author's sensitive instincts about human behaviour, as well as his mischievous sense of humour. The book is partly a distinctive travelogue featuring solitary filming treks through jungle, mountains, deserts, and oceans, as well as in slums and dangerous traffic. It also offers intriguing historical anecdotes that set a useful context for the larger stories, including the author's meetings with an array of global activist citizens.

McKee's early chapters can serve as insightful introductions to the history of the international volunteer movement and to some of the most illuminating examples of the realities faced by young Canadians working in Asia and Africa under the auspices of CUSO in the 1960s and 1970s. His chapters covering his time with Canada's International Development Research Centre also provide a powerful reminder of why and how this agency, in the 1970s and 1980s, became a global leader in pioneering new approaches to the field of international development.

Surprisingly, the book is also a beautiful love story. I so enjoyed the tales of meeting his partner, Elizabeth, their ability to sustain a love affair at a distance, and their incredibly special and unusual marriage in Zambia. Throughout the book, the challenging stories of poverty and conflict are balanced by examples of Elizabeth's poetry and her artwork.

For me, the most exciting output and outcomes from McKee's design skills are represented by the animated life stories of *Meena* and *Sara* and their impact on young people across Asia and Africa. The stories behind their creation make extremely compelling reading. I highly recommend this book to a wide range of readers who care about supporting leaders who balance a focus on high performance with an altruistic focus on humanity and the sustainability of our planet.

–DON SIMPSON, Ph.D., Chief Explorer of the Renaissance Expedition

My University of the World

Other memoirs by Neill McKee

Finding Myself in Borneo: Sojourns in Sabah (2019)

Guns and Gods in My Genes: A 15,000-mile North American Search Through Four Centuries of History, to the Mayflower (2020)

Kid on the Go! Memoir of My Childhood and Youth (2021)

My University OF THE World

Adventures of an International
Film & Media Maker

NEILL McKEE

NBFS CREATIONS, LLC
Albuquerque, New Mexico, USA
Books: www.neillmckeeauthor.com
Digital media library: www.neillmckeevideos.com

NBFS Creations, LLC
Albuquerque, New Mexico, USA
neillmckeeauthor.com
© 2023 Neill McKee

All rights reserved. No part of this publication may be reproduced, stored in a retrieval system, or transmitted, in any form or by any means—electronic, mechanical, photocopying, recording, or otherwise—without prior written permission, except as permitted by U.S. copyright law.

Note: This book is a work of creative nonfiction reflecting the memories of the author's career as an international film and media producer. The dialogs contained herein have been recreated to the best of his memory and are not intended to represent word-for-word transcripts of the many conversations that took place. Many of the photographs, especially in Part Two and the cover photo, were contributed by the International Development Research Centre (IDRC), Canada.

Literary and Copy Editor: Pamela Yenser, NM Book Editors
Photographs: By the author unless otherwise credited or noted
Book and cover design: The Book Designers, bookdesigners.com

Publisher's Cataloging-in-Publication data

Names: McKee, Neill, author.
Title: My university of the world: adventures of an international film & media maker / Neill McKee.
Description: Includes bibliographical references. | Albuquerque, NM: NBFS Creations, LLC, 2023.
Identifiers: LCCN: 2023913577 | ISBN: 978-1-7329457-8-4 (paperback) | 979-8-218-24317-3 (hardcover) | 978-1-7329457-9-1 (ebook)
Subjects: LCSH McKee, Neill. | Motion picture producers and directors--Canada--Biography. | Sustainable development--Developing countries. | Documentary films--Authorship. | Documentary films--Production and direction. | Interactive multimedia--Authorship. | Canadian University Service Overseas--History. | International Development Research Centre (Canada)--History. | UNICEF. | Johns Hopkins University. | BISAC BIOGRAPHY & AUTOBIOGRAPHY / Personal Memoirs | BIOGRAPHY & AUTOBIOGRAPHY / Adventurers & Explorers | TRAVEL / Special Interest / General
Classification: LCC PN1998.3 M35 2023 | DDC 791.4302/32/092--dc23

To Elizabeth, my partner in life
who shared many of these adventures with me.

Acknowledgments

I would like to thank my wife, Elizabeth, an artist with a portable career, who reviewed the manuscript and corrected details of our life together. I also wish to thank our children, Derek and Ruth, for their feedback, corrections, suggestions, and encouragement. I very much appreciate the input and reviews provided by Mehr Khan Williams, Gary Saffitz, Crystal Casavant Otto, Chris Smart, Jane Bertrand, and Donald Simpson, as well as the excellent suggestions of reviewers Jeanette Panagapka and Bruce Williamson. Many former colleagues also reviewed and gave excellent feedback on particular chapters: Fred Harland, Barbara Hoffman, Richard Carothers, Elaine McNeil, Peter Westaway, Doug Miller, Brian Davy, Cherla Sastry, Gordon Banta, Gordon McNeil, Jean-Marc Fleury, Trevor Chandler, Paul Stinson, Bob Forrest, Sylva Etian, Edson Whitney, Nuzhat Shahzadi, Sanjeeda Islam, and Mark Rasmuson. Thanks also goes to Pascale Vaudrin, who assisted me in accessing IDRC's photo collection in Ottawa, Canada. In addition, I much appreciate the early reviews by and feedback from Gaye Lauradunn, an Albuquerque writer and poet, as well as Ken Frey's help in proofreading. Finally, I want to thank Pamela Yenser, my literary and copy editor, for her usual good work on the manuscript.

Table of Contents

Acknowledgments xiii

Part One: Learning to Make Films and to Love 1

1. An Itinerant Cinematographer in India 3
2. Making My First African Films 21
3. An Engaging Trip to Papua New Guinea, Malaysia, and Japan 37
4. A Lettered Love Affair 55
5. Forty Days in Ghana 69
6. Our Marriage and Travels in Southern and Eastern Africa 85
7. Serendipitous Transitions 107

Part Two: Juggling Filmmaking and Homemaking 113

8. Stretching the Earth, and the Filmmaker 115
9. Healthy Filmmaking at Home and Hearth 145
10. Getting an Education on Education 159
11. Making Films on Food for Africa 167
12. Documenting Oysters in Mangrove Swamps and Seas 181
13. Filming Fish from the Earth's Vast Oceans 193

14. Meanwhile on the Homefront........................209
15. Harnessing the Monsoons in Sri Lanka.................221
16. Clean Water and Sanitation for the
    Developing World 239
17. Finding Solutions for Campesinos in
    South America 263
18. Filming Multipurpose Trees Around the World........291
19. Adventures in the Forests of China and Southeast
    Asia 311
20. Uprooting and Retooling in Tallahassee, Florida..... 325

Part Three: My Years as a Media Producer
    and Facilitator 339
21. Becoming a Multimedia Producer in Bangladesh 341
22. Creating Our Own Kenyan Village.................. 367
23. Travels and Creations in Eastern and
    Southern Africa................................... 377
24. A Brief Sojourn in Uganda 395
25. Finding Myself in America 409
26. Russia: Life and Work in Our Last Overseas Posting...431
27. Our Final Period in Russia and Travels Thereafter.... 453
28. Last Post in Washington, D.C.......................471
Epilogue...483

Chapter Notes 489
Repeated Acronyms 501
About the Author.......................................504

PART ONE

LEARNING TO MAKE FILMS AND TO LOVE

An Itinerant Cinematographer in India

As I rolled across the plains of northern India in December 1970, on a rickety old train, rumbling between station stops and passing many smaller ones, I soon got into the stride of things by listening to *Santana Abraxas* through the earphones plugged into my compact reel-to-reel tape recorder. From that time on, the song *Black Magic Woman* became forever embedded in my mind as a part of India. The time was magic for me because I was on the road, filming and photographing Canadian volunteers in Asia. It was exactly what I wanted to do with my life—an answer to my prayers, or I should say to my meditation sessions. I was more in touch with Zen Buddhism than Christianity in those days, like other North American youth—many of whom were hippies, or what we then called "flower children," who traveled to the East in search of answers to life's mysteries and their future paths.

But I had a different goal. I had left Canada in August 1968 to be a volunteer high school teacher in the small town of Kota Belud, in the state of Malaysia called Sabah (formerly British North Borneo). I only had a B.A. and no teaching experience, but was somehow accepted and became a pretty good teacher, connecting with my students and the community, learning the Malay language, and so much more. My two years in Borneo were the driving force for the rest of my life. It's there that I literally and figuratively "found myself" in a magical land populated by people of many Asian ethnic groups. At the time, it was a land of tropical jungle and mountains, rice fields, and coastal plains—a place where horses, cattle, and water buffalo roamed beside uninhabited beaches with sharks, attracting only adventurous swimmers like me and my volunteer friends.

The agency that recruited me to teach in Borneo was CUSO, which then stood for "Canadian University Services Overseas," but now is known as Cuso International. Through a lot of exaggeration about my past filmmaking experience, CUSO took me up on a proposal to make a 16mm film on our program in East Malaysia—Sabah and Sarawak. After I left Malaysia, I stayed for two months in Japan, where I sent them my Borneo film with soundtrack incorporated, and waited for a reply on a new proposal to shoot more films during a long journey home through Asia and Africa. I had spent most of my repatriation funds in Hong Kong, buying a new zoom lens for my 16mm movie camera, a Super-8 movie camera, a new still camera, and then I burned up more money traveling around Japan. If CUSO didn't want more films from me, I would have to stay in Japan and teach English to earn my way home, eventually. I had never studied filmmaking, nor worked in a film studio, but I had access to a few books on the craft and I spent many hours watching documentaries in the National Film Board's screening room at the Canadian Embassy in Tokyo.

After seeing all those films, I knew mine was pretty shoddy. What made me think I could do this job? Was it pure hubris on my part? Was I doomed for failure? Why did they take me up on this second proposal? I had no clue at the time that this assignment would lead me to a career in international development communication, traveling the globe, living and working in other developing countries and emerging economies, while having the privilege of meeting so many interesting, knowledgeable, and wonderful people.

In retrospect, my success in securing this great job was probably due to the fact I was willing to act as a cheap "one-man film crew" who could slog around on local transportation with my movie cameras, tripod, tape recorder, film and tape stock, while also taking still photos of almost everything I covered. When the good news of my new contract arrived, I also received a letter of instruction from the head of CUSO Information, in Ottawa, to take shorter and more varied shots—including sequences with mid-shots and close-ups, as well as cutaways to people watching the main action. These were important points, which I internalized immediately.

My first stop was in Thailand, where, due to its relaxed culture, I saw some of those wandering flower children. They stayed as long as they could—mainly because of cheap food and lodging. Also, drugs like marijuana and hashish were cheap and easily accessible. I indulged a little, but I had to stick to my mission of photographing various volunteers and completing a 16mm sequence on a Canadian woman by the name of Joan Tuck. She worked at Bangkok's Chulalongkorn University on a study of rural manpower utilization, unemployment, and underemployment, helping to formulate policies on the need for rural industries and jobs for youth. Her work involved inputting data on a mainframe computer, using those old-fashioned punch cards. I was impressed with Joan. She spoke fluent Thai and I filmed her interacting with her community in a lively market setting.

Back on that slow-moving train in India, as *Santana Abraxas* played in my ears, I gazed at endless dry plains dotted with people carrying buckets of water, squatting to talk in groups or to defecate in solitude, while others drove bullock carts loaded with produce to and from small market towns. Whenever the train stopped at a station, a crowd of vendors would rally to offer fruits, various flatbreads with curry, and cups of sweet milky tea. I had a choice of consuming what was thrust at me through the train window or going hungry. I threw caution to the wind and chose the former, not knowing, or maybe not wanting to know, that I was also ingesting the eggs of long intestinal worms, which would journey with me all the way home to Canada—at least helping to keep my weight down.

Indian Railways passenger cooling himself, Source: Lilibaba[1]

AN ITINERANT CINEMATOGRAPHER IN INDIA

I spent most of December on trains, stopping to photograph and interview CUSO teachers, nurses, and agriculture workers in places such as Patna, Bihar, and Calcutta, West Bengal—some of the poorest cities on Earth, where smallpox was still raging at the time. I found it hard to navigate streets with camera equipment without drawing a crowd of children and numerous beggars, some pockmarked. I began to feel depressed by the filth, confusion, harassment, and unrelenting stares I drew as I captured scene after scene. To survive and get the job done, I had to ignore the onslaught of people with missing eyes, arms, and legs. Children, children everywhere—no wonder Indian's Prime Minister Indira Gandhi prioritized family planning.

The author filming a CUSO agricultural worker -Photographer unknown

My job was to capture the energy and diligence of CUSO volunteers as they interacted with this impoverished population. I also photographed a volunteer in a more prosperous

CUSO nurse talking to a local pharmacist –Photo by Neill McKee

place called Chandigarh, a center for the Sikh community, surrounded by farms that produced the bulk of northern India's staple food—wheat. The various forms of delicious breads I consumed kept me energized. I managed to travel by myself because most people I met spoke English, thanks to the former British Empire, of which India was once the "Jewel in the Crown."

In late December, I was slated to film Alex Ritchie, a farm boy from Saskatchewan, who was helping to set up a tractor unit at the Nibkar Agriculture Research Institute in Phaltan, Maharashtra, to the east of Bombay, a city which has now been renamed "Mumbai." This was planned as my main 16mm sequence in India, but it turned out to be rather difficult to achieve because of miscommunication in planning and scheduling.

After an arduous journey with all my luggage, I arrived at Alex's institute just before Christmas, only to find he had taken off on vacation. His Indian manager was away too, and I received a cool reception from the manager's wife, so I decided to travel to where Alex was staying north of Bombay, with some other CUSO volunteers. When I arrived on Christmas eve, I found that the two women there had planned a cozy Christmas with Alex and another male volunteer, and they made it clear I wasn't welcome to crash their party. I returned to Bombay in the early morning to spend Christmas alone. I entered a cinema to see a stupid movie starring Jerry Lewis, *Don't Raise the Bridge, Lower the River*, and then took a boat to Elephanta Caves—ancient ruins devoted to the Hindu god Shiva. But I was never a good tourist. I preferred to sit in cafés and restaurants, talking to local people and watching the world go by—picking up the rhythm of life, rather than wandering through temples and mosques.

In the evening, I wrote a letter to my parents in Canada and another to Elizabeth, an American woman I had met in Tokyo. These letters acted as a substitute for a diary. My mother kept all of them. But how did I retrieve those I sent to Japan? Well, the woman I wrote to, Elizabeth Ann Diemer, who went by the diminutive "Beth," would become my wife in 1972. I had met her the evening she arrived in Japan to teach English as a volunteer in a Lutheran-supported school. Through a friend's connection, I was staying in a Lutheran volunteer hostel in Tokyo, Beth's first destination. We hit it off immediately, but she had to attend her scheduled orientation and language lessons, so we could only spend time together in the evenings and on a couple of weekends.

When my filming contract came through, we met once more and parted without offering promises to each other. But in that letter to her from Bombay I wrote, "Being in Tokyo with you was the happiest time in recent memory for me, and I do love you. I don't know where you are in your feelings toward me, so...I guess we either wait until we meet again, or meet again sooner, by plan."

Our letters to each other would provide a sort of anchor for me during the following months.

Alex Ritchie and I managed to meet up in Bombay and travel back to Phaltan together. It was a delight working with this practical, down-to-earth man. I filmed him interacting with his Indian boss and counterparts, as well as with local farmers—helping them to maintain equipment and learn new mechanized cultivation and planting methods to improve production of food for their families and increase their incomes. A cooperative facility like this seemed sensible to me because few farmers could afford to purchase such farm equipment by themselves. I interviewed Alex and took shots of him in community settings, at the local outdoor market, and then on his motorcycle, which I thought would make a great musical film sequence.

After a few days, it was time to move on. I boarded an old bus, which took off in the direction of Poona (now spelled "Pune"). My aluminum suitcase, containing all my exposed and unexposed film stock, had to go on the roof of the bus—and I remained alert at every stop, making sure it wasn't off-loaded when we picked up and dropped off passengers and their possessions. As we bounced along, I balanced my camera equipment and tape recorder on my lap. The journey was interrupted at a railway crossing, where there was no one around to lift the barrier gate. This resulted in a half-hour, on-the-bus, off-the-bus argument-cum-scuffle between the bus driver and another man, all of which was entirely incomprehensible to me because I understood neither Marathi nor Hindi.

Arriving in Poona, I bought a first-class sleeper compartment ticket for the night train to Bombay with the help of a "coolie," a colonial term then still used by Indians for porters. We managed to get my luggage to the station's designated platform for the train. It was late and I sat there for an hour. By the time the train finally arrived, I could see a line of about 20 first-class ticket holders for each first-class compartment. When I purchased the ticket, I wanted to ensure I had a place to sleep, but the clerk told me reservations for compartments would be available on the platform. This seemed odd to me.

An attendant guarded the entrance to my designated space. Other travelers were lined up there as well. I'd heard about this scam, so I waited until he walked away, followed by all the other ticket holders who, I assumed, wanted to bribe him for the compartment. Then, I simply loaded all my luggage and sat in it. The attendant returned to ask me to move out, but I refused. I had a first-class ticket and I didn't want to pay the bribe. He must have realized I had beaten him at his game, for he soon gave up—this foreigner refused to play by Indian rules. A couple of other foreign travelers, in the same boat, asked if they could share the small space, and we all fitted in somehow. The train soon departed for Bombay, putting me to sleep between station stops with the rhythmic clunking of steel-against-steel on ancient tracks.

After about eight hours, we arrived in Bombay—a journey which was supposed to take only five. But how could I complain? I had enjoyed being rocked through a half-decent sleep. With the help of another coolie, I headed through a mass of money changers, vendors, and beggars to "Reservations," where I bought a first-class ticket on an evening train to Bangalore.

I immediately found a taxi to go to a cheap hotel and checked in, securing all my belongings in the room. With the whole day ahead of me, I decided to send my exposed film stock to Canada for processing. I'd been told about the difficulties of sending anything from India and wanted to get it right. I asked the hotel clerk where I could get my film package prepared for sending by registered airmail. This pleasant lady sent me to a nearby shop, where in no time my items were nicely wrapped up in a white cloth, all stitched up according to Indian regulations. I thought to myself, *I'll have this in the mail in an hour and go for a leisurely lunch at a good restaurant.*

I must digress a little to explain that when I entered India at New Delhi airport on November 30th, I was required to write down the details of my cameras, tape recorder, and my film and tape stock, including the value of all items, on a Tourist Baggage Re-Export (TBRE) form to be shown on exiting India. But it wasn't explained to me that if I couldn't produce all items on departure, I'd have to pay 100 percent duty on those missing.

After a short walk to a post office, I waited in line, only to be told I had to take my package to the General Post Office in the center of the city. So, I hailed a taxi—a clanking and smelly yellow and black car made in India—and headed downtown. When I arrived, I entered the parcel section, where an idle clerk seemed to be waiting for me. *So easy*, I thought, *All I have to do is fill out the customs form and have the package sealed with one of those old-fashioned red wax jobs.*

But the clerk asked, "Is its value over five rupees?"

AN ITINERANT CINEMATOGRAPHER IN INDIA

Bombay taxi, Source: The Wire[2]

"Yes, it's exposed film. Very important it gets to Canada."

He said, "Then you will be requiring permission from the Bank of India."

"But this is film stock I brought into India."

"Do you have proof?"

"Yes. My TBRE form, but it's at my hotel."

The clerk said pointing, "You must show the TBRE form at the Foreign Parcel Counter over there."

I'd already experienced a good deal of Indian bureaucracy during the past month and knew I had reached an impasse, so I went outside to find the same taxi and asked the driver to take me back to my hotel. *Just a little set back,* I thought. *Since the clerk knew about the form, all I have to do is show it to his colleague.*

Returning to the post office, package and TBRE form in hand, I walked to the designated counter where a short male clerk weighed my package and started to glue the form to it.

I shouted, "Please stop! I need that form. My cameras, tape recorder, and unused film and tape stock are on it."

"You cannot separate the shipment. All must be sent at once," the man said.

"But I'm going on to Africa from here to do more filming."

"I must ask my supervisor. Please wait here," the little man said.

After ten minutes, a much larger Sikh man in a turban arrived to inspect my package and TBRE form. After repeating my explanation, he said authoritatively, "What's the commercial value of the package?"

"It has no commercial value since it's exposed film. I'm sending it to Canada for processing and it only has value for my agency, a non-profit volunteer organization."

"How much value?"

"None, commercially. It really can't be sold to anyone."

"Can I open it for inspection?" the supervisor asked.

"If I open it, I can only show you the cans of film. They can't be opened and exposed to light or they'd be ruined."

The supervisor was getting suspicious. I think he saw the frustration in my eyes, so possibly he tried another ploy to get rid of me, "You will be needing a Re-Export Certificate."

"Okay. Can you give me one?"

"No."

"Can't you just mark off the items I'm shipping on the form and sign and stamp it?" I knew I was getting more creative than Indian bureaucracy would ever allow, but it was worth a try.

The Sikh replied with a slight smile, "No. You must go to the New Customs Office for the correct certificate." He wrote the address on a slip of paper and I returned to my waiting taxi.

We headed through the increasingly filthy and smoky city air to the designated office, where I bought the required form for ten rupees from a silent clerk. I filled it out and handed it back to him. By this time, I only had about five hours left before my night train to Bangalore was scheduled to depart.

The clerk said, "You must take this for validation to the Export Office at Church Gate Station."

I stared in disbelief, but tried not to show my dismay. I knew I had hit another roadblock, so I went outside to hail my patiently waiting taxi driver. Arriving at the Export Office, I approached a nice-looking lady who directed me to another woman with a mocking smirk. I started my explanation over, as she rocked her head back and forth in that Indian way of signaling a non-committal "I hear you," which looks like a "no" to Westerners when they first come to India. As I explained my situation, I laid my TBRE form and the Re-Export Certificate on the counter.

The lady stopped me in the middle of a sentence, "Are you sending it airmail or post?"

I replied, "I want to post it by registered airmail."

She said, "You should send it air freight."

"Through whom? I asked.

"Send it by BOAC air cargo. They will take care of the re-export procedures. Their office is on the next block. It's not hard to find." (Note: BOAC was the acronym for British Overseas Airways Corporation, the precursor to British Airways.)

As I thanked the lady and left the office, I could have kicked myself. *Why didn't I think of that alternative route in the first place? It would be much safer and more efficient.*

It was a quick walk to BOAC. I'd already paid off my faithful taxi driver, not knowing how long he'd have to wait. But he followed me to the BOAC office and parked, waving at me as I disappeared inside. The interior looked much cleaner and more efficient, a good omen. I approached a pleasant-looking clerk and started to repeat my story. He listened patiently, with his head rocking back and forth as if it was mounted on a single large ball bearing in his neck. When I stopped for his reaction, he smiled and handed me another form, saying, "You will please fill this in."

I was more than pleased with this fellow, a man of action and few words—unusual in India. I carefully filled in the new form and handed it back to him. *That is that!,* or so I thought.

The clerk inspected the form carefully, then said, "You must now take it to a shipping agent."

"Aren't you a shipping agent?" I asked.

"No," he replied. "We are the shippers. You'll need an agent. They will take care of the re-export procedures."

"Can you tell me where?" I asked.

"At the New Customs Office."

"Yes, I know the place," I said, keeping my cool as I left to find my smiling driver. By then, his smelly taxi was a welcome refuge in my ever-more-absurd adventure.

When I reentered the New Customs Office, a clerk directed me to the shipping agent's office where I began to repeat my story. I told him right up front I had a train to catch in three hours.

The clerk looked at my TBRE and my Re-Export form and said, "That's the wrong form. You need to fill in this one."

I quickly filled in the new form and handed it back to the man, who inspected it carefully, then said, "Okay. Follow me to the TBRE customs man next door."

"Oh yes, I know him. Met him this morning!"

As we walked into the office, the TBRE customs man

didn't look so happy, probably thinking he'd gotten rid of me. He looked closely at my TBRE form and said, "Your problem is the customs people in New Delhi should never have entered the film and sound tapes on the TBRE form. The only people who can regulate this mistake are at the Export Office. Tell them the whole story and I'm sure they will understand."

I nodded, remembering that office very well. It's where I had met the lady with the mocking smile who directed me to BOAC air cargo. I headed back there with my faithful and ever-growing-richer taxi driver, where I followed the custom man's instructions, throwing in even more detail as instructed, "It's about a Canadian volunteer working at the Nibkar Agriculture Research Institute in Phaltan. He's helping improve agriculture production in India."

The lady was not too impressed with my new line of narrative. I assumed she knew her BOAC detour had driven me in various fruitless directions. So, she tried something else, "You're only allowed to export 120 meters of film footage."

No one had mentioned this rule before, so I countered, "But I brought all this film into India unexposed and so I should have the right to send it out if it's on my TBRE form."

"Well, if you want, you can see the Export Superintendent," the lady said. "He may be able to help."

I agreed, and she led me to his office. I estimated the man to be about 45 years old—his lips and teeth red from chewing betel nut. He spat into the spittoon beside his chair before taking a good look at my papers. After a tense minute, he said, "Can you show me your permission from the Government of India for making this film?"

The CUSO field staff officer (FSO), in New Delhi, had told me not to bother trying to obtain such permission because it could take months, and may never be granted. As a one-man crew, I could probably get away without official permission. Realizing I had been defeated, I picked up my papers and package and walked out of the place. My taxi driver, who was still waiting for me, cheerfully took me back to the hotel to retrieve my baggage, and drove me to the train station. He was a pleasant enough fellow, but I began to think he had seen a good thing coming when I told him in the morning where I wanted to go, package in hand. He'd probably taken other foreigners on such ride-abouts before. An all-day customer was a lucrative proposition in a city flooded with taxi cabs. When we reached the station, I paid off my happy driver and hired a coolie. I already had my ticket in hand, so we headed directly to the platform marked "Bangalore."

I can't recall how I managed to get a sleeping compartment that evening. As the train pulled out of the station, I thought about my day. I wondered if the British had set up this system within their policy of "divide and rule"—keep everyone so busy, going around in circles, so they would never have time to rebel. If so, it didn't work. The rebellion came to a climax in 1947 when independence was granted, but by that time the Brits had so entrenched such systems in the country that Indians knew no other way of life. I was starting to believe they were all condemned to go around in such circles for eternity, or at least through many reincarnations.

Despite these difficulties and frustrations, my first experience in India ended on a high note. When I returned to New Delhi, the CUSO FSO invited me to attend a garden party at the residence of the Canadian High Commissioner (the term used for ambassadors in and from Commonwealth countries). The occasion was in honor of Pierre Trudeau, our Prime Minister. It was January 12, 1971, and he was on his way to Singapore to attend the Commonwealth Heads of Government Meeting. I recall talking to him briefly about my present filming mission and my time in Sabah, Malaysia, as a CUSO volunteer teacher. I recommended, if he had the time, he should visit Borneo. I'm not sure if my recommendation helped, but I found out later he did fly to Sabah to meet and greet orangutans—and humans too, including the CUSO volunteer sub-species.

In a letter to my parents I wrote, "Trudeau appears much older and less powerful than you'd expect. He's sort of a shy and quiet-toned person." I suppose I had different expectations about this famous 51-year-old bachelor, who had enthralled most of Canada's younger generations when he was elected in 1968. He had dated Barbra Streisand in 1970, and when I met him, he was about to marry Margaret Sinclair, a woman three years younger than me.

I never recorded the exact details of how I finally managed to send my film package to Canada. I believe that after the FSO asked the Canadian High Commission for

Pierre Trudeau in New Delhi, January 1971 –Photo by Neill McKee

assistance, I got a letter from them and simply took the parcel to BOAC in New Delhi. They must have shipped it off, no questions asked. But I do clearly remember all the details of that day in Bombay, for one evening before I departed, I wrote a short story, which remains in my files. I called it "A Day in the Life of a CUSO Cinematographer in India." Under the title, I added a fitting line from a then-popular song by the group known as Blood, Sweat & Tears:

"What goes up, must come down. Spinning wheel got to go round."

2. Making My First African Films

I arrived in Addis Ababa, Ethiopia, on a flight from New Delhi on January 26, 1971. It was the first time I'd stepped onto African soil, and after India, the feeling was elating. Instead of New Delhi's thick winter air, containing smoke from millions of home fires and exhaust from thousands of inefficient combustion engines, in Addis I saw blue skies, brilliant white buildings, and boulevards dotted with green trees. The city, situated at only 8.9 degrees north of the equator but at 7,700 feet (2,347 meters) above sea level, is graced by gentle breezes and adequate rainfall—a purifying effect. The postcard I wrote to Beth in Japan reflected my new state of mind.

I had imagined and dreamed of going to Africa as a child, while growing up in my industrially polluted hometown of Elmira, Ontario, Canada. I ended up in Borneo instead—a wonderful substitute. But now I had arrived on the so-called "dark continent," which appeared brilliant to me.

Emperor Haile Selassie held onto power at the time, desperately trying to usher in a few reforms to save his skin. In 1963, the Organization of African Unity (OAU) had established its headquarters on a hill in Addis Ababa, occupying shiny new buildings—a symbol that helped to drive and sustain African countries' new independence. Ethiopia is the only Sub-Saharan African country that managed to avoid colonization by European powers, although it had been briefly occupied by the Italian Army from 1936 to 1941.

At the time of my quick stopover, Rastafarians from Jamaica and elsewhere were living amongst the people, some idealizing Haile Selassie as a kind of second coming of Jesus Christ, the incarnate of *Jah*—their concept of God—who would usher in a new age of Pan-Africanism on the continent and throughout the world for the benefit of black people. Rastafarians helped to popularize marijuana consumption as a way of life and reggae provided the background music for their social movement.

Less peaceful movements were, however, also afoot on African soil. The day before I landed in Addis Ababa, General Idi Amin had overthrown the elected government of President Milton Obote in Uganda. I was due to travel there, but had to change my plans. When I left Addis Ababa, I stopped in Nairobi, Kenya—another modern high-altitude African city—long enough to photograph a couple of volunteers working in tertiary education. Then I flew to Zambia, a country that had gained its independence from Britain in

1964. It had been a British protectorate known as Northern Rhodesia, but was now run by the independent government of President Kenneth Kaunda. To me the bustling city center of the nation's capital, Lusaka, gave off an air of newness and prosperity, but I knew I was only getting a brief glimpse of the city—growing urban slums would tell a different story.

CUSO had built up a large education and health program in Zambia, and the FSO, Dave Beer, welcomed me on my arrival. Dave and his spouse, Irene, a black Zambian woman with a fiery spirit, oriented me on CUSO's Zambia program, as well as on the country, the region, and its politics—especially the struggle for black majority rule in Rhodesia, where the racist white settler government of Ian Smith remained in power. I knew something about this because I had talked through the early days of that struggle with a friend from Southern Rhodesia, Naison Mawande, when we were together at the University of Western Ontario during 1965-66. On November 11, 1965, Smith declared unilateral independence from Britain, refusing to share power with the majority black population. In my talks with Dave, it was evident he wanted CUSO to be involved in education about this struggle for what would become Zimbabwe a decade later, after a protracted bush war.

Between Dave and CUSO-Ottawa, it was decided I would do 16mm filming of Volker Budziak, a young Canadian electronics and mathematics teacher in Ndola, a small city in Zambia's copper belt. Mining copper was the main source of foreign currency for the country, and remains a main source today. At the time, the industry was run by white mining specialists and businessmen, mainly Brits or people of British descent, some of whom came from Rhodesia and South Africa.

My assignment took me directly to Ndola to film and photograph Volker as he went about teaching, mixing with his fellow teachers, and buzzing around on his Honda 350 motorcycle. I found him to be a congenial and adventuresome man. He had taken up membership in a gliding club and invited me to experience his extracurricular activity. I had no qualms about it since I had joined a parachuting club in university and had no fear of such heights. Volker explained his glider had no parachutes, but I shouldn't worry for he was a good pilot. I sat in the seat behind him to capture an excellent sequence, as the tow plane released us to slowly and silently glide in the clouds above the green forests, red soil farms, and hills—my first good overview of this land.

In my filming, I wanted to show how volunteers lived, both on the job and in their spare time. Eventually, I learned how to edit these leisure sequences to local music, giving some spice to the volunteers' lives, hoping this would attract more Canadians to join the service. I also photographed and interviewed a few other volunteers in Zambia. Some taught general subjects such as African colonial history—educating students on how their continent and cultures had been exploited.

Michael Murphy gives the middle finger to the British East African Company -Photo by Neill McKee

MAKING MY FIRST AFRICAN FILMS

Next, I flew to Dar-es-Salaam, Tanzania, for a CUSO regional conference—and to meet my boss from Ottawa, Iain Thomson, the head of CUSO Information. He was the man who had not only accepted my idea of making my first film on CUSO in East Malaysia, but also my proposal to do more filming in Asia and Africa. Although I had only known him through letters and telegrams, he turned out to be just as I expected—a warm personality with a great sense of humor. He had emigrated from Britain to Canada and had also spent time in Australia. He had worked in television news, which then used 16mm film. I had been getting pointers from him and a film editor in Ottawa on how to improve my cinematography and, by then, he'd seen my Thailand and India footage. He told me I'd improved and I might be hired on as regular staff to do more films and photography after this trip. This was a relief since he'd taken a chance on me and CUSO never actually used my Borneo film because it was not well-crafted and contained some controversial statements about Malaysian politics.

I don't recall much about the actual CUSO conference, except that there was a big debate on whether, and to what extent, CUSO should be involved in the Southern African liberation movement—mainly in development education on such matters in Canada. The discussion interested me, but my focus was on making films to recruit volunteers. At the time, the Canadian International Development Agency (CIDA), then a branch of the Department of Foreign Affairs, gave CUSO grants to run its operations, based on the number of volunteers it recruited and placed.

By this time on the trip, my old Bolex 16mm movie camera, purchased in Borneo from my U.S. Peace Corps buddy, Peter Ragan, was giving me problems, and Iain agreed to take it back to Canada for repairs and then ship it to me in Nigeria, where I would need it next to do the final coverage of volunteers for the main film I was making. I still had my new Super-8 movie camera with me. I had proposed to make a "groovier" impressionistic film with it, setting it to youth music, and another short film focusing on just one volunteer. Iain didn't show much interest in the former production, but it was decided I should shoot the latter one on a volunteer in Tanzania.

I did some general photography in and around Dar-es-Salaam, which seemed much more authentic to me than Lusaka. "Dar," as we called it, was a blend of black African and coastal Swahili Muslim culture, dotted with Indian- and Arab-owned stores. Julius Nyerere was President, an African socialist who was introducing changes such as land reform and communal organization of farming, as well as other economic policies that would benefit the poor. Unlike Nairobi and Lusaka, whites were almost missing from the scene in Dar. Its mixture of humanity reminded me of Malaysian cities, and I felt more at home.

Then one evening, when returning to my hotel with CUSO's Deputy FSO, Jack Titsworth, we passed a commercial area where we witnessed a scene of "instant justice." Some man had been accused of theft and was being beaten to death on the side of the road. Jack, a man who normally drove at a frantic pace, doubled his speed to "get the hell out of there." As we sped away, he explained there was nothing we could have done about it, which wouldn't have led to our beatings or deaths. Education and the rule of law would eventually erase most of such killings from the African landscape. For centuries on the land known as Tanzania today, black Africans had been enslaved and/or ruled by other African tribes, Arabs, Germans, and the British. Colonialism runs counter to the concept of human rights, and Tanzania had been granted its independence from Britain only a decade earlier. I concluded it would take time to change.

My next assignment took me on a flight to Tanga on the northeast coast of Tanzania, to do Super-8 filming of Richard Carothers, a CUSO volunteer teaching at a government secondary school. I found Tanga to be an interesting place and Richard friendly and cooperative. My experience as a volunteer teacher in Kota Belud, Sabah, and his in Tanga, were similar. First of all, the majority of Tanga residents are Muslim Swahilis—a culture and language that blends black Africa and Arabia. Kota Belud's population is also an ethnic and cultural mix, dominated by a local Muslim group called "Bajau." Richard had become quite fluent in Swahili, as I was in Malay, and he moved easily about town in different social circles, as I had done. I stayed with him in his teachers' quarters, much like my government-issued bungalow in Borneo. We visited the seaside and dined in local restaurants, as I had done in Sabah. We both had rickety old motorcycles—instruments of freedom and mobility, which we maintained with our similar mechanical skills.

One big difference was I had taught English and geography, whereas Richard taught math and science. Also, his school was better resourced since it was located in a larger town and had been operating for a much longer time. In addition, Richard was musically talented, so he had helped to resurrect the school band and to start a guitar club. His music, and the interview with him I taped, made up most of the soundtrack. No need for a separate narrator—his voice told it all. He had made a multi-color light machine, which rotated with heat generated by a lightbulb, and later I edited

Images from my film on Richard Carothers in Tanga

a dreamy sequence, dissolving from its lens into clouds from arial shots I had taken while landing at Tanga. This sequence went well with Richard playing his guitar and his anticipated nostalgic thoughts about how it would be to return someday. I found my week with Richard to be a creative and energizing time—exactly what I needed at this point in my long journey—and I used up a lot more Super-8 film stock than intended. In a way this film combined my proposal to make both a film on the life of one volunteer, plus the more impressionistic one.

By the time I was wrapping up filming in Tanga, I had been in Africa for about five weeks but had never seen a wild African animal. Through a stroke of luck, I caught a ride with some volunteers to a game park near Mount Kilimanjaro, a dormant volcano rising 19,340 feet (5,895 meters) above sea level. It is often capped with snow, despite its location just south of the equator. The nomadic Masai people call it the "House of God" in their language. There, I photographed and filmed the wild animals of my childhood dreams—elephants, rhinos, giraffes, mixed with herds of wildebeests, impalas, zebras, dik-diks, and kudus. Most of my efforts were too touristy to ever use, but I thought, *How could I leave East Africa without capturing this?*

Elephants grazing on the plains below Mount Kilimanjaro
-Photo from Alamy[1]

From Kilimanjaro, I made my way by bus to Nairobi, where I caught a flight to Lagos, Nigeria. There my infatuation with Africa ended. On arrival, I was met by the CUSO driver and taken to the office to meet Ian Smillie, the FSO. After a brief discussion, he brought up the subject of my 16mm camera, which had arrived at Lagos airport after being repaired in Canada. Smillie didn't smile about that. He said, "Do you realize what difficulties we could encounter to get it out of customs?" Why didn't you bring it with you along with the rest of your equipment?"

"It broke down and needed repairs," I told him.

"Couldn't you have rented a camera here?"

"That's unlikely. It's 16mm, not a tourist item."

Smillie frowned and explained I had landed in Nigeria a year after the Biafran Civil War had ended. The country was still suffering from that disastrous and complicated conflict. It was difficult to get things done.

The next day, he took me to the customs house, where my camera was being held, to begin negotiations. I was hoping I could retrieve it and get to work right away, but the process of getting it out took four days. Smillie had to be there with me every day, since it required his skills in talking with officials. Each day we returned to take a new approach. On the last day, we somehow succeeded, but I counted 12 steps, which had to be taken by 12 different people. One clerk held the stamp to be placed on a document, while another held the ink pad. It was a mind-bending exercise that reminded me of my experience in Bombay, trying to ship film footage out of India. *The British had been here as well,* I mused, *setting up all sorts of regulations to pit one minor official against another, possibly to prevent corruption.*

After finally succeeding in taking possession of my camera, I was driven to Zonkwa, a small town in the middle of the country, south of Kaduna. There I met Bill and Grace Bavington, a doctor-nurse, husband-wife team involved in rural health services. It was one of the most challenging postings I had seen on my travels so far—the poverty so acute and needs so great. I filmed a sequence of Bill removing a huge goiter on a woman's neck, and another of Grace and her staff servicing a long line of malnourished women and children with just about every disease in the book. But their main focus was supposed to be preventative rather than curative healthcare. I filmed the Bavingtons traveling around in their Volkswagen bug, supervising outreach services, setting up health committees, and carrying out home visitations and health education interventions, including messages delivered through a puppet show. I also accompanied them to a village where Bill addressed all the people through an interpreter, standing beside an old chief in a large chair—a king among his subjects. He had four wives and at least 20 children, many of them running around naked. I was finally seeing and documenting the true state of much of Africa in 1971, and I admired the Bavingtons for their fortitude in sticking it out here for two years.

From Zonkwa, I was taken to Kano in northern Nigeria, to catch an evening flight to London on April 4th. As we passed over the dark Sahara, I drank a little wine with an okay meal before falling deeply asleep, satisfied but exhausted at the end of my first African journey. I had originally planned to stay in Europe for a month, traveling around and seeing different sites; but counting Japan, I'd been on the road for eight months, so I grabbed a cheap charter flight to Montreal and another to Ottawa, arriving on a mid-April day to see the last snow melting away.

I'd left Canada in August 1968, nearly three years before, and was happy to be in my home country again—especially at the beginning of spring.

After an emotional visit to my hometown, Elmira, to see my parents, siblings, and friends, I traveled back to Ottawa in an old Volkswagen bug I'd bought, after I spray-painted it bright red at my father's farm equipment manufacturing factory. My next step was to move into a cooperative living arrangement in a two-story house inhabited by a group of university students, where I had a room to myself and lots of company whenever I wanted it. These guys and gals were cool—an appropriate living arrangement for me as I re-entered North American culture. There were only a few basic rules such as contributing to grocery money and taking turns shopping, cooking, and cleaning. They smoked a bit of pot, and I joined them occasionally on weekends. But by that time, I had pretty well given up such recreation.

To explain further, I had had a transformational experience in Sabah taking LSD with my American Peace Corps friend, Peter, the effects of which led to our creation of the North Borneo Frodo Society (NBFS).[2] The title of our club was based on the belief that North Borneo and J. R. R. Tolkien's Middle-Earth, as described in his trilogy *The Lord of the Rings*,[3] are one and the same place. Surprisingly, Tolkien had joined our society, so that summer I followed up with a letter to his publisher in the U.K., proposing to write a book titled "A History of the North Borneo Frodo Society and its Latter-Day Manifestations." The publisher expressed no interest, unfortunately—or perhaps fortunately, since I could have been "found out." The NBFS had no real history.

It wasn't until 45 years later, when I was engaged in writing my first memoir, *Finding Myself in Borneo: Sojourns in Sabah*,[4] that I used my old papers and memories on the NBFS to write its history. In this memoir, I also described a "bummer trip" I had experienced on an overdose of hashish—the exact opposite of my one and only LSD experience in Borneo. So, along the way, I had grown wary of drugs, though not fundamentally opposed to them. I had to stay focused on the task at hand—making films.

I started to spend around 10 hours five or six days a week learning how to edit at Crawley Films, an independent studio in Ottawa. I worked under the supervision of Sarah MacDonald, a film editor in her 50s, who went by the nickname "Sally." She loved detail, as much as I did. She had a degree in engineering from the University of Toronto and usually edited technical films such as documentaries on mining or engineering projects. But she also loved the opportunity to work on something so inspiring as young Canadians trying to do good in the world. I had edited my first film for CUSO in Sabah, using the camera-original film in a house on stilts built over the South China Sea shore. Now, working with Sally, I was learning the basics. She was a good teacher and conversationalist, and I digested the proper processes quickly, editing with a workprint—a copy of the camera-original footage—so it would be protected from scratches, tears, and fingerprints.

I put in many happy hours cutting and splicing, while learning how to match movement and build sequences. I learned the process of doing musical sequences and how to mark up the workprint for fades, dissolves, and picture mixes, using a white crayon, which gave instructions to the negative cutter—the person who matches the workprint to the camera-original film, while wearing clean white gloves to ensure no damage.

All my work was done on a bench using a simple viewer and synchronizer with sound heads, or sometimes on a Moviola machine. I included the volunteers' taped interviews, background sounds, and the local music I had recorded, to construct the soundtrack. My camera equipment didn't have the capacity for synchronized sound, but I soon learned how to match "wild" sounds I had recorded, or stock sound effects, to picture. I didn't want long and potentially boring on-camera interviews anyway.

Through this process, I ended up with six or seven 16mm magnetic soundtracks to match the picture and then supervised the sound studio personnel as they mixed them, rocking back and forth on large 16mm sound tape machines, until the result was perfect. Hands-on production of films came quickly to me at Crawley's and interacting with Sally and others reintroduced me to Canadian culture. Few of my co-workers were like Sally. Most saw me as a do-gooder, not a real filmmaker. In fact, most people I met outside of CUSO circles would never engage with me in conversations about my overseas experiences, nor could they understand why I would want to go to hot disease-ridden countries.

We decided to title my first film *Four Times CUSO*.[5] It starts with the volunteers I filmed in Thailand, India, Zambia, and Nigeria eating breakfast in their four different locations, with radios playing the news in national languages or local music. Each of the four main sequences follows a pattern of showing the volunteers working, mixing with their students, counterparts, clients, and their communities in leisure activities—a good way to demonstrate the wide variety of locations where prospective volunteers might be posted.

My boss, Iain, and others in CUSO loved my first professional effort and used it widely in Canada for recruitment purposes. But when some in the African section saw it, they were dismayed with the sequence of Volker Budziak in his glider. It was obvious to them, if not to all viewers, that membership in such a club would be for whites only and CUSO personnel shouldn't join such organizations. It's not that black Zambians were forbidden to join if they really wanted to, but at the time, it was unlikely they could have afforded the fees or would have seen gliding as a desirable thing to do, when they were having a hard enough time establishing their place in the economy on the ground. Iain didn't pay much attention to these sentiments, fortunately, but it was a good lesson for me on my future filming choices of recreational activities.

The Super-8 footage on Richard Carothers in Tanga, Tanzania, proved to be a winner. We blew it up to 16mm for editing and produced a short film titled *Tanga Man*.[6] It begins with Richard walking out of a cave, as our original ancestors did in Africa (my idea), mounting his old *piki-piki* (motorcycle), and heading into Tanga. In the activities I filmed and in his own narration, Richard caught the spirit of the international volunteer movement. He has a low-key, honest-sounding voice, which would make Canadians pay attention. He mentioned he was probably gaining much more than he could ever give to the people of Tanga. Today, *Tanga Man* remains my favorite of the CUSO film series I produced, and it brings back my fondest memories of Africa.

An Engaging Trip to Papua New Guinea, Malaysia, and Japan

In September 1971, I left Canada to shoot two more films, stopping in Hong Kong to buy a brand new 16mm Bolex camera paid for by CUSO. My old camera from Borneo days had "given up the ghost." Then I flew southeast for 3,000 miles (4,828 km) to New Guinea. I didn't know a lot about the place, only that its people were Melanesian and they live on the second largest island in the world, located north of Australia.

During the past century, various portions of it had been colonized by The Netherlands, Britain, and Germany; then the Japanese took over parts in World War II. After their defeat, the western half, West Irian, briefly went back to The Netherlands, then to Indonesia with that country's independence. The southeastern part, Papua, remained under Australian administration and the northeastern half, New Guinea, became a United Nations Trust territory. But in 1949, the whole eastern half of the island became the "Territory of Papua New Guinea," and was administered by Australia. When I traveled there, the territory was preparing for full independence as Papua New Guinea (PNG) in 1975.

Arriving in Port Moresby, the capital, I met Fred Harland, as well as Peter and Barbara Hoffman. I had met Barbara before. She was an excellent resource person at my orientation in Vancouver before I left for Malaysia in 1968. She and Peter had both been CUSO volunteers in Sarawak, Malaysia, at different times, and later married in Canada. Fred was the head FSO of the CUSO program, and Peter the deputy.

I filmed a volunteer by the name of Thelma Howard, a social worker from Saskatchewan who trained local people in a community development group on how to assist rural-urban migrants who were squatting on unoccupied lands around Port Moresby. This was contributing to the growth of urban slums. Among other duties, Thelma's job was to advise the group on best practices in resettlement schemes.

Fred accompanied me on some of my travels outside of the capital. He also did the narration for the film, which I used as a voice-over for the introduction, transitions, and wrap-up. I filmed him during one of our flights, looking out at the mountainous country below, and again while visiting volunteers, George and Margaret Ney from Vancouver. This couple was involved in teaching self-reliance skills in Popondetta, on the southeastern peninsula of the island.

The established curriculum included industrial arts such as woodworking, metalworking, baking, marketing, and growing rice to earn cash from richer urban dwellers. Rice was not a traditional food crop for New Guineans, who preferred yams, taro, cassava, and sweet potatoes.

George also taught geography with an emphasis on overall world development and urbanization, which was rapidly taking place in PNG. Margaret taught a social science course specially designed for PNG. It focused on traditional communities and how they changed with exposure to the industrialized world. She also taught simple skills like making sandals out of old tires—important for students who had never worn shoes and couldn't afford them.

I flew into the highlands to film Cliff Wiebe, an agriculture extension teacher at Kamaliki Vocational and Technical School near Goroka. He had joined a movement to try to stop the aimless rural-urban drift of youth, which was contributing to unemployment and crime. At the school, students had to live in traditional thatched-roofed houses and learn new farming skills, as well as bookkeeping and banking. They were given plots of land to work and could keep a portion of the proceeds from the sale of the crops they grew. This gave them incentives to return to their own communities, where they had pre-arranged agreements for farmland. Cliff spent two days a week following up on how his graduates were doing, giving further assistance, as needed. The program had been requested by village elders and the young men's practical education gave them added status in their communities, allowing them to earn a "bride price"

Fred and the Neys in Popendetta – Images from the film

(usually paid in pigs), get married, and become a contributing part of the village structure.

Traditionally, a New Guinean native male had to gain status through fighting endless wars with other communities. I had seen the 1963 documentary titled *Dead Birds* about such a warfare cycle between two highland tribes in West Irian (West Papua), Indonesia. Retribution for an attack by a raiding party might not happen for months and could involve the killing of an old woman or a child in a garden. Payback followed, but rarely in a predictable way. The fighting might continue for decades, although many of the clashes using traditional spears or bows and arrows, appeared to be more about form and posturing, rather than all-out aggression.

Melanesians first settled on the island around 40,000 B.C.E. and started farming 7,000 to 10,000 years ago. When I visited in 1971, the mountainous interior was still made up of fractured communities. From the air, I could see densely populated land with gardens and terraced hillsides. Their methods included irrigation and crop rotation; use of local refuse, ash, and rotting vegetation for fertilizer; and even intercropping with nitrogen-fixing trees—sophisticated farming sustained for thousands of years without the help of western missionaries and outside experts, who didn't enter the interior until the 1930s.

I was told people in the highlands may understand the dialect of the tribe in the next valley, but not the dialect two mountain ridges away. There are an estimated 800 distinct indigenous languages on the island, but fortunately New Guinea Pidgin—the *lingua franca* called "Tok Pisin"—gradually developed, and continues to be used. It primarily draws on vocabulary from English, as well as German, Malay, Portuguese, and local languages.

I filmed Dan Hooper, a Civil Engineer from Grand Manan Island, New Brunswick, who was helping this fractured and divided country by building roads in the interior. I flew with him into Tari and Mendi in the Southern Highlands to capture his work in some of the most remote places in the world. Landing in these outposts was treacherous—clearing mountain ridges of 10,000 feet (3,048 meters) and then suddenly swooping down onto airfields hidden in valleys, often with a one-and-only chance of landing safely. Aborting an attempt at landing could easily crash a plane into the mountain on the other side of the valley. Fortunately, the mainly Aussie pilots were well-trained blokes.

Dan Hooper with assistant– Images from the film

Joining Dan and his crew in their four-wheel-drive vehicles, I filmed and photographed them giving technical assistance to local government personnel as they surveyed, laying out routes the construction crews would follow, joining villages with zig-zagging roads to unite people who had been strangers, if not enemies, for thousands of years.

I captured shots of some of the onlookers and laborers—Huli men sporting bones or sticks in their noses, and some with large colorful wigs topped with feathers and other decorations. Despite their fierce appearances, Dan said he found the local people friendly and cooperative, and they provided essential manpower for the road-building process.

MY UNIVERSITY OF THE WORLD

Huli man, Source: Alamy[1]

AN ENGAGING TRIP TO PAPUA NEW GUINEA, MALAYSIA, AND JAPAN

In a taped interview with Dan, he told me he and his men had to camp out in the wild for five or six nights at a time, but he claimed it was in no way a hardship. It just added to the greater enjoyment of his job. His assignments gave him a broad experience in different aspects of civil engineering, compared to what he would have been exposed to in Canada at the beginning of his career. It also changed his outlook on the world in general. He claimed, "The person who is gaining the most from this experience is myself."

I also was learning a lot by making this film. For example, I included one explanation for New Guineans' eventual acceptance of modernity and Christianity. Cliff Wiebe, the agriculture extension teacher in Goroka, described above, mentioned in his interview—which became part of the soundtrack—that most of his students believed their ancestors would come back to them as white men. This belief was part of "cargo cults," a system of thinking that involved performing certain rituals, including rigid copying or impersonating something seen or experienced in the past, in order to bring it back.

During World War II, for example, many New Guineans saw Americans and Australians with planes and machines enter the land to defeat the Japanese. Local people copied the behavior of the departed soldiers by parading and drilling, using fake wooden rifles. They believed such rituals would cause more white people to arrive with power shovels and scrapers to construct airports. Then more airplanes would come with even more goods for them, and men and equipment to build houses, churches, and hospitals. Many New Guineans saw their first wheels on military and missionary airplanes. Some believed that these white people were perversely withholding the secret to accessing all these goods, and equality in financial and social matters, and that they may someday get over it and hand them the key. These beliefs and symbols of change persisted, so when Lyndon Johnson was running for President of the U.S. in the 1960s, many coastal New Guineans cheered for him because of all the Johnson outboard motors left behind by the American armed forces when they departed. They wanted to vote for Johnson too!

New Guinea man with World War II airplane –Photo by Max Diemer

CUSO volunteers were well aware of these collective myths, a product of colonialism in many parts of the world, but probably stronger in Melanesian cultures than anywhere else in the mid-20th century. Volunteers were told not to get involved in politics and religion—no proselytizing about Christianity nor any other religions allowed—just stick to the job. And their jobs were growing more technical. All

AN ENGAGING TRIP TO PAPUA NEW GUINEA, MALAYSIA, AND JAPAN

of the volunteers I filmed in PNG had specific specialized training and skills to offer. I realized how lucky I had been to be selected to teach English and geography in Malaysia during 1968-70, without much knowledge of those subjects, nor teacher training. The trend toward specialized volunteer placements would be clearly demonstrated in my next assignment on this trip.

From Port Moresby, I flew to Kuala Lumpur, the capital of Malaysia, where I felt much more at home, having left the country only 15 months earlier. During my two years of teaching high school in Sabah, I didn't take the time to venture into the deep jungle. On this return trip, I made up for that missed opportunity. I filmed CUSO foresters Bill Dumont and Ron Burrell, alongside their Malaysian counterparts, as they hacked their way with long knives called *parangs* through tropical rain forests, to carry out an inventory of tree species and to start replanting schemes for the Government of Malaysia's Forestry Service. These CUSO foresters were fulfilling a gap in specialized personnel until more Malaysians could be trained. As fresh graduates, they had the challenge of applying everything they had learned at university in a fast-track manner.

During a three-week period, traveling by Land Rover, airplane, boat, and on foot, I filmed jungle overviews, logging operations, the exporting of logs, sawmills, plywood factories, charcoal production, tree nurseries, reforestation, surveying growth, camping scenes, and computerization of data in offices. I also took shots of the volunteers' living quarters and recorded interviews with them for the soundtrack of my film. In Bill Dumont's interview he explained:

> Many of my friends in Canada thought I was nuts coming over here to a snake-infested, malaria-ridden jungle, the image perpetuated by Tarzan movies. Actually, I found the forests here have less vegetation than some I worked in, in British Columbia. The forest here is fairly open, especially virgin forest, and quite easy to get to. On my first day in the jungle, I was quite apprehensive about the problem of running into a nice big python. I mentioned this to the rangers who accompanied me and they laughed. So, I didn't bring the subject up again.

As a one-man film crew, I found the work both challenging and invigorating. Fortunately, the Malaysian forest rangers helped to carry my equipment. They also gave me a chance to reimmerse myself in Malaysian culture, speaking my second language, Malay. My favorite sequence was filming another volunteer, Michael Clarke, as we glided in small boats powered by outboard motors through the coastal mangrove forest in the State of Johor, in the south of the Malayan Peninsula. Mangroves, while traditionally viewed as unhealthy and unproductive places, prevent coastal erosion, improve water quality, and provide habitat for many species of wildlife and birds. They are also nursery grounds for our oceans' commercial fish and shellfish, thereby providing nutrition and income for millions of people around the world. My job gave me the opportunity to learn so much—each assignment like a mini-university course.

AN ENGAGING TRIP TO PAPUA NEW GUINEA, MALAYSIA, AND JAPAN

I also filmed these Canadians eating their favorite Chinese and Malay dishes in a colorful outdoor night market. The contrast with New Guinean highland culture could not have been starker. I'd traveled from the Stone Age to modern Southeast Asia in a matter of days.

In early November, I flew 900 miles (1,448 km) northeast to Kota Kinabalu, Sabah, to do a little more filming of CUSO foresters, and then took a Land Rover taxi through the hills and valleys to Kota Belud, my Malaysian hometown. I found everything just about the same. What could I have expected? I had left only 16 months earlier. It remained the sleepy little burg I remembered, populated by Chinese, Bajaus, and Kadazans—ethnic groups who all spoke different languages but also spoke Malay, the *lingua franca*.

I stayed with CUSO volunteers, Paul and Evelyn Gervan, who lived in my former bungalow on a hill overlooking the town. Evelyn had taken over my teaching duties, while Paul taught math and science. They had purchased my old motorcycle as well, and it was still getting them around. The only big change was they had adopted a monkey—an unusual thing to do in Malaysia, especially one that roamed around free in the house.

I met some of my former students, who were surprised to see their former teacher, now with longer hair and a goatee. I knew from my experience in Kota Belud that they thought beards were only worn by old men. Despite this, they were all so welcoming. They went out of their way to thank me for making sure Paul and Evelyn had been posted to Kota Belud before I left.

Continuing my correspondence with Beth Diemer in Japan, I told her about all the changes in my life, including becoming a real filmmaker when I reached Ottawa. I even wrote her about the women I met and dated along the way, since we had both agreed to continue with no commitment to each other—to just see how things turned out. That had suited her fine, for she was getting over a love affair with a U.S.-based, Lebanese-born gynecologist by the name of Munir. Earlier on the same trip, on my way to PNG during a flight change at Tokyo airport, I had written and mailed a postcard to Beth, giving her my address in Port Moresby and offering to stop over on my way back to Canada, if she wanted to see me.

Postcard mailed at Tokyo airport

AN ENGAGING TRIP TO PAPUA NEW GUINEA, MALAYSIA, AND JAPAN

During our brief time together in Tokyo in 1970, I had learned Beth knew PNG well because she had been born there in 1948, in the coastal town of Finschhafen. Beth's father, Max Diemer, was an American Lutheran missionary in New Guinea, and Beth had spent the first three years of her life in a place called Raipinka, in the highlands. The family, including Beth and two boys, Joel and Dan, had to return to Iowa when their mother, Darlene, became ill with tropical sprue. She got better but became ill again and died of cancer when Beth was only seven. In 1958, Beth and her brothers returned with their father to PNG, where he married another American woman from Iowa. The young children were sent to a boarding school for missionary kids at a place called Wau, in the highlands, and then to high school in Brisbane,

Max Diemer with New Guineans, around 1947 –Family photo

Australia. Beth and her brothers returned to Iowa for university, while her father, stepmother, and two half-brothers remained in PNG.

Beth and her brother Joel with a New Guinea guard in front of the local jail, circa 1951 –Photo by Max Diemer

On a Friday evening in Kota Belud, I went to the verandah of my old bungalow, overlooking the valley and town center—one of my favorite places in the world—where I had prepared lessons, marked papers, listened to Bach or Bob Dylan, watched the setting sun, and observed people ride by on water buffaloes. I wrote a letter to Beth at her home address in Japan to be sure she knew I would be coming.

> Dear Beth,
>
> I'm sitting on the verandah of my old house in Kota Belud as a rainy Friday afternoon filters into euphoria, with Sam the monkey at my back. All is

the same but different here. "You can't go home again," wrote Thomas Wolfe. This is just a note to say that I will be in Tokyo on the 22nd of November at 7:50 pm on JL062 and would love to see you at the airport and spend some time with you until the morning of the 24th, when I fly away unless you keep me there.....If your place is too difficult, I can stay at a hotel in Tokyo and hope you will find an excuse to spend most of the time with me, if you need one.

Love, Neill

Later, Beth told me she wasn't at the airport to meet me because the 22nd was a Monday and she had to teach during the day. She was living in Omiya, a city 50 miles (80 km) to the north of Tokyo. I had learned to navigate the Japanese train system in 1970, so somehow I made it with all my luggage to her tiny apartment. Her landlord had prepared bedding in a separate room for me, but I didn't use it. We were so overjoyed to see each other again that we only needed one bed on her *tatami*—a woven straw mat floor. At least in my memory, our lovemaking was the climax, so to speak, of a great trip.

During those years of traveling as a CUSO filmmaker, I had a flexible schedule—like being my own boss. No one back in Ottawa questioned where I was at any time. No trip reports were needed, just the results on celluloid. I felt so welcomed by Beth that I decided to stay for most of the week. We had only spent a short time together in that Lutheran hostel in Tokyo the year before, so we needed more time to get to know each other. Fortunately, November 23rd was

Japan's national holiday for celebrating labor and production, a replacement for the traditional harvest festival. We walked and talked, patronizing coffee shops and restaurants. Most memorably, we visited a Japanese garden and took photos of us together, using my tripod.

The author and Beth Diemer in a Japanese garden
—Photo by Neill McKee

Beth had been pretty skinny when I first met her, but now had rounded into full womanhood, and had longer hair. I preferred her that way. She had become fluent in basic Japanese, and I loved the way she was able to navigate her community. She said she only spoke a simple form—children's language—dropping most of the honorific word endings, which Japanese have to use, according to the status of the person with whom they are speaking. But it seemed to me even her body language had become Japanese when interacting with the local community.

AN ENGAGING TRIP TO PAPUA NEW GUINEA, MALAYSIA, AND JAPAN

I can't remember, but at some point, I must have said we should get married. She replied with words something like, "Let me think about it. I'm going home to see my parents in PNG at Christmas time. They are really angry with me over my affair with Munir."

When her parents left Beth in Iowa at university, and returned to PNG, they told her she was on her own and had to earn a living after university, intimating she couldn't come home again except for vacations. After her first year, she had transferred from her father's *alma mater*, the small Lutheran Wartburg College, to the University of Iowa to study speech therapy, not knowing the course was so technical—full of math and science. So, she switched to Comparative Religion because she had to have a major and wasn't sure what else to study. She really didn't know why she was at university. Her father had written her about her new major, wondered if she was thinking of following his footsteps to become a Lutheran minister. But that was not to be. Her father had let her know he was displeased with a previous engagement she had broken off and her recent romantic adventure. Beth didn't want to blow it again, in a possible failed relationship with me.

For the rest of the week when Beth was teaching, I explored her city and read. I met her at her school to accompany her home. I also met her American friends, Dick and Jeannine Helmstetter, and babysat their small daughter. Dick was a young businessman making a living by manufacturing billiard tables and cues, and I was impressed with his vision and drive. I really liked them. Fortunately, after I left they told Beth I was a winner. Beth was supervised by an American Lutheran missionary in Omiya by the name of Cliff Horn, but I can't remember meeting him—probably better that way for he might have wondered whether we were sleeping together.

During my visit, Beth and I discussed how we could get together again soon. I had at least two more films to do for CUSO in Africa, in 1972, and I mentioned the possibility of returning to Japan after that, circumnavigating the globe. But then, just before I left, I said, "Come to Africa with me."

She answered quickly, "Sure I'll marry you."

I said something like, "Okay. Let's do that."

Beth accompanied me to the airport and saw me off. As we looked at each other through the airport's glass window for the last time, we both wondered what we had gotten ourselves into—did it actually happen? We had to write detailed letters to try to figure it out. Postcards would no longer do.

All and all, my trip had been very fruitful and engaging, so to speak.

4. **A Lettered Love Affair**

When I returned to Ottawa on December 1, 1971, I moved my belongings from the students' cooperative housing place to an apartment I had arranged to rent before leaving on my trip. I'd planned to move in with a woman I was dating in the summer but our relationship had to end. It was a fatality of international travel, with letters not arriving on time, no fax machines, let alone computers, emails, cell phones, or social media connections. In those days, few people, including me, could afford international phone calls. At any rate, my feelings for this woman could not compare with my renewed love for Beth.

I began working long hours at Crawley Films to edit and produce my Papua New Guinea film. I'd return home to read one or two letters from Beth, usually waiting for me. I'd cook something, eat, and then reply to her, while listening to classical music and glancing through the front window to watch snow falling around streetlights and people trudging home with parcels. Christmas was in the air and I no longer felt so alone.

In a way, Beth and I completed our engagement by mail—almost like an old fashion arranged marriage. We hardly knew each other, but later when people asked why we decided to get married, having spent so little time together, our reply was, "We had a hunch and sometimes a hunch pays off." We exchanged ideas on where and how to hold the ceremony, who to invite, her wedding dress, my plans for attending film school, and what she wanted to do with her life in Canada—study French or speech, drama or art, get a teaching certificate, become a children's book writer and illustrator? She didn't know what path to follow besides marrying me. I accepted this because she was three years younger than me and had not really "found herself" in Japan, in the way I did in Borneo. With the Christmas mail slowdown, due to volume, letters arrived late and sometimes not in the right sequence. We started to number them but remained loose about it, and also about putting dates on them. Our communication became confusing.

I had to plan for the two films to shoot in Africa, and my boss, Iain Thomson, also briefed me on the possibility of doing a development education film on the life of a typical farmer in Thailand, on the same trip. So, I wrote to Beth about meeting up with her again in Japan. She replied, proposing a wedding in Omiya—a Lutheran affair officiated by Reverend Horn, the missionary who supervised her. She even wrote about the possibility of my staying in Japan to work for Dick Helmstetter in his billiard equipment manufacturing business, until her two years were up in September. Beth felt she couldn't leave her students early, and I was sympathetic to that because I felt the same way, until I found the Gervans to replace me in Sabah. But I was far from sympathetic about the idea of a Lutheran wedding. Besides, after Africa and Thailand, I would have to spend the summer editing in Ottawa. I had to explain to Beth that over 50 percent of filmmaking takes place after the camerawork.

While I was in Japan, I had told Beth all about my North Borneo Frodo Society and she borrowed Tolkien's trilogy, *The*

Lord of the Rings, from the Helmstetters, writing to me that she considered the books "essential reading for her new career." She was winning points with me in an important department—her sense of humor.

We exchanged impractical and impossible ideas, like her coming to Canada for Christmas, and me going to Africa by way of Japan, a hugely expensive detour. Our letters were frank and open. Beth had written to her former Lebanese lover about our engagement, but had not heard from him. She had not completely flushed him from her system and we exchanged lines on this. I understood her feelings since we had spent much less time together than she had spent with him. I sent her a copy of *The Prophet* by Kahlil Gibran[1]—all the rage with free thinkers in the 60s and early 70s, and Gibran was Lebanese to boot!

Beth sent a description of an engagement party the Helmstetters had held for us, marking my presence by a photo of me holding their baby daughter. That seemed official enough, so I wrote my mother about a bet I had made with her when I was 20—that I wouldn't marry until I was 30. (By this time, I was 26.) I sent Mom my copy of our signed wager, along with a ten-dollar bill and a copy of one of the photos I took of Beth in that Japanese garden. This was a fantastic Christmas present for my parents. They were overjoyed with the news about this exotic American girl who would soon join the family—the daughter of a "man of the cloth," just like my mother's father.

Before Beth's Christmas break in PNG, she wrote a letter to my parents, enclosing an artistic book she had created with a typewriter and a pen:

Beth Diemer in a Japanese garden —Photo by Neill McKee

Dear Mr. & Mrs. McKee,

Most young girls have the privilege of meeting their prospective in-laws face-to-face and saying little while looking sweet and coy. This business of writing letters is far from satisfactory in this situation but there is little that can be done to remedy it at this point. The main problem which has arisen here is that I have forgotten all the suitable English words to describe just how sweet and coy I really am. Besides, it is best that I not be the one to do the telling. On the other hand, I could tell you about Neill, but you already know more than I do, or at least as much as he probably wants you to know.

More than anything else, I would like to hear more about you, from you. How you feel about anything and everything, what you're interested in. When we've been together, Neill and I have always been so busy that we haven't done a whole lot of talking about the in-laws. I only know how he feels about you and that is only half the story.

So, I've gotten this far without saying anything (which is as it should be). Let this book say what I would like to say if I could meet you in person, and, as we in Japan say (...Japanese script...)—which means, "Please look benevolently upon my humble being and bestow upon me your gracious favor." It gains a little in the translation.

> I am looking forward to...
> .. hearing from you ...
> .. meeting you ...
> .. being related to you.
>   With love and trepidation.
>   Beth

The poetry book Beth had made for my parents with comic illustrations of her, me, and them, read like this:

> Waiting is a Time of Mixed Emotions
> Waiting is a time of sadness ....
> ...And a time of fear;
> A time of impatience ....
> ...And a time of wondering just how long one can stay on cloud nine.
> It's a time of nostalgia ....
> ...and a time of hope;
> A time to watch one's cup running over without being able to drink.
> But mostly ....

> ...waiting is a time of thankfulness for what has happened ....
> ...and joyful anticipation of what's impending.
> It's a time when almost everything one touches comes out happy ....
> And even the most trying days can't get one down for long.
> It's a time to run and jump and do double somersaults Just because there's so much good ahead ....
> .... And someone worth waiting for.

My mother was a homemaker and loved to do weaving and other crafts. Beth hit the mark with her letter and illustrated poem. She had written to tell me she feared not being accepted. But I had replied that my parents would have accepted anyone who married me and wouldn't have been surprised if I brought back a native girl from Borneo.

I went home for Christmas with my large family—my parents and five siblings, a new sister-in-law, a brother-in-law, and a nephew. It was a happy but overwhelmingly materialistic experience for me after what I had seen of poverty in the world, but I tried as hard as I could to participate. On Christmas eve, I retreated to my bedroom to write a long letter to Beth, who had reached PNG by then. It began:

> My soul is in New Guinea captured like the snowman outside my picture window at 39 First Street with carols on the stereo and the tree looming over other material representations of love and joy and nostalgia, with my father perched in his favorite well-worn chair, sitting silently reading while others watch *The Christmas Carol* on TV for the sake of

A LETTERED LOVE AFFAIR

....and a time of fear;

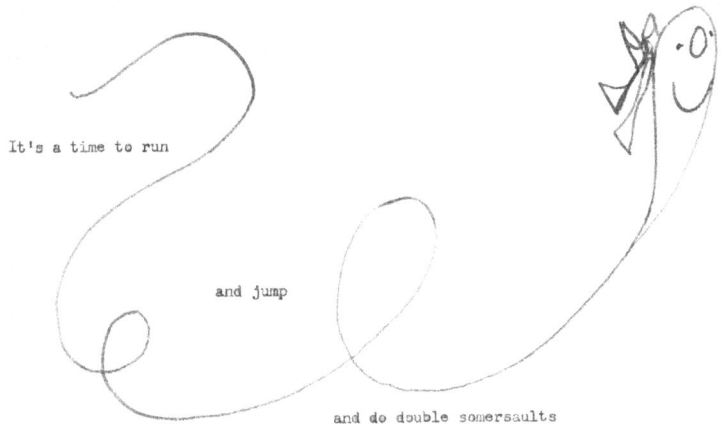

It's a time to run

and jump

and do double somersaults

just because there's so much good ahead ....

Scrooge and his ghosts...but my mind is with you. I love you so much and you are definitely absent. Scrooooo...ge! All is well in Elmira but the flow of mental vibrations takes me to flower out spontaneously on tracks ending only in some South Pacific island where it's already X-mas day and all are warmly wrapped in tropical non-Christmas air.

Beth, you are beautiful. The more mail the better—each letter unrolls another aspect (just like each of Frodo's steps—but not to evil—not to the gloom of Mordor—to a good.) My mother jumped on me at the door—happy to tears about us. She received the pictures and announcement, the old wager plus $10.00, and needs no other gift. Your book excited her even more—she's showing everyone who comes through the door and I don't mind it.

I realized that, for Beth, the biggest hurdle to get over was my lack of Christian belief. She had been born into and nurtured by the Lutheran Church and Lutheran schools. The church had even given her a scholarship for university. She still retained a strong faith, and wanted to really know what I believed. After putting it off for a long time, I finally wrote to her about it in my long letter. I began at the beginning and outlined my whole life so far, including my thoughts on religion, right up to my university days. To summarize, I had a relatively liberal protestant upbringing, not caring much about religion at all. I was a rebel in the early 1960s, but in my late teens, through mentors, I was introduced to good literature and theological books such as Paul Tillich's *The Eternal Now*[2], Dietrich Bonhoeffer's *Letters and Papers from Prison*[3], and Martin Buber's *I and Thou*.[4] Around the same time, I started to read about Zen Buddhism, but not in a serious way. I was just curious. At age 19, I decided there was no such thing as an all-powerful loving God, heaven and hell, or an afterlife.

During my time in Malaysia, living in a Muslim Bajau-dominated town, with Christian Kadazans, and so-called Buddhist Chinese, who really only worship their ancestors, I became even more disillusioned about any form of organized religion. It all seemed too formalistic and divisive—each one excluding all the souls who do not follow their own religion's path to salvation, heaven, or nirvana. Few people I met had any real understanding of their own creed—they just repeated its doctrine.

After I sent the letter, I wondered if I had blown up our engagement. If so, I thought it was better to do it before we went any further. I had to be honest about my beliefs, or lack of them. My letters to Beth in PNG didn't reach her until she was about to leave. With no mail arriving, she had grown a little frantic. Somehow my Christmas parcel containing a letter, some cloth, and *The Prophet* by Kahlil Gibran made it through to her. Beth read the book and left it on the coffee table to see what her father would say. When she asked him, his only word was, "Ugh."

However, Beth also wrote that her parents were happy for us. She had arrived just after her father had completed supervising the building of his modern well-ventilated church in Rabaul, on the island of New Britain, and he was quite pleased with this accomplishment. But he didn't want to discuss her previous misadventures in love or anything much about me. Beth wrote me saying "my father is just a tough old man who hasn't learned to express his own emotions. He seems to have lost the joy of life. His whole life is so well-ordered and perfect. His joy is creating things, but he can't create perfect people." But later she wrote that her going home was good, "a kind of reconciliation without going through the words."

Her father told her he would marry us in his new church, but thank Buddha that didn't happen! I sent a letter to Beth's parents, as she advised me to do. When it arrived, her father called her to his study to question her about this marriage. She admitted I was not a Lutheran and not even a church-goer. As mentioned in Chapter 3, before she left home for university, he had told her she was on her own and couldn't come home again, except for holidays. But after reading my letter, he said she was welcome to return home if her plans with me didn't work out. In other words, they didn't have a lot of confidence in her choice of this young non-Lutheran filmmaker—possibly another disaster in the making.

Before she left PNG, Beth received some reassurance about me when she stopped in Port Moresby overnight. She telephoned first and then visited the CUSO office, where she met Peter and Barbara Hoffman. They said they were expecting her since I had written them about her. Beth was somewhat relieved to hear this, needless to say. They also told her I was a "real winner" in CUSO—a former volunteer who had made a solid contribution and was now a filmmaker, and that I had all the luck in the world. For instance, it had been raining in the highlands for weeks before I arrived, but when I flew into the mountains, the rain stopped and the sun shone just long enough for me to complete all my filming.

When Beth returned to Japan, she read outdated letters from me, including the one on my religious beliefs, and some others forwarded from PNG, as well as new ones from me in Ottawa—out-of-order letters causing more confusion. Fortunately, she received a letter from my mother containing such emotion and joy that Beth no longer had fears about the in-law issue. Then other positive "reference letters" arrived from some of my married friends in Canada, and Beth started to feel overwhelmed and inadequate. I didn't know about this until late January, after a Canadian air traffic controllers strike ended, which had caused further havoc to our communications. But finally, I received a letter, which Beth had written to me before leaving for PNG, that reassured me:

> Dear Neill McKee,
> Once I said, "Wait till Christmas.
> I'll tell you then."
> Knowing what I'd say
> and yet afraid to say it
> Knowing that I've rushed into this before
> and knowing you too well
> To want to do a repeat performance
> Knowing, knowing but fearing speed
> You work so fast
> You knew so soon
> Why? Why? Why couldn't I feel the same?
> How can you accept me as I am?
> <u>Never</u>. Never in my life has this happened before
> Never have I not had to prove myself
> Do love me as I am
>   As I don't understand.
> Let this be the gift from my heart—
> And let my life prove it
> Move where you want to
> I will go with you
> Fight for what you will
>   And I'll stay by your side.

I may not always believe
   what you believe
But I shall always believe in you.
Change—but do not change without me
I shall change
   But I'll try not to change alone
I cannot promise not to wander
But I promise not to try to make it without you.
In short—I promise to love you
As I have never promised before
With all its implications
And in all my humility
Because, Neill McKee—I too know
What you knew first
I'm beginning to understand
This thing I thought I understood before
Only to find there is no understanding
   No definition
   No parenthesis
There is only You and Me and
"that has made all the difference."
Forever & ever. Amen. Love, Beth

Beth's poem came on two aerograms, which she numbered 8G-1 and 8G-2. When I absorbed her words, any small speckle of doubt that she would be my life partner disappeared. She was spontaneous, expressive, open, honest, beautiful, and loving. What else could a man ask for? I wondered, quite frankly, how on earth I had found this woman. *More good luck*, I thought. I also finally received the letters she wrote while she was in PNG, indicating she'd done her homework well, finishing Tolkien's trilogy during her trip.

With no mail arriving from me, she had written, "Where is my Gandalf in my hour of weakness?" and a few days later, "You shall be my Tom Bombadil and I'll be your Goldberry." She also wrote that her dad had told her my lack of religious affiliation was her problem.

On January 20th, Beth wrote a letter telling me she had read *Siddhartha* by Hermann Hesse[5]—a book I had also boldly sent to her in PNG. It's a novel based on life of Siddhartha Gautama, Prince of Kapilavastu, who became the Buddha: a philosopher, meditator, and spiritual teacher who lived in ancient India, leading to Buddhism in all its forms, including Zen.

Beth wrote, "Will try to do more thinking (about the book) while I'm waiting—probably wouldn't do too much harm to take up fasting too. On principle, I believe in trial marriages just because they have no bonds beyond the couple's will to live together. Vows can be a terrible crutch." But another letter indicated she still had not given up on the idea of our having a Christian wedding in Japan.

My evolving love life was the good news; the bad news came when I was called into a meeting to be told CUSO was running out of money due to overall budget cuts from the government. They could pay for my Africa trip, but I had to go on contract—no longer a staff member with benefits. I would be advanced funds for travel costs, but my fee would only come when I returned.

I worked extra long hours through January and part of February to complete my present film, which we simply titled *CUSO in Papua New Guinea*.[6] My colleagues loved it, but it was decided to put off completion of the Malaysia forestry film until I returned from Africa. Around that time, I was asked if I wanted to apply for a CUSO field staff job in Malaysia. I decided not to because my chosen career path was filmmaking. Since I would now be on contract, I negotiated an agreement with CUSO, which would allow me to look for other filming and photographic work to do in Africa for other non-governmental organizations (NGOs), and hence cut down on CUSO's part of the expenses for the trip. CUSO could not decide on the Thailand film we had discussed until the new budget was approved in April.

I wrote a proposal to make a development education film on Lesotho in Southern Africa, documenting how this tiny independent African country was successfully making progress, despite being surrounded by the racist apartheid regime of South Africa. I received a commitment from CIDA that they would put up 50 percent of the money needed, but I had to raise the balance from NGOs. I created a letterhead for a company I called "Econofilms" and began meeting various people to sell my services. This was an exciting time for me and I wrote Beth about it. I was thrilled about the prospects of getting funding for this additional work. But most of the filming would have to be done in Africa, and that clouded plans for the time and place Beth and I would meet up again—and where we would marry.

Ever the optimist, I sent a telegram to Beth about my original proposal, "Come to Africa with me." I added it could also be somewhere in Asia. I followed up with a short phone call and a detailed letter, including my tentative travel plans. Then, I flew off once more to that immense and challenging continent, Africa.

Forty Days in Ghana

I stopped in London to talk to Voluntary Service Overseas (VSO), about doing photography for them in Africa, and then took a train to Grenoble, France, to visit Canadian friends. When I arrived in Accra, Ghana, I was met by Peter Westaway, CUSO's deputy FSO, and he invited me to stay at his place. There, waiting for me, were 13 letters from Beth. Many of them were outdated by my telegram, letters, and my recent phone call to her—more confusion. But within them, I learned she had found a replacement. Her school principal, fellow teachers, and friends all agreed that, of course she should leave her job early and meet me in Africa.

She told me she wanted lots of children and asked me what clothes she should pack. She also mentioned she didn't want a diamond ring from racist South Africa—a good sign, I thought, and I couldn't afford one anyway. She admitted the fantastic religious wedding in a Japanese garden was all in her head and not in mine at all. She recognized it was best if our marriage took place on "neutral ground," but she still hoped for a Christian ceremony of some sort. I had suggested getting married in Lusaka, Zambia, where I would be around the end of April. I told her I'd ask Dave Beer, CUSO FSO in Lusaka, if he knew how such a marriage could be arranged.

More letters arrived from Tokyo and I answered all of Beth's concerns, questions, and her affectionate words. We agreed to send out a wedding invitation for April 29th in Lusaka. I sent her a long invitation list of relatives and friends from Canada and elsewhere.

I had planned five weeks in Ghana and CUSO had tentatively scheduled me to spend two more weeks in Nigeria—a return trip I dreaded. I was already experiencing a big difference between the two countries, although they are near neighbors and both former British colonies. Ghanaians seemed much easier, happier, even joyous in their philosophy of life.

On the negative side, Ghana had just gone through a military coup. The country had gained independence from Britain in 1957, and started as a multi-party democratic nation under Prime Minister Kwame Nkrumah, a pan-Africanist who many on the continent looked up to. He was a socialist who believed in central planning and receiving aid from the Soviet Union. Peter took me to a place beside Accra airport, where I could take a shot of rusting snowplows. Soviet-style planning dictated all airports should have snowplows, even in a city only 5.6 degrees north of the equator—a package deal, all or nothing.

In 1964, Nkrumah had engineered a constitutional amendment to make Ghana a one-party state and declared himself President-for-Life. But he was overthrown in a military coup in 1966. The military allowed a parliamentary government to form again in 1969, but on January 14, 1972, Prime Minister Dr. Kofi Busia and the parliament were overthrown by Colonel Acheampong—just a month before my visit. As an indication of how easy Ghanaians are, Peter Thompson, the head CUSO FSO, told me to come anyway. After I arrived, it only took a few days to obtain permission to film and get a press accreditation card.

It also only took a few days for me to come down with chills and a fever. I figured it was malaria and since I had to get to work, I decided to hit my body with five chloroquine tablets all at once. That did the trick. I stayed on the tablets for the rest of my time in Africa. I'd been lucky never to have been struck by the disease before, throughout my sojourn in Borneo and previous travels through Asia and Africa.

On my first trip out of Accra, I hitched a ride with a couple of volunteers who were heading north toward the Afram Plains. They dropped me at a mission station, where I stayed overnight. I managed to get a peanut butter sandwich for supper and a cup of instant coffee for breakfast. I had intended to photograph a CUSO volunteer stationed there, but found he had just left for Accra. Dissatisfied with his placement, he wanted either a different job or to return to Canada. It must have been frustrating for him, but I was also frustrated. Telephone networks were rudimentary in those days—few landlines and no cell phones.

The next morning, an American Peace Corps volunteer gave me a ride in the mission's Land Rover to a dock on Lake Volta, where I skirmished with two tsetse flies while boarding a rather rickety-looking boat. I knew these pests sometimes carried trypanosomiasis (sleeping sickness). They finally grew tired of my waving arms when we reached open water bound for Kpando, a small city on the other side.

The Volta Dam, now called Akosombo Dam, is a hydroelectric project, which opened in 1965, to provide energy for aluminum smelters and much of the country's electricity. It created the lake, a huge body of water, displacing many villages and wreaking havoc on the environment and human health in the surrounding population due to water-borne illnesses, such as schistosomiasis (bilharzia). These were the

Visiting the Campbells at Kpando —Images from the film

kind of choices many developing countries had to make in their rush to modernize during the 1960s and 1970s.

When we docked at Kpando, I bought a can of meat and a loaf of bread in the nearby market to fill my stomach, and then caught a taxi to the technical school to see a CUSO couple, Bill and Jean Campbell from Halifax, Nova Scotia. I found them to be practical and stalwart souls who would never abandon their posts despite all the poverty and diseases around them. Bill had been an auto mechanic in Halifax and now taught auto mechanics. He focused on practical experience, using basic tools to train the students on how to repair cars and trucks—nothing fancy because they wouldn't find any special tools on the job when they graduated. He told me in his interview the students posed a lot of questions, which made him think a lot. He said the experience would improve his work when he returned to Canada.

Jean had been a secretary and taught typing, stenography, bookkeeping, and other office procedures—skills the country needed rather than more unemployed university graduates. I filmed her teaching rows of young women in purple dresses and young men in white shirts and short pants—uniforms that hid the different income levels of the families they came from. I also took sequences of Bill and Jean in the community, including shopping in the open market. There was nothing pretentious about the Campbells—my first good subjects for the film on Ghana. On my last day at Kpando, I was lucky to be able to film and tape the sound of a celebration, complete with Ghanaian music and dancing—the highlight of my brief stay.

From Kpando, I grabbed a "mammy wagon"—a brightly decorated truck with slogans painted on the back—to the town of Akosombo near the dam, where I photographed another CUSO volunteer. I also negotiated with security guards to take a shot of Volta Dam and the lake from the verandah of deposed President Nkruma's villa. Achieving this without being jailed as a spy was tricky. I continued to find Ghanaians to be accommodating and spontaneous people. If they wanted to dance, they danced, and if they wanted to sing, they sang. Sometimes they could be overwhelmingly extroverted but seldom argumentative. On my travels through their country with CUSO volunteers, I only once ran into drunken soldiers at a roadblock carrying Soviet AK-47 semi-automatic rifles. They gave us a hard time but we kept our cool because they were intoxicated with more than military power, following the coup.

At Akosombo, I was picked up by two volunteers who were heading north in a Volkswagen van. They were a godsend since I didn't have the time or energy to take mammy wagons or rickety buses, guarding my equipment all the way. After a day of driving, we reached Tamale, where I stayed overnight with a volunteer, Brian O'Dwyer, and arranged to film him the following week.

At Tamale, I received a pile of letters from Beth, forwarded to Brian by the CUSO office in Accra. I'd written her on my travels but our letters took at least two weeks to reach each other—a time gap of a month for reactions to each other's thoughts. Most of her letters were on travel details, issues in her school and community. I couldn't tell her any more about our planned wedding since I hadn't heard from Zambia. I just wrote that she should try to arrive in Zambia around April 21st and I'd be at the airport. *What more assurance did she need from me?*, I thought in jest. I did receive another poem on her upcoming last 15 days of teaching, which reinforced my thoughts that she was the woman for me:

> Let us consider the last 15 days
> and are they worth it?—
> The consideration and the time?
> Will I be happy to see them pass?
> I am such a silly lass.
> It's not teaching I abhor,
> teachers' meetings are a bore,
> and getting up at half-past four.
> Apart from those, a couple more...
> But taken by a greater quest,
> my eyes turn ever to the west.
> Still 15 days of toil and stress,
> till I shall join my happiness.

The next day, I traveled by means I never recorded and can't recall—perhaps I hitchhiked—for another five or six hours to the village of Wiaga, about 42 miles (68 km) west of the northern city of Bolgatanga. Wiaga is located only 50 miles (80 km) from the border with Burkina Faso, then called the Republic of Upper Volta. I had entered a scorching dry land in the hottest season of the year.

At Wiaga, I filmed and photographed four CUSO volunteers—two agriculturalists and two nurses—stationed at a small mission. For the work in agriculture, I focused on George Martin from Manitoba, but used the interview with Bob McDonald for the sound track. They were teaching the local farmers to grow better crops and how to market their surplus, and to improve traditional grain storage systems—cost-effective methods of preventing insect and water damage. Bob said Ghanaian farmers were collaborative and

Volunteering at Wiaga Mission —Images from the film

75

happy to receive help and advice—probably more so than their counterparts in Canada.

On the medical side, I focused more on Heather Raymond, who was running child welfare clinics funded by Catholic Relief Services, but also filmed Hélène Bricole, a nurse-midwife from Montreal, who was operating antenatal and post delivery services. These volunteers had a difficult posting. My experiences in Wiaga and the surrounding countryside are best recounted in excerpts from letters I wrote to Beth:

> Wed. March 15, 1972
>
> The last three days I've been in a very different world. The savanna—dry grassland and semidesert. I just had a bath using half a bucket—while I had visions of you in your local public bath. I have been filming in temperatures up to 130°F, and at night in the CUSO bungalow, it creeps down to 95°F. The people here are very poor, with disease all around. It really blows your mind. The CUSO volunteers here have a hell of a job to do.
>
> Fri. March 17, 1972
>
> Yesterday was a day to remember. Went with one of the nurses to a bush clinic to film. On the way, one of my microphones and my light meter got shook up and have ceased to function. Must do without. The clinic went on for so long—people coming from all around with every disease in the book. The line never dissolved until 1:30 pm. I

admire this CUSO nurse, Hélène, who just stayed on the job, taking it all in.... Then, we headed back and the car broke down four miles from the nearest water. It was 120°F in the sun and 103°F in the shade, so we trudged along the road with dry mouths. A government vehicle passed and we called it every name in the book—bastard didn't stop. A sorcerer's curse was certainly put on us. After a couple of hours, we made it to a small town where I downed four warm Cokes—well water not to be trusted. Finally, we made it back to the mission and I drank four quarts of water and a quart of beer, ate, and relaxed in the not very cool evening. God, in a week I'll be back in the cool tropical south by the sea. Really need green trees around me to be happy. Hey, I've lost 10 pounds in three weeks—all sweated away!

Sat. March 18, 1972

Just sitting here in the "cool" of the evening with the CUSOs, and a group of people came along to ask for milk. A man and a woman carrying a three-month-old baby for 36 miles (in this temperature) to get help because the mother had died. What a tremendous respect for the right to live! As I write, warm milk is entering its tummy. Tears in my eyes. But I know there are so many like this around here just the same.... Tomorrow I will leave this place. It's too easy to forget the reality. The Government of Ghana has forgotten these people. Only a few missions with limited resources.... It may seem kind of crazy that we are so close in time to being together and yet I say little about it. All I can say is that it will be good. We are now in such completely different and opposite worlds, but we will soon be in body and mind in the same world and will experience it together. I hope that will be a lasting experience.... As the time gets nearer, I'm more anxious. I want and need your love. I will give you mine.

From Wiaga, I returned to Tamale to film and photograph Brian O'Dwyer from London, Ontario, an affable fellow who was teaching at a business college. In his interview, he said that a lot of his work involved imparting skills in logical thinking—organizing thoughts on paper and in speeches, writing telegrams, and using the telephone. There was only one telephone in town at the time, located at the post office. Few of the students had practice with this element of modern society since they came from poor urban and rural backgrounds.

Brian's classes were full of bright smiling faces and especially attractive girls. He loved teaching here—no sulking North American adolescents. He was so uplifted by the keen attitudes of the students and his work, in general, that he said in the interview he was considering teaching as his vocation when he returned home to Canada, in spite of the differences in attitudes. He claimed, "Ghanaian people effervesce and that's certainly the most enjoyable part of being here."

I filmed Brian casually interacting with his Ghanaian colleagues, then riding around town on his motorcycle. I took a sequence of him in a market buying a traditional Ghanaian shirt, and another of him patronizing his favorite restaurant called "Old Man's Chop Bar." The old man who ran the place served roasted guineafowl, which had the taste and texture of tough chicken. This rudimentary facility was such a shock compared to the Chinese, Indian, and Malay restaurants I had frequented during my volunteer days in Malaysia. I tried *fufu*, made of yams or cassava pounded into a fine flour and then boiled into a sticky glutinous mass. It's dipped into groundnut (peanut) stew, and eaten with your hands. The problem was that I couldn't chew it, so when I tried to swallow, it discharged out of my throat. I can't recall exactly, but I believe someone brought me bread.

I also filmed Brian drinking with the locals—an essential cross-cultural exchange, he told me. This episode in a *pito* bar became an interesting finale for my Tamale coverage. After

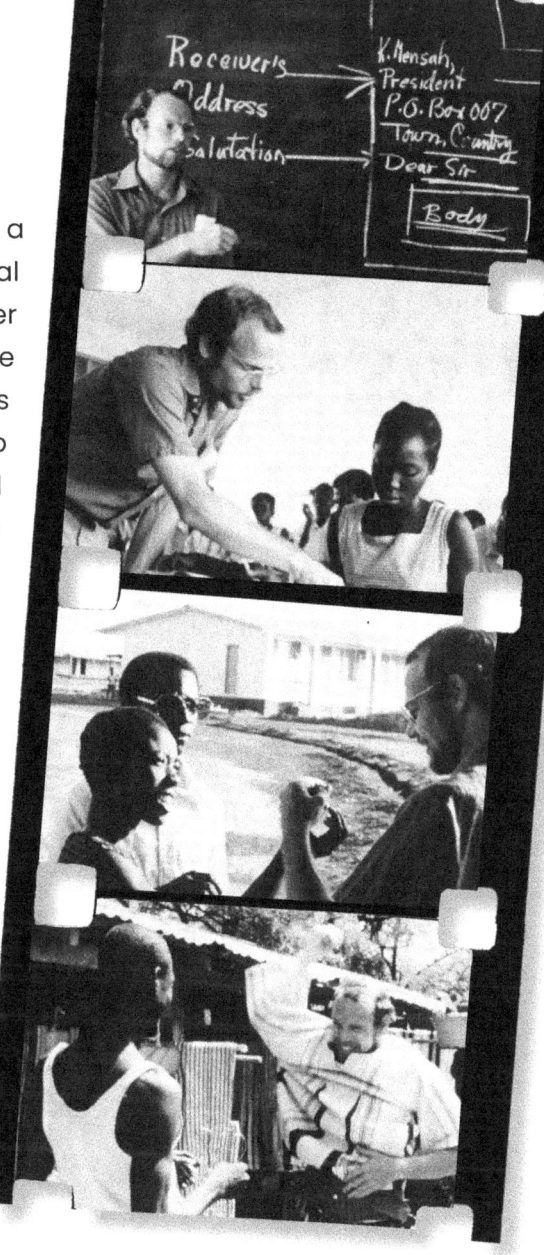

Brian O'Dwyer on the job – Images from the film

Episode in the pito bar
—Images from the film

putting down my camera, I sampled the *pito*—a beer made from fermented millet or sorghum. It was made in the bar and served to us in calabash gourds, while we sat on benches placed around a dirt floor. Local minstrels provided entertainment for tips, or a calabash or two of *pito*. That evening, I wrote to Beth about my experience:

> Men and women sit around in a village-type place and drink *pito* from large calabashes. Of course, I had to drink it too and my head started to float. One man sang a beautiful song for his share of *pito* and I was able to film and record him. Then another man invited me to film and tape him playing his xylophone, called a *gyil*, with wooden bars and resonating gourds hanging below. Ghanaians are not modest. Every minute someone shouts, "take me" when they see the camera.

Their photo studios are full of posed pictures of people beautifully dressed, wearing seven watches, and holding a transistor radio—really funny stuff.

On March 24th, Brian must have managed to get me to the airport for the flight to Accra, which I can't recall at all. My mind remained foggy due to all the *pito* I had consumed. When I arrived, I found a deluge of letters, including an important one from CUSO-Nigeria. I was told to cancel my trip there because school holidays would last for most of April. I was overjoyed with this news. I would finish up my business in Ghana by photographing a few more volunteers and shipping my exposed film to Ottawa.

I also took many busy market shots for the opening of the film. Ghanaian urban scenes were so vibrant and colorful. I was especially attracted to the slogans on trucks and buses, so I captured an action sequence for the film's finale.

Ghanaian vehicle slogans –Images from the film

I had many letters from Beth to answer. There was one about her Rev. Horn trying to find a Lutheran minister to marry us in Zambia. I pushed back:

> As for your mention of a Lutheran minister—choke! I don't particularly want Cliff to arrange anything. He probably won't know the man personally and he may be a real shithead. You must remember I don't even know Cliff, for that matter. Sorry if this makes you angry at a time when I only want to make you happy, but I am not a Christian in any sense of Lutheran or Methodist or whatever.

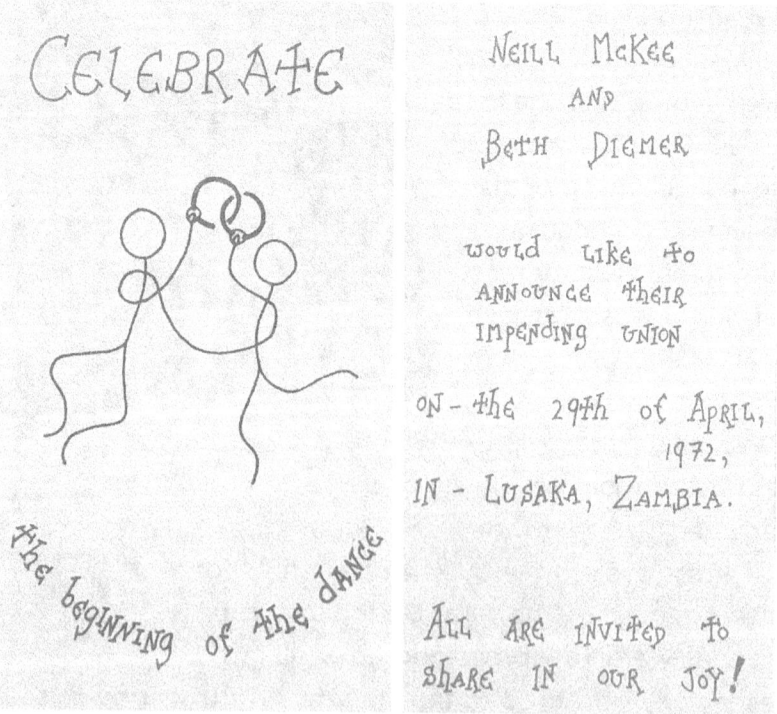

Our wedding invitation

I made it clear neither of us would know what our wedding would be like until we reached Zambia. A few days later, I found out Beth had already accepted this, when I received a copy of our wedding invitation, which she had sent out to 300 people. There was not a traditional religious word on it. Yippee! I liked the "beginning of the dance" idea. This woman was reading my mind—mental telepathy over 13,000 miles.

While watching Ghanaian children playing on the beach the evening before I left, a warm feeling came over me about my productive forty days in Ghana, and our coming union.

Our Marriage and Travels in Southern and Eastern Africa

On Easter Sunday, April 2, 1972, I flew from Accra to Johannesburg, South Africa, to reach my next stop, the Republic of Malawi. After gaining some time from the cancelation of my Nigeria stop, I decided to attend a CUSO regional staff meeting in Malawi and get started on my second film before Beth would arrive in nearby Zambia. The FSO for CUSO-Malawi, Don McMaster, wasn't too happy to learn I would be traveling through South Africa, where the policy of apartheid remained in place. But I have never been a purist in such matters, and I chalked it up to my necessary first-hand education. Besides, the immigration people at Johannesburg gladly stamped my arrival on a separate slip of paper, not on a page of my passport, so it would not stop me from entering Zambia and Tanzania later, where evidence of being in South Africa would prohibit entry.

I stayed at the airport's Holiday Inn overnight and tried to board a flight to Malawi the next morning, but was informed I needed a visa. I had no choice but to turn back and go to the Malawi Embassy, where I was told I didn't need a visa because Malawi is part of the Commonwealth, like Canada. So much for South African efficiency. The delay at least allowed me time to buy a new light meter so I wouldn't have to guess at lens aperture settings. I also had a chance to see apartheid up close. Everything was segregated: buses, parks, restaurants, public urinals—those for whites had smart signs

"Here Gents," while those for non-Europeans were just labeled "Toilet." Signs reading "Europeans" and "Non-Europeans" were posted just about everywhere. I took some photos of them, while frequently checking if I was being tailed. I thought to myself, *What a quick transition I've made from singing and swinging Ghanaians to this place of racial oppression.*

The next day, I flew to Blantyre, the commercial capital of Malawi. From there I sent another postcard to Beth.

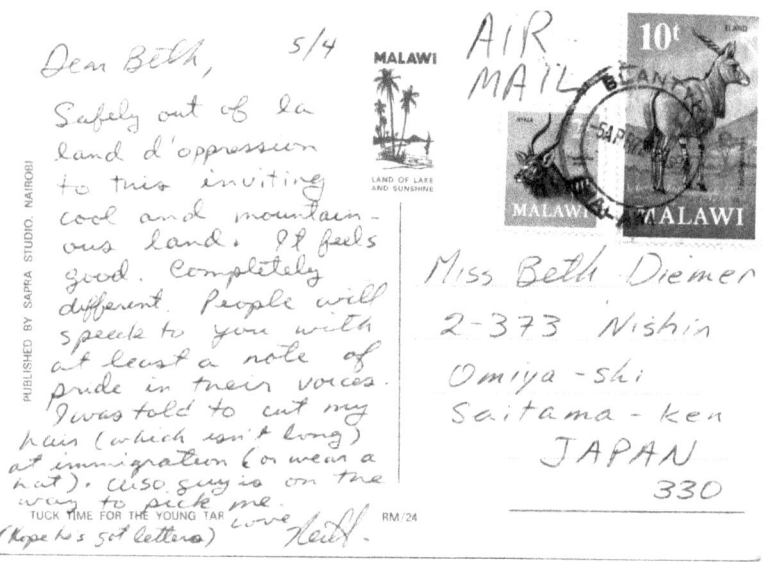

Postcard from Malawi

Actually, compared to Ghana, Malawi gave the air of being a conservative place, where longish hair and beards were not welcome, as noted in my postcard. Formerly the British protectorate of Nyasaland, Malawi gained its independence in 1964. The constitution was revised in 1966 to make the country a one-party state and a republic, at which point Dr. Hastings Kamuzu Banda became President. In 1970, the Malawi Congress Party revised its own constitution, making Dr. Banda its life-president, and the following year he managed to get Parliament to change the country's constitution once more, to make him President-for-Life—a growing trend on the continent. When I arrived in Malawi, it was starting to operate like the personal property of Dr. Banda, a renowned anti-communist who maintained diplomatic relations with South Africa. At the time, his government was just beginning to use detention without trial, torture, and assassination to suppress all political opposition.

I saw no "singing and swinging" Africans here—mostly men in old-fashioned threadbare European suits, sporting white shirts and ties. Most women wore what we called "missionary dresses"—boring Western garbs—rather than the colorful flowing robes and headpieces, which adorn the women of Ghana. One of the best things about Malawi is its climate. Much of the country is perched on a plateau of rolling hills and mountains—perfect for photography. The rainy season had just ended and I learned CUSO's regional meeting had been postponed, so I got right into filming the work of Maitland and Elaine McNeil, a photogenic doctor-nurse couple from Saskatchewan, working with the Ministry of Health. They invited me to stay with them in their small bungalow.

With two small children to look after, Elaine didn't have a formal CUSO job, but she volunteered three mornings a week at the Queen Elizabeth Hospital, in Blantyre, and pitched in to help her husband whenever she could, assisting nurses and midwives in outreach clinics. I took a brief sequence of Elaine at work but fully documented Maitland as he traveled through the undulating green countryside, holding village meetings with chiefs and political leaders, advocating to villagers through a translator on the importance of

Film images of Maitland McNeil advocating with local leader and Elaine attending a child at an outreach clinic

health care, so they could understand the causes of their children's illnesses and deaths. The area was filled with rundown outreach clinics, which had been built during British times, 20 to 40 years ago. Each clinic was staffed by only one medical assistant, who previously had received little support or supervision, while attending up to 300 patients per day, with a limited supply of medicines.

I became inspired by the McNeils' dedication to making the situation better. A consortium of NGOs, including CUSO, contributed to building new clinics, along with efforts by the communities themselves through their labor and donation of materials. Besides educational sessions in communities, Maitland spent his hours supervising building projects, plus retraining and supporting health assistants on clinical diagnosis. He also taught students at the College of Medicine and visited them in clinics after they graduated.

While filming the McNeils, listening carefully to all their discussions, recording interviews with them, and talking informally in the evenings, I gained knowledge about health issues in Malawi. They had arrived in the country when health outcome statistics were grim. But the system the McNeils helped to set up was the beginning of a sustained national and international multi-agency effort that gradually reduced under-five mortality and contributed to a leveling off of population growth. In 1971, under-five deaths of children were very high—203 per 1,000 live births. That was reduced to 29 per 1,000 live births by 2020.[1] In 1971, population growth was escalating with a fertility rate (births per woman) of 7.32, and this also was reduced to 3.98 by 2022.[2] Today, it's well established that couples around the world will practice family planning if they are confident their children have a better chance of survival. (While writing this book, I learned Elaine's volunteer work ignited a fire in her, for it led to a career in international development, managing Canadian-funded health and education projects in Malawi and other sub-Saharan African countries for decades to come.)

My time in Malawi with this couple also included some fun. Compared to the CUSO workers in northern Ghana, on weekends the McNeils had a chance to hike and explore mountainous terrain. I filmed them in their small car, heading to an area near the scenic Mount Mulanje with their older son Colin, Maitland, and Elaine in the front, and baby Sean with their Irish Setter called "Pumpkin" in the back with me. We reached a waterfall where Malawian children swam and slid down natural slides into pools of fresh clean water, and I took shots of the family joining in the fun.

On a cloudy Sunday morning, Maitland, Elaine, and Colin went to church, leaving me to babysit Sean and Pumpkin. I read my letters from Beth, containing her plans to fly from Tokyo to Lusaka, Zambia, via Cairo and Nairobi. In my last letter to her during this long separation, I told her that, so far, none of my plans for doing work for other NGOs and neither the film on Lesotho, nor the one in Thailand, had worked out. I hadn't given up, but it looked more and more like I'd be completing the CUSO filming and then we'd head to Europe and Canada by mid-summer.

I also mentioned Dave Beer, in Lusaka, had reported to me that in Zambia there was a required waiting period after posting marriage banns, inferring she had to be prepared for changes. By then, I think Beth knew to expect just about anything. I thought about our coming life together, inspired by the married life that I was witnessing in the McNeil home:

> GRAY BUT HAPPY SUNDAY—April 9, 1972—Month of our becoming:
>
> My Dear, Doctor McNeil, his wife, lovely she be, Colin and car have gone to church. It's 8 am and Bob Dylan sings *I Want You* and makes me drift lightly over the hills of Malawi to the hills of North Borneo where I first heard the tune. I want you indeed. The time gap closes. Sean, four months old, sucks his bottle between smiles beside me. Pumpkin, the big Irish Setter licks his balls while looking for tidbits of attention. A very human dog. I'm in a lovely little house in Blantyre....Another baby smile comes my way with Dylan's words, *Your brand-new leopard-skin pill-box hat*....Sure hope all our babies (all!?) smile like this one.

On April 21st, a few days after I had arrived in Lusaka, I went back to the airport to see Beth walk through the arrival doors. She came running and hugged me, saying, "You're here!"

"What did you expect?" I said after we kissed. "It has all gone as planned, sort of, no?"

Beth, looking even more beautiful than I remembered her, now with longer hair, said something like, "You don't know what I was going through. It all seemed like a fantastic dream, which could have turned into a nightmare if you weren't here to meet me."

She told me later it was the kind of marriage that just happens in crazy movies. She only had about $1,000 and a ticket to Rome in her purse. Her parents had even sent her $300 in case she needed it—something they would never have done if they trusted all would go well with this strange filmmaker in Africa. But I thought, *How could I have led her on from afar through such an elaborate scheme, and for what purpose?*

We stayed with Barrie Fleming and his partner, Jalna. Barry was the deputy FSO of CUSO-Zambia. I had applied for

Beth and the author the morning after her arrival
—Photo by Neill McKee

a marriage license at Lusaka's District Office for April 29th, but Beth brought some news—our friends, Dick and Jeannine Helmstetter, were going to fly in from Tokyo, arriving after that date. Ha! Exactly my point of being flexible. These were the only international guests who accepted our invitation, so we had to change our plans. After all, they were coming at their own considerable expense.

The next day, Beth and I went back to the District Office to change the date to May 2nd, a Tuesday. Then we shopped for wedding rings. We had over a week to wait before the Helmstetters would arrive. I had a brilliant idea, and said to Beth, "Let's go on our honeymoon first. We can stay at Victoria Falls."

Beth looked at me and said, "You had all of this planned, didn't you?"

"Not really, but why not have our honeymoon first? We're already sleeping together."

"Yes, let's go!" Beth replied.

She was getting the hang of it—a good sign of things to come. Gone were all of the elaborate visions she had written to me about—a religious marriage ceremony in a Japanese garden. I must admit neither Dave Beer nor I had done any real scouting for a Lutheran minister, or any other kind of preacher who could hold a religious service after the civil one. Beth seemed to have accepted this new reality.

We took a bus to the town of Livingston to stay in a hotel right beside the Zambezi River. It featured *rondavels*—circular African-style houses for rooms. We cooked outside on an open-pit fire. We hiked along the bank of the river upstream and sat for hours watching vast quantities of water tumble 354 feet (108 meters), producing a mist stretching high above the river. At the time, there were no guard rails along the river bank. One slip and you'd be swept over the falls in seconds, possibly making the mist faintly red as your body hit the rocks below. In the local African language, Lozi, the falls are known as *Mosi-oa-Tunya*—"the smoke that thunders."

Beth gazing into the rapids above the falls –Photo by Neill McKee

We spent our time by the river getting to know each other better, and laughing at our reckless decisions. As the week progressed, I could see this hunch was paying off. Beth was the woman for me, and it was a good decision to get married on neutral ground, far from family expectations and pressures. In Japan or Papua New Guinea, I would have been a stranger. In Canada, Beth would have been surrounded by my family and friends, and would have worried she was not living up to their expectations as a good match for me. Yes, this exotic neutral ground did the trick.

When we returned to Lusaka, we went to meet the Helmstetters at the airport and then we all checked into Ridgeway Hotel. I laughed when Dick told me he was charging his trip to a search for new exotic hardwoods for his billiard tables and cues. Dick and Jeannine both possessed a sense of humor and adventure I much enjoyed, and we became good friends during their brief stay. They acted as witnesses for our marriage. Another volunteer, Dirk Jol, an artsy CUSO architect with longish hair, who worked for Lusaka town planning, acted as our official pro-bono photographer. Everything happened as planned, almost. I described the whole affair in a letter to my family, the day after the wedding:

> Dear Folks, May 3/72
>
> Well, Elizabeth Ann McKee, my bride of 29 hours and 4 minutes, washes my wedding shirt out in the bathtub as I sip a cup of tea and write you a letter before we take off tomorrow for a second (post-marriage) honeymoon-cum-photography trek. The marriage went off smoothly except for a few minor hitches—like the ceremony had just started when the District Secretary began to look closely at our marriage license to find it had expired, at which time we all swallowed our tongues. The clerk had assured me 15 times it had been amended, but the District Secretary didn't seem to know about it. We waited 14 minutes, listening to a loud ticking clock on the wall as he made many phone calls. Permission to proceed was finally granted.

Then our photographer asked me to stand when the official told me to sit. Back on my chair, he asked, "Will you, Nelly McKee, take this woman to be your husband?," to which I, of course, answered, "Sure!" He did get the words right on the question posed to Beth and she also agreed. We officially became man and wife at 11:54 am. My wedding ring fit well, but Beth's had to be held on by a band-aid and some string because she wanted a plain one and they only had men's plain style and couldn't fix it in time. Anyway, the bride wore a short white wedding dress—a vogue fashion she had ordered to be made in Japan—with a white band in her hair and sandals—very classy. The groom sported a brown $6.00 jacket made in Hong Kong, a lovely white shirt with golden patterns and puffy sleeves,

Our wedding was like a crazy movie –Photos by Jol Dirk

the tie Marg made and gave me at Christmas, and sandals with a pair of old brown socks covering up the hair on my feet—yes, Hobbit hair.

After we finally escaped the throngs of people (joke), we went for lunch in a coffee shop, and then Beth and Jeannine went shopping in the afternoon, while Dick and I went to arrange things for dinner. Dick and Jeannine are these fantastic people who live in Japan where Beth lived and they came to Zambia for three days to be our witnesses. I didn't believe it until I saw them step off the plane. Not only that, Dick is a connoisseur and gourmet cook (and an owner of a pool cue manufacturing business). He arranged and paid for a wonderful meal for 10 in the hotel we are staying in. The dinner included some CUSO people: Dave Beer and Irene, Barry Fleming and Jalna, and Dirk Jol and Josette. We gorged ourselves on *pâté maison* and champagne, *sole bonne femme* and white wine, *fillet mignon* with croquette potatoes and vegetables in season with red wine, plus baked Alaska (with wedding cake trimmings) and liqueurs and coffee. The food, the people, and the music were all excellent. The party made up for the disjointed ceremony in the morning. But the day ended when Neill McKee fell into a deep slumber while Elizabeth was brushing her teeth…. Great way to begin! Glad we had our honeymoon first.

We have just seen Dick and Jeannine off at the airport—life-long friends, I believe—and now have a few hours to relax before we travel. Our plan is to be in Zambia until the 15th, when we will fly to Botswana for two weeks.

Love, Neill and Beth

By this time, my parents were prepared for such news from their wandering "prodigal son" and I'm sure my letter provided lots of laughter for my family. They were probably just relieved to hear we were legally married. Beth wisely treated her own parents to very few details of our non-Lutheran honeymoon and marriage.

Back row L to R: Beth and Neill, Jeannine, Josette, Jalna, Dick;
Front row: Barry, Irene —Photo by Dave Beer

We hitchhiked around Zambia to photograph more CUSO volunteers, and for some reason had no trouble getting rides. It was an anomaly to see white people hitchhiking in Zambia, especially a white woman.

Beth trying her luck at attracting rides –Photo by Neill McKee

Next, we flew to Gaborone, the capital of Botswana. There we were met by Helmut Kuhn, CUSO FSO, who took us to photograph some volunteers and sites, before we boarded a train to journey through this comparatively dry and cold southern African land. It was mid-May, with winter fast approaching in the Southern Hemisphere. We arrived at Shashi River School located near the isolated village of Tonota, in the northeast of the country, where I filmed CUSO teacher Janis Kazaks.

The secondary school had about 600 students—450 in the academic program and 150 in the brigade or vocational stream. It had been established by disenchanted white South Africans who left their own country to build a relevant system of education, which they couldn't create at home. Janis concentrated on teaching English, mathematics, and development studies—the three subjects taught to the brigades in their academic section. He also taught economics, imparting skills to allow students to constructively criticize development trends in their own country, and compare developments in the neighboring racist regimes of South Africa and Rhodesia.

Beth and I stayed in a guest room and we shared some meals with Janis and his partner, Angela, in their *rondavel*. Living conditions were primitive with no refrigeration. One time, Angela had to scrape a green film off a cow's liver before cooking and serving it to us. One principle of education at Shashi River was that conditions for both teachers and students should be the same—very basic. If students became used to modern facilities it could inhibit their return to rural areas.

Beth did some sketching, but froze half the time, even while wearing all the clothes she had with her. I joked she had thin blood and poor circulation from growing up in Papua New Guinea. She told me she hoped my Lesotho film project wouldn't come through, since that mountainous country is even further south, with snow in winter. I asked her with a smile, "So you're coming with me to live in Canada?"

I filmed Janis and his students in a classroom, and then followed the brigade students through their day. The young men were learning new carpentry and building skills, while the young women worked in textiles: weaving material and making handbags, placemats, rugs, and bedspreads. Others learned tie-dying and sewing skills. All their products were sold through Botswana Craft, a government-run retail outlet. Other brigade students worked on a cooperative

Film images of Janis Kazaks and Shahi River School

farm, set up by the school, to help them learn agricultural methods. Even the academic students had to get their hands dirty by taking "development practicals," fancy words for gardening and other activities, in which students learned the necessity of doing physical work to build their country. I also filmed students and teachers doing voluntary work, digging an irrigation ditch on Saturday morning, as well as a recreational activity—female students playing basketball.

The experience at Shashi River allowed me to think more deeply about the overall role of education in development. But what I remember most about the school is the determined faces of these students and their joyous voices, for they sang in harmony while they worked. This would become good background music for the soundtrack of my film. I also took some shots of Janis on his motorcycle. He reminded me of Peter Fonda in the movie, *Easy Rider* (1969)—all the rage at the time.

My next assignment took us to Tanzania to film Trevor Chandler, a CUSO volunteer teaching biology and apiculture at the Forestry Training Institute at Olmotonyi, a few miles outside Arusha on the slopes of Mount Kilimanjaro. He was tasked with upgrading the training on beekeeping in the country and initiating a long-term research program. He mentioned in his interview that beekeeping in the area probably goes back to the dawn of the first *Homo sapiens* and mankind and bees evolved together in Africa. Humans probably learned how to harvest honey here, thousands of years ago.

He spent a good deal of time working with Tanzanian instructors, upgrading their knowledge and the curriculum, and giving them access to new information sources. Trevor said during colonial times, many Tanzanians saw education as the key to escape physical work, allowing them to become bureaucrats in government offices, so he emphasized the importance of practical duties. He wanted his students to spend as long as possible "getting to know bees, getting to like bees, getting to think like bees."

I also recorded a statement he made, which I knew I had to use: "Research on the African bee is one of the most exciting frontiers of research in the world today." I didn't know what he meant by "exciting" until I filmed him opening beehives at one of his experimental sites. I wore a protective hat with a wrap-around screen, a full-body suit, and gloves, but the sound of my whirling movie camera excited the bees so much that I had to run away as quickly as I could, while carrying the camera and tape recorder. These aggressive insects followed me, hitting the sleeve of my suit, as well as the underside of a leather belt holding a monopod, on which

The author suited up for filming African bees
—Photo by Trevor Chandler

my camera was mounted. I received about 10 nasty stings on one arm, but fortunately, no stingers lodged in place. My arm swelled for some time, but then just felt itchy.

Trevor thought the whole episode was hilarious. He said the African bee is the meanest of bees in the whole world. He told me he had plans to capture a much milder species, further up the slopes of Kilimanjaro, and bring it to the research station to breed a less aggressive bee—his plans too late for me!

Film image of Trevor teaching biology of bees

Beth and I were guests of Trevor and his wife, Dale, in their English-style country cottage, where we sampled his experiments in making a new type of mead, available for export someday, or so Trevor hoped. Beth had access to the tennis courts and other recreational facilities at Olmotonyi, but by this time she was getting pretty tired of her new role of washing our clothes, helping in the kitchen, doing a little sketching, and being a cheery guest in other people's homes. She must have wondered about her decision to leave a busy teaching job in Japan to become a traditional wife. Frankly, at this point I was glad none of my other filming projects had come through—one more stop in Africa is all she and our marriage could bear.

At the end of June, we flew to Entebbe, Uganda, to film Ed Tingley, a hard-driving, no-nonsense, 50-something mechanic who opened his interview for the film by stating, "My coming to East Africa is a paradise compared to Port Churchill, Manitoba. I was there for 15 years and before that at Eskimo Point, Rankin Inlet—pretty well all over northern Manitoba and Ontario in isolated territory. So, coming to East Africa was just another posting to me."

I directed him to say East Africa instead of Uganda because CUSO didn't want it widely advertised that we were still operating in Uganda during Idi Amin's horrific military rule. Unlike the U.S. Peace Corps, CUSO (an NGO), made its own decisions on when to close down a program with a change in the political situation or other factors. Field staff and volunteers stayed as long as their physical safety was not at risk.

It took us three days to get five separate ministries to okay my mission and I must say, I never felt safe. Roy Fischer, the CUSO FSO, put us up in his house and drove us around. One time our vehicle was trailed by aggressive soldiers looking for someone to stop and extract small monetary rewards for their "service" to the country. Roy sped us into his driveway and his guard closed the gate.

Ed Tingley was the kind of volunteer who didn't care who ruled the country; he just wanted to make sure everything was running properly at the Mechanization Unit of the Department of Agriculture. He was in charge of workshop operations, training of mechanics, and keeping bush clearing machinery running up-country. In his interview he said:

> "I have quite a bit of paperwork. That's something I never did agree with—me and paperwork don't get along too well, and the telephone and radios. If I can dodge 'em I do, but most of the time somebody catches me and I have to perform on them. The radio bugs you all the time. You just get busy with something and then something's broken down somewhere, or there's no fuel or money, so you madly try to take some action at it. No coffee breaks in bush clearing."

I think Ugandan employees actually liked this rough and tumble guy, who loved to pitch in and get his hands dirty, compared to their former British overlords. When I asked Ed what aspect of his job gave him the most satisfaction, he simply stated, "What I like mostly about my job is that I am succeeding in getting several employees their mechanical certificates, which in turn will help them in making their living."

I figured Ed could be a tough boss but would also love to share a few beers in the evening with his colleagues. I'd known this class of hard-working, hard-drinking, skilled laborer while working in my dad's agricultural machinery factory during the summers of my teenage years. I just didn't expect to find one in Africa.

Finishing filming in Uganda, I reflected that I'd seen and documented a wide variety of CUSO volunteers working in several countries under much more difficult circumstances than I had ever encountered during my two years in Malaysia. I had also gained a good deal of knowledge about various issues in international development.

When Beth and I flew out of Entebbe on Sunday, July 9th, 1972, we had no idea we would return one day to spend seven years in East Africa, including Uganda. Our future moves were certainly not on our minds. We only wanted to put our feet on the ground in Canada.

Serendipitous Transitions

After a brief stop in London to see a play or two, and obtain a Canadian immigrant visa for Beth, we flew to Ottawa. I dropped off my gear and film for processing, and we took trains to Guelph, Ontario. Then we hitchhiked to my hometown, Elmira. When we arrived at my parents' home, they were away. But I knew where they kept the spare key, so we entered. When they returned, Beth greeted them at the door by offering tea. Needless to say, they loved their new daughter-in-law. She was quickly adopted by my family.

My friends, a married couple by the name of Ed and Toni Panagapka, who had plenty of children, also were enchanted with Beth and held a party for us at their house. It was there that Beth finally broke down in tears. The trigger was a married couple—strangers to me too—who argued over whose job it was to throw out the leftover pizza from their refrigerator—an enormously trivial thing to be bickering about, Beth thought. Is this what eventually happens in marriages? After our lengthy journey and staying with so many people, she longed to be in a mental and physical space for just the two of us, so we soon headed to Ottawa in my old Volkswagen, piled high with her belongings shipped to Elmira from Japan. We set up house in a small third floor apartment at the edge of Ottawa's small Chinatown, with its Asian restaurants and grocery stores. Beth had a few Japanese dishes in her repertoire, and I had only done basic bachelor-type cooking.

I suggested to her she should learn to make more Asian dishes, my favorite.

Besides learning to cook, Beth began to explore what she had started in Japan—Japanese painting and calligraphy, under the instruction of a local Japanese-Canadian artist. Our apartment also followed a Japanese theme, including a simple low-level plywood dining table I made, which required us to sit on the floor. When we invited friends over for dinner, including my film editor friend Sally and my CUSO colleagues and their wives, the table proved too uncomfortable for some. My boss, Iain, expressed his level of discomfort by flopping over on the floor halfway through the meal in feigned agony. Later, I found a few old chairs with backs in the basement, and removed the legs. I painted them blue and Beth did a professional job of covering the seat pads in bright yellow and orange cloth. At least older people would have a backrest, even if they had to figure out what to do with their legs, while trying to avoid playing footsie with others.

I got down to editing my two films, which eventually we titled *CUSO in Ghana*[1] and *CUSO in East and Central Africa*.[2] I worked at Crawley Films with Sally again, learning even more. I'd already given up the idea of going to film school. Before departing for Africa, I had visited Ryerson Polytechnic College in Toronto and showed them *CUSO in Papua New Guinea*. They told me there wasn't much they could teach me about film production, which I didn't already know, and I wasn't interested in becoming a film critic or film historian. I was already enrolled in the best film school of all—an actual working studio. But I began to wonder how I was going to earn a living after these two films were finished. None of my freelance film proposals had come to fruition, and CUSO had enough recruitment films for now.

SERENDIPITOUS TRANSITIONS

As I considered our future means of livelihood, I received a serendipitous letter from Peter Hoffman, the CUSO FSO I had met in Papua New Guinea. He and his wife Barbara had moved to Malaysia to take over the program there, but Barbara was now pregnant with their first child and had a complication, which prohibited her from traveling. So, they were looking for a deputy to help Peter with the now large CUSO program in the country. It would mean being based in Kota Kinabalu, Sabah, my old stomping grounds, and frequently traveling to Sarawak and West Malaysia—an attractive offer for me to be back in the country I loved. Beth only wanted to settle down in Ottawa and stay there, after living in, and traveling to, so many different places. But I reminded her of the lines in her poem, as reported in Chapter 4:

> Let this be the gift from my heart—
> And let my life prove it
> Move where you want to
> I will go with you
> Fight for what you will
> And I'll stay by your side.

Now a married man and feeling the need for more security, I decided we should return to Malaysia. CUSO's personnel director wanted an interview with both of us, knowing some marriages can fail when subjected to the stress of living and working in developing countries. I was a bit nervous in the interview, probably because my preference would have been to continue making films. But Beth, having been born and spending part of her childhood in New Guinea, passed our interview with flying colors. In addition to Peter's recommendation, I figure Beth's honest answers probably got me the job.

In February 1973, after only six months in Canada, we flew to Kuala Lumpur, the capital of Malaysia, to begin a new chapter in our lives. There, we were welcomed by Peter and Barbara and I was briefed on my new job. Then I had to take over while they flew off to Canada for medical care.

My time as a CUSO FSO is fully documented in my memoir *Finding Myself in Borneo*, so I won't go into it in detail here. I can't say taking this job was a completely wrong choice, for I have always found whatever choices you make, you usually learn something new, and something about yourself, which leads to personal growth. I liked working with the Malaysian government people I met and scouting new jobs for volunteers, running in-country orientations for new arrivals, supporting volunteers in the field, editing our CUSO in-country newsletter, and rekindling the North Borneo Frodo Society by recruiting new members. But the overall job wasn't exactly my cup of tea. It involved too much paperwork and bureaucracy, as well as counseling unhappy volunteers and sorting out their problems. In university, I had studied psychology and had counseled some gay friends who were in distress, but I had given up that idea of a future for me when I headed to Borneo as a teacher and began to make films.

CUSO's Information Section agreed I should take the filming equipment with me to Malaysia in case they had some work for me to do while based in Asia. It wasn't until late 1973, in Kuala Lumpur, that I had a chance to get my creative juices flowing again, when I had time to complete the film I had started on my visit to Malaysia in 1971, *CUSO in Forestry...Malaysia*.[3] I had to do some more filming of volunteers in the field, more shots of the forest industry, and an introductory sequence, which I set to music. I worked in a studio to complete the editing, happily cutting, splicing, and viewing for hours on end, often losing track of time.

In early 1974, CUSO-Ottawa asked me to travel to Laos to film a silkworm project. CUSO volunteers were assisting in restarting the silk production industry as the war in Indochina began to wind down. A peace treaty had recently been signed between warring factions in Laos, and on April 4, 1974, the Provisional Government of National Union was established. I was there on a street in the capital, Vientiane, the day the communist Pathet Lao (Lao People's Liberation Army) entered the city. As I raised my movie camera with its long zoom lens for a good shot, two soldiers across the street raised their semi-automatic rifles, so I graciously lowered my own imposing "weapon." I don't remember what CUSO did with my footage of the silkworm project, but I have a clear memory of those soldiers and their guns.

From Laos, I traveled to Bangladesh, formerly East Pakistan, a country still recovering from its brutal 1971 war of liberation from rule by Pakistan. Arriving in the capital, Dhaka, I recall being put up in a small hotel where I found it impossible to sleep due to the noise all around me, including frequent calls to prayer broadcast over a loudspeaker system on the mosque right beside my room.

I traveled southeast to Comilla District to film a rural health care extension project, but I don't remember how CUSO used that footage either. I do have an indelible memory of a senior CUSO volunteer driving me around Dhaka. On a lark, he took me to the gates of a prison where there was a small concrete building surrounded by ravens. He flung open the wooden doors and then roared with laughter when a flock of ravens flew off the half-eaten corpse of a former prisoner. It had been placed there for his relatives to collect. I didn't take a photo to commemorate my guide's weird sense of humor.

In mid-1974, Peter and Barbara, with their daughter Janne, left Malaysian and I took over the whole program, based in Kuala Lumpur, while waiting for the next director, Roger Campbell, to arrive and be fully briefed. By December 1974, my second two-year stint in Malaysia was coming to an end and Beth was pregnant with our first child. I didn't want to continue as an FSO, but I wasn't sure what to do next to earn a living for my family. The world closed in on me; I became depressed.

Then a second serendipitous event occurred. A Canadian journalist by the name of Clyde Sanger visited us in Kuala Lumpur. I'd known him from my first stay in Ottawa when I attended some development education film showings. Clyde was now the public affairs head for an interesting international research outfit in Ottawa, which I had heard good things about. He told me his organization may be interested in hiring a filmmaker like me—one who could work economically, taking still photos as well. After he left, I applied in writing and received a warm reply to come and see him when I reached Ottawa. The job was coming together and I was the most likely person for it.

My depression lifted.

PART TWO

JUGGLING FILMMAKING AND HOMEMAKING

Stretching the Earth, and the Filmmaker

On a snowy March day in 1975, I entered the offices of the International Development Research Centre (IDRC) in downtown Ottawa, where I met Clyde Sanger and his division's director, David Spurgeon. Within a couple of days, I was signed on. After most of a two-year pause, I happily went back to full-time filmmaking.

Beth and I rented a small apartment in Lebreton Flats, a working-class neighborhood of Ottawa, just downhill to the west of Ottawa's commercial center. In early June 1975, we managed to put a deposit on a house at 136 Irving Avenue in the Hintonburg neighborhood west of center.

136 Irving Ave, Ottawa –Photo by Neill McKee

It was only 2.3 miles (3.8 km) to IDRC, and I kept in shape walking to work, even in the dead of winter with icicles growing from my mustache and goatee. It was our good luck to find this house located one block away from Crawley Films, where IDRC rented facilities for me, making my commute only one minute on foot when I was editing. For the first year, we kept the tenant who lived on the second floor so we could afford the variable rate mortgage, which floated upward to 19.5 percent—the astonishing cost of inflation in the late 1970s and early 1980s. Nevertheless, this old brick house became our happy home for our years in Ottawa.

IDRC was created in 1970. It's a Canadian public corporation funded annually by a vote in Parliament and is overseen by an international board of governors. It was the brainchild of former Prime Minister Lester Pearson and Maurice Strong, an entrepreneur who also became a United Nations diplomat. These visionaries assembled the board and hired the organization's first president David Hopper, an agricultural economist with a background in the Ford and Rockefeller Foundations in India. The main idea of IDRC was, and remains today, to build the research capacity of developing countries so they can solve their own problems.

When I joined the organization, it was rapidly expanding. By the end of the 1970s, it employed about 500 people of multiple nationalities in Ottawa and offices in almost every region of the world. IDRC was loaded with Ph.D.s in social science, education, agriculture and nutrition, as well as M.D.s and public health specialists. Quite a few other former CUSO volunteers had also joined the organization. Dr. Hopper made it clear to employees that we were not civil servants, a classification which would make hiring and employment contracts too rigid, although we all earned civil service pensions and other benefits.

STRETCHING THE EARTH, AND THE FILMMAKER

The organization's program divisions then included Agriculture, Food, and Nutrition Sciences; Population and Health Sciences; Social Sciences; and Information Sciences. The Communications Division, in which I was housed, supported all these program divisions through the production of scientific and corporate publications, as well as popular accounts on IDRC's work through the quarterly magazine *IDRC Reports*, and in newspapers and magazines.

IDRC has its own hiring procedures, which circumvent a lot of the government's red tape. I was hired without even a competition for my job. If IDRC was forced to apply typical civil service job descriptions to my post, it would have had to be broken down into at least five separate functions: photographer, cinematographer, sound recordist, film editor, and production supervisor. The organization never could have afforded such a team. I was not given a job description—just asked to get on with it. So that's what I did. On my advice, IDRC purchased CUSO's 16mm movie camera and sound equipment, still in my possession, and after familiarizing myself by studying descriptions and reports on the most interesting and photogenic research projects, on June 22, 1975, I was off to Latin America and the Caribbean, a part of the globe I had never seen before.

During the next seven weeks, I shot sequences for a general film on IDRC's work, and took 35mm still photos to expand our collection. Susanna Amaya and Jaime Rojas from our regional office in Bogota, Colombia, took turns joining me for various parts of the Latin America portion of the trip, acting as my interpreters. Jaime also took some stills and assisted in sound recording, when needed.

We were asked to write trip reports and I became good at that, detailing my travels, sometimes in an entertaining way.

Luckily, I saved these over the years and through our many moves. I found Latin Americans to be warm and welcoming. Most people addressed me by adding the honorific "Doctor" to my name, although I only had a B.A. We started in Mexico and made our way south through Guatemala, Costa Rica, Panama, Colombia, and Venezuela; then I continued by myself to Trinidad, Guyana, and Haiti. I took background film sequences and photos of people in cities and rural areas going about their daily activities. I also taped interviews with researchers for film script material and filmed and photographed them in labs and in the field, as they carried out:

- research in Mexico on sorghum and triticale, the latter a wheat-rye hybrid, then touted as a "miracle" grain of the future;
- experiments in Guatemala with coffee pulp by-products as cattle fodder, (Quite naturally, the coffee pulp made the beasts pee a lot!);
- studies in Colombia and Venezuela on the best models for improved low-cost housing and other services for slum dwellers;
- research in Colombia on cassava, also called manioc (*yuca* in Spanish), a root crop grown in almost all regions of the tropics, from which a starch is extracted known as "tapioca" in English;
- investigations in Trinidad on appropriate biological crop pest control methods—an alternative to pesticides;
- saving and processing fish by-catch caught in nets while trawling for shrimp off the coast of Guyana; and
- a study on the effects of a comprehensive rural development scheme near Cáqueza, Colombia.

STRETCHING THE EARTH, AND THE FILMMAKER

Children near Cáqueza, Colombia – Photo by Neill McKee/IDRC

The most memorable portions of the trip were visits to the health care delivery projects in Haiti, Venezuela, and Panama, especially in the latter two countries. Before I left Canada, I had already begun talking to Dr. John Gill, who would soon become the director of the Population and Health Sciences Division, and Dr. Yolande Mousseau-Gershman, about doing a film on rural health workers to accompany the 1975 IDRC monograph titled *Doctors and Healers*.[1] It describes the interesting concept of "barefoot doctors," a movement started in China during the 1960s. It spread to many different countries and was further popularized in the 1977 book *Where There Is No Doctor* by David Werner.[2] The main idea was that, around the world, doctors and health ministries were setting up big hospitals and research facilities with expensive equipment, and focusing on curative rather than preventative medicine and community health care. Establishing these high-tech institutions made doctors, bureaucrats, and pharmaceutical companies richer, while they neglected people living in rural areas or urban slums, who had little or no access to such facilities due to physical or monetary barriers.

When I arrived in Panama, I rolled my camera to document a revolutionary project. At the time, the country had about 9,000 small and scattered communities, making it difficult to deliver health care to most of the population. I concentrated on Marciane Jurado, a health worker in the Province of Colón, on the isolated and poorer Pacific Ocean side of the country. With only basic training, she monitored the growth rate of children; organized community health meetings to formulate plans of action; gave advice to villagers on food and nutrition; and addressed sanitation and hygiene problems, as well as clean water supplies. She and 39 other rural health workers, at the time, had become an integral part of the provincial health team. The system continued to expand, thereafter.

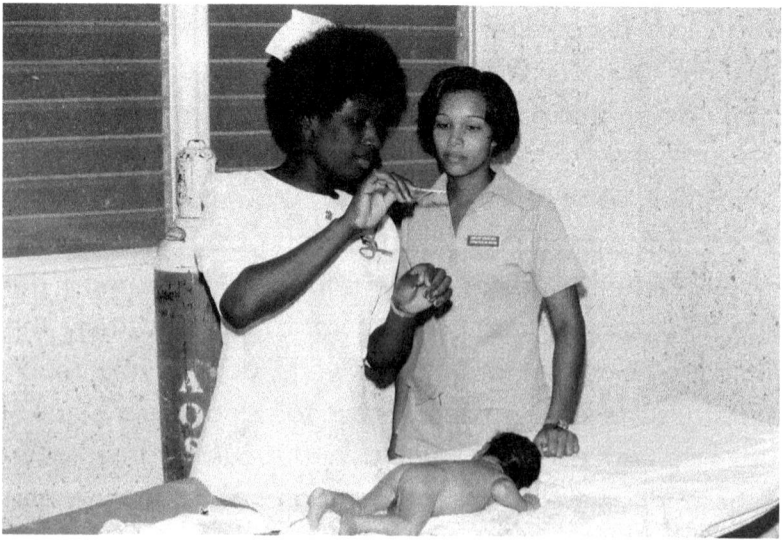

Marciane Jurado in training –Photo by Neill McKee/IDRC

STRETCHING THE EARTH, AND THE FILMMAKER

This pilot project was the brainchild of Dr. Hugo Spadafora Franco, an Italian-Panamanian physician and former guerrilla fighter. But political turmoil in the country eventually led to his murder, in 1985, by the American-backed government of Manuel Noriega. Despite this, improvements in health continued in Colón Province, where the infant mortality rate dropped from 81.4 per thousand live births in 1960 to 13.5 in 2003, beating the national average.[3] I'm sure there were many causal factors, but giving communities more responsibility in—and ownership of—their health care delivery was likely a major factor.

On our visit to Venezuela, we flew south from Caracas to Puerto Ayacucho on the Oronoco River in the Amazonas Region. From there we joined a health team and made our way over rough roads to a small village 60 miles (97 km) upriver to film Omanyo Prato. He was an Amerindian medical auxiliary who traveled by dugout canoe, powered by a 30 HP outboard motor, to reach scattered communities living in large thatched grass houses along the river bank. He had received only six months of training and worked alone, taking and checking malaria swabs, offering basic medicines, and giving health and hygiene talks to the people. Only the worst cases were transferred to the regional hospital at Puerto Ayacucho, a long boat trip through many dangerous rapids in crocodile-infested waters. Movement is always more dramatic on film, so I followed him in another boat to get the shots I wanted. Fortunately, we stayed afloat and met no crocodiles.

At the time, this project was promising. But Venezuela gradually descended into political and social chaos, while infant mortality rates increased, and many other health indicators declined. Today, the Amerindian population continues to grow, but remains at the bottom of a heap of broken promises. At least I caught, on celluloid, a much happier time when it seemed the indigenous people of the Oronoco had a chance for a brighter future.

Omanyo Prato delivering health services to his people
—Photos by Neill McKee/IDRC

After six weeks on the road, I returned to Ottawa on August 10th, and just in time. Beth was about to give birth to our first child. Like an empathetic modern husband, before leaving on my travels I had attended evening classes, practicing rhythmic breathing. The idea was to breathe along with Beth during contractions, to help her overcome the pain. But when the day of reckoning came, after six hours in our local hospital, breathing deeply and pushing, Beth finally gave up and accepted an epidural. Our son Derek was born soon afterward and Beth fell asleep with him cradled in her arms, while I watched over them.

Beth has always been a plan-ahead person, and she knew the delivery of hospital food followed a strict schedule, so she had packed two hard-boiled eggs to eat as soon as she could after giving birth, to help restore her strength. She'd missed dinner and looked forward to those eggs when she woke. Unfortunately, I was so exhausted from my recent long trip, and all that breathing, I ate them during her slumber. At least those were my excuses, although not justifiable according to Beth. As I recall, I went out immediately to look for hard-boiled eggs but came back empty-handed. Most stores were closed and she had to settle for some toast. To this day, Beth continues to mention my sin in conversations with friends. Fortunately, our marriage didn't end over a couple of eggs and we had a healthy son to raise together.

I write "together," but six weeks later I was back on the road—this time to West Africa. I was accompanied by Bob Stanley, our senior writer. We began in Dakar, Senegal, the location of IDRC's West Africa Regional Office. Bob was an easy-going companion throughout the trip. His French was better than mine, so he acted as an interpreter in Senegal and Mali, formerly colonies of France. My method was the same as on the previous trip, covering all I could in 16mm film and photos:

- improving sorghum cultivation and small farmer grain storage methods at an agriculture research station in and around the town of Bambey, Senegal;
- research on resolving rural land tenure issues near Kaolack, Senegal;
- recording the beginnings of an oyster culture pilot project near Freetown, Sierra Leone;
- documenting family planning improvements in Bamako, Mali.

Malian women at a family planning clinic
–Photo by Neill McKee/IDRC

Our trip went smoothly except for an unlucky incident. One late afternoon a week into our travels, our driver from the IDRC office in Dakar, a Muslim man we all called "Pap,"

STRETCHING THE EARTH, AND THE FILMMAKER

was in a hurry to get home from our final rural location. He explained the youngest of his four wives was about to deliver his latest offspring and I, as a new father, had empathy for him. IDRC's Deputy Regional Director, Tim Dottridge, had told us he was a trustworthy driver, and Pap, a hefty man, stood about six-foot-five (almost two meters), so who could argue with him about our speed on a gravel road? Suddenly, our Toyota Range Rover hit an ungraded washboard patch as we rounded a curve, and the wheels lost traction. The vehicle glided sideways and hit a small bank on the opposite side of the road. Then we went flying into the scrub bush, turning upside down and landing back on all four wheels.

Fortunately, I had just told Bob, sitting in the front seat, to buckle up his seatbelt a couple of minutes before the accident. I had mine on and also had the habit of holding my camera equipment on my lap over rough roads. We all miraculously escaped injury—only a few scratches. Pap and Bob got out to inspect the situation. They discovered one flat tire, but the jack was nowhere to be seen. Probably it had flown into the bushes and it was growing dark. I remained in the vehicle, testing all my equipment, and thankfully found no damage. But there we were, stuck in the middle of nowhere, about 60 miles (97 km) from Dakar, among thorn trees.

Pap was distraught but not defeated. He went out along the road and soon returned, accompanied by a whole group of villagers with a long hardwood pole, which they used to lift the heavy vehicle to change the flat tire. Then Pap proposed we should slowly drive back to Dakar in the wounded vehicle, which no longer had a windshield or windows. Bob and I glanced at each other and opted to hitchhike back to Dakar. We were soon picked up by a fellow in a small truck. Unfortunately, he drove at the same speed as Pap, even on curves. Fortunately, we all made it back to Dakar that evening. I remember hoping Pap would at least learn a lesson about washboard-type gravel roads, which I knew a thing or two about from my youthful days of driving in rural Ontario.

Bob and I had intended to cover some projects in Nigeria. But the regional office had asked the Canadian High Commission in Lagos to seek permission to film. I knew this had made it a government-to-government affair, and that approval would be difficult and delayed. After my earlier experience in Nigeria, when filming for CUSO in 1971 (see Chapter 2), I was not disappointed to miss returning to that country, but knew I'd have to make it up to cover IDRC projects there on a later trip. Bob and I returned from West Africa on October 20th.

It was great to be back with Beth and our infant son Derek. He was now seven weeks old and could focus his eyes on his father. I spent as much time with him and Beth as possible, while sneaking over to the studio to see the results of my filming, and going to the office to start the photo sorting. Then, in less than a month I was off again, this time to Egypt and East Africa with Clyde Sanger, the man who had hired me. In formal terms, he was my supervisor but he was the most informal non-hierarchical boss I ever had. We traveled well together for five weeks through Egypt, Ethiopia, Kenya, Malawi, and Tanzania, gathering film footage and photos, as well as information for stories Clyde wrote for our quarterly, *IDRC Reports*, and English language newspapers in the capitals of the countries we visited. He knew most of the editors and senior journalists.

Arriving in Cairo on November 15th at 4:00 am, a pre-arranged car and driver took us to Alexandria, where I filmed and photographed a university-based research program on restoring old shelterbelts and planting new ones.

An Egyptian farmer ploughing next to casuarina shelterbelts
–Photo by Neill McKee/IDRC

In this case, the shelterbelts were rows of casuarina trees, which were planted alongside farmland to protect crops from heavy winds. On the Nile Delta, they help to keep back invading sands from the Sahara Desert. I took shots of farmers plowing fertile land beside rows of more mature trees, as well as nursery operations and planting of seedlings.

Returning to Cairo by train, we boarded a flight to Addis Ababa, Ethiopia, foregoing a visit to the pyramids. We were purposeful travelers, not tourists. On arrival in Addis Ababa, we were immediately invited to the Canadian Ambassador's house for lunch. We had informed the embassy of our coming, but were surprised by this invite. We surmised the man was lonely because few people visited the country. A drought and famine in 1972 led to the ousting of Emperor Haile Selassie in 1974, by General Mengistu Mariam, who ran the country through the so-called "Derg," a socialist-military *junta*. Few western countries wanted to help his Soviet-leaning government, but IDRC was independent enough to remain loyal to the scientists and research it was supporting.

One of the reasons for the famine was that, for thousands of years, Ethiopians have eaten *teff*—pronounced properly by practically spitting out the "t"—a very small grain. It's loved for its taste, especially in the form of *injera,* a fermented flatbread with a slightly spongy texture. But the problem with this staple food is that it kept Ethiopians poor and hungry because up to 50 percent of *teff's* minuscule grains were lost before and during harvest. For a few years IDRC had been sponsoring projects on collecting and cross-breeding sorghum, another native African drought-resistant plant with larger seeds, which don't blow away in the wind and are easy to recover if they do drop to the ground.

We traveled by road to Alem Maya and Dire Dawa, over 300 miles (500 km) east of Addis Ababa, to film and photograph sorghum research. I captured on film the dry landscape, with high ridges and deep valleys.

STRETCHING THE EARTH, AND THE FILMMAKER

Village and landscape near Dire Dawa, Ethiopia
—Photo by Neill McKee/IDRC

A typical house near Dire Dawa, Ethiopia —Photo by Neill McKee/IDRC

Mrs. Brhane displaying her injera —Photo by Neill McKee/IDRC

Dr. Brhane and an assistant looking over new sorghum varieties —Photo by Neill McKee/IDRC

Dr. Brhane, our project leader, and Dr. Melak, Dean of Agriculture at the university, ensured we filmed typical village life, including processing and cooking sorghum in the form of *injera*. I recall tasting a sample made by Mrs. Brhane, which she served in the traditional way—a pile of spicy meat with sauce placed in the middle of the large pancake. All of us dug in with our hands.

Dr. Melak took us to the ancient walled city of Harar, further south, where for the past 500 years the inhabitants have sanitized the city by feeding its organic refuse to hyenas. That evening, we witnessed one of the famous hyena men sharing pieces of meat with a hyena, teeth-to-teeth, while I snapped photos, or so I thought. I had not properly attached the roll of film to the crank handle, so the film never advanced—the first and last time that happened in my career! I blamed this lapse on the excitement and fear the beast induced in me, especially when Dr. Malek fed the hyena with his hands.

Clyde and I documented what was being done to establish sorghum's proper place in Ethiopian diets. It takes a long time to change human eating habits, but today, in Ethiopia, sorghum is the third most important cereal crop after *teff* and maize. It is a staple food millions of poorer Ethiopians depend on, especially in drier areas of their country. It's used for foods such as *injera*, bread, porridge, infant food, a snack called *Nifro,* and local beverages known as *Tella* and *Areke*. Also, the leaves and stalks are used for animal fodder and cooking fuel, while the stalks can be employed for the construction of houses and fences. The work IDRC supported in the 70s and 80s, was instrumental in this success.

Next, we flew to Nairobi, Kenya, where IDRC's Eastern Africa Office is based. Clyde had been a journalist in Nairobi in the 1960s and knew his way around. He managed all the permissions we needed through his friends in the Minister of Information. The Regional Director, Tony Price, and his deputy, Trevor Chandler (the former CUSO bee biologist I'd filmed on the slopes of Kilimanjaro in 1972, as described in Chapter 6), facilitated our visits to film and photograph several Kenya projects:

- research on breeding disease-resistant strains of triticale;
- a pilot project using eucalyptus trees to prevent soil erosion;
- a community-based gravity water supply scheme to reduce the daily workload of women and girls, who have the main burden of delivering water to households in Africa.

A community-based gravity water scheme built by villagers in Kenya
–Photo by Neill McKee/IDRC

In addition, we visited the International Livestock Research Institute (ILRI) to film and photograph research on

Researchers at ILRI studying trypanosomiasis
—Photo by Neill McKee/IDRC

preventing various animal diseases, including trypanosomiasis (sleeping sickness), caused by bites from tsetse flies that have been infected by a parasite of the genus *Trypanosoma*.

Trypanosomiasis can be fatal to all vertebrates, including humans. Infections in wild animals easily transmit to domestic animals, leading to their sickness and death. Domestic animals are like a bank for small farmers—an investment they depend on for protein and income. This time, I had an excuse for filming African animals in the wild and in captivity, for they act as a reservoir for the type of trypanosomiasis (*Trypanosoma brucei gambiense*) most harmful to humans. It starts with severe headaches and insomnia, enlarged lymph nodes, anemia, and a rash. Later stages involve progressive loss of weight and damage to the central nervous system. Without treatment, the disease is invariably fatal.

During our stay in Kenya, I had a chance to see parts of the country from the air, flying with researchers to a sheep ranch, then driving to the land of the famous Masai tribesmen to film cattle being inoculated and dipped in a bath of insecticide to help prevent transmission. Clyde and I wanted to film tsetse flies in action, infecting humans. After many failed attempts, we caught two in a forest near the border with Tanzania, using Clyde's bare arm as bait. Somehow, we managed to get the little beasts into a brown paper bag, and carried them with us across Kenya, until they were good and hungry. Then we released them in my hotel room and I got some good shots of them gorging on Clyde—anything for science!

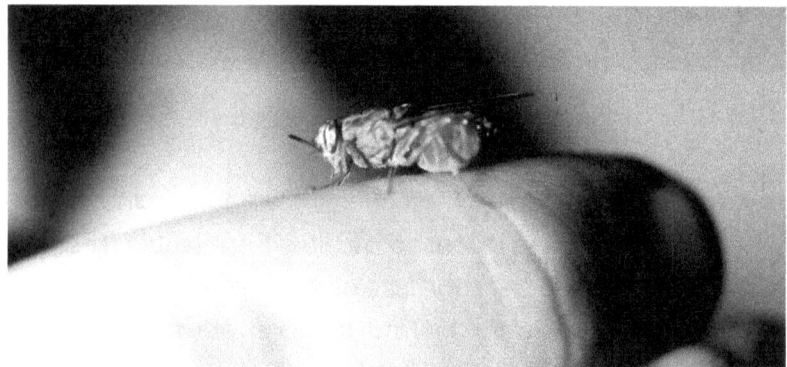

Tsetse fly filled with Clyde Sanger's blood —Photo by Neill McKee/IDRC

Clyde before being bitten —Photographer unknown

STRETCHING THE EARTH, AND THE FILMMAKER

Flashing forward, trypanosomiasis, which caused devastating epidemics, is now a rare human disease due to international coordination on tracking, diagnosis, and treatment, although it continues to infect wild and domestic animals.[4] Much progress has been made, but the struggle continues.

We also had photographed the beginnings of a project on triticale in Ethiopia and were interested to see how longer-running trials were working out in Kenya. Earlier in the year, I had filmed IDRC-supported research on triticale in Mexico, and I wanted to record the process of adaptation to Africa. It's a perfect crop for Africa's periodic droughts and the fragile state of African soils, which are severely and continually degraded by desertification, leaching, and erosion.

When writing this book, I found that African farmers rarely adopted the cultivation of triticale, whereas utilization and harvests in Mexico and other parts of the world increased exponentially: 167,000 metric tons by 1980 and 14 million metric tons by 2013.[5] Sometimes in some places research pays off, sometimes in other places it doesn't.

Ethiopian researcher and farmer inspecting a triticale trial on his land
—Photo by Neill McKee/IDRC

Likewise, sometimes our arrangements worked, sometimes they didn't. We flew to Blantyre, Malawi, to film a water gravity scheme on Mount Mulanje, the place I had filmed the McNeil family on an outing in 1972, when I was making films for CUSO (see Chapter 6). On arrival, we found out another film crew had recently covered the project, and the government had clamped down on such permissions, so we failed to achieve our objective. Clyde, who had sensed it might not be possible, had organized the filming of the similar scheme in Kenya, briefly listed and pictured above.

People in Malawi evidently had become more and more paranoid since my visit in 1972. Dr. Banda, the anti-communist president, had spies everywhere. Our contact, a British expat giving technical assistance to the water project, was terrified when we showed up without filming permission. He was even more paranoid about an IDRC health bibliography he'd received in the mail. It was in English, but the cover was designed in cardinal red with some Chinese characters because many of the sources within came from China. It was as if IDRC had sent him a copy of *Quotations From Chairman Mao Tse-Tung*—the famous "Little Red Book." He gave the bibliography back, asking us to take it off his hands. We laughed at his gesture, but he didn't appreciate our levity on the matter. We gladly took the book from him, but wondered why he had not simply shredded or burned it.

Next, we made a brief visit to Dar-es-salaam, Tanzania, a country that had no problem with information or lessons from China. President Nyerere, a socialist, remained in power. We covered an experimental intercropping program, an adult education class, and an attempt to adapt a compost toilet model from Indochina, which kills bacteria and parasites in human feces with solar radiation. The objective was to use the output as manure—a pretty "far out" attempt, I thought. How could you convince Africans to carry their own feces and dump them on their fields?

We arrived home on December 22nd, just in time for Christmas celebrations, but my son, Derek, didn't have a clue who I was, for I had been gone for most of his short life.

Candles more fascinating than strange people
–Photo by Beth McKee

We took Derek to Elmira, to see his McKee grandparents, and then to Iowa in early January 1976, where he was baptized "Derek Daniel McKee" by his maternal grandfather, Rev. Diemer, who was on home leave from Papua New Guinea. Beth remained a Lutheran and I was doing my fatherly duty. Rev. Diemer and I never discussed my religious beliefs. I'd first met him, in Iowa, during Christmas of 1972, before Beth and I moved to Malaysia, and I thought it was wise not to bring up the subject of religion.

On our return to Ottawa, I prepared for my longest trip of all, crossing the Pacific Ocean to Asia and continuing around the world through Iran and West Africa. Fortunately, the journey was broken in the middle by a visit from Beth and Derek, who flew to Singapore to join me, courtesy of IDRC, while I covered projects there and in Malaysia and Thailand. At the time, the organization had a rule that if an employee traveled for work over 100 days in a year, it would cover the cost of the spouse going on the next business trip. By then my son was getting the hang of things and not playing strange as much when the funny man with a dark mustache and goatee popped up, even on the other side of the world.

I had a daunting task to achieve in Asia, due to the expectations expressed by Nihal Kappagoda, IDRC Regional Director. Besides agriculture, aquaculture, health, and family planning research, I was asked to cover new studies in slum rehabilitation, resettlement projects that provided sites and services—fancy words for water supply and toilets—and low-cost housing and transport for the massive influx of Asian populations from rural areas to cities. Rather than providing a tedious list, let me express my work during those weeks in a less detailed, more entertaining way:

> Arriving in Singapore, Nihal assembled his legion,
> who fired off cables to project leaders in the region.
> Then I flew to the Philippines to cover small-scale
> industries, cropping systems, milkfish aquaculture,
> and other fisheries. Not to forget plant varietal screening and processing of beans, jeepney transportation,
> improving slums, and resettlement schemes.
>
> Next to Hong Kong for low-cost housing and an information center, then to Indonesia for research on making village life better. More on transportation by trishaws and three-wheel scooters, cassava processing for

use in various animal fodders. Back to Singapore to meet my wife and son, and to rest a few days halfway through my run.

Then to Malaysia but with no time for browsing, while filming family planning and low-cost housing. A visit to a cassava microbiological project organized, and then to another one on rural water supplies. But gladly in Kuala Lumpur, we toured old haunts, and dined at some of our favorite restaurants.

Next to Khon Kaen, Thailand, to cover health volunteers—villagers trained to deliver basic services to their peers. In Bangkok, a national youth corps, and boating on klongs, for shots of slums, temples, factories, and fish ponds. Then a nutrition project and contraception distribution, ending on affordable transport, and another housing solution.

Some scenes I filmed: low cost transport and housing, plus a rural health worker in training —Photos by Neill McKee/IDRC

MY UNIVERSITY OF THE WORLD

From Bangkok, Beth and Derek flew back to Singapore to pick up two daughters of a Chinese-Malaysian family, the Yaps—friends from Sabah, whom we had helped to emigrate to Canada. It was an exhausting trip for Beth because Derek hardly slept until he got home. I continued on my mission, traveling to Bangladesh to film a rural health project in Companyganj, a sub-district southeast of Dhaka, and then to Teknaf, at the very southern tip of the country. I was accompanied by Dr. Mujibur Rahman from the International Centre for Diarrhoeal Disease Research, Bangladesh. There, I filmed the operations of his new *Shigella* dysentery project.

Bangladesh researcher surveying woman in Companyganj –Photo by Neill McKee/IDRC

From Bangladesh I flew to Hyderabad, India, to cover an agriculture project, and then headed to Tehran, Iran, where I caught a flight to Shiraz, Fars Province, in the south-central part of the country. There I met Dr. Hussein Ranaghy, a visionary medical doctor based at Pahlavi University. He was training female primary health workers to focus on children's respiratory diseases in the winter, and diarrheal diseases in the summer. They also monitored children's nutrition and growth, delivered advice on feeding and hygiene, inspected water supplies throughout the year, and gave talks on health in schools. In 1976, there were 12,000 doctors in Iran for a population of 33 million, with half of them in the capital, Tehran, and most of the rest in other cities or large towns.

Iranian rural health workers in action
—Photos by Neill McKee/IDRC

I focused on Mrs. Bonar, one of 46 such health workers in the area. Their services were linked with a cadre called *bedar*—health technicians who could deal with 90 percent of cases referred to them, sending only 10 percent to physicians, including new graduates doing obligatory national service in small towns all over the country. Only a small percentage of patients ended up in hospitals.

This seemed like a very well-designed, forward-looking system—the sign of an advanced and organized ancient culture. I had time to visit and photograph Persepolis, situated 37 miles (60 km) to the southwest of Shiraz, ruins which date back to 515 B.C.E. This was, unfortunately, my only visit to Iran, for less than two years later, the Islamic Revolution began. At the time of my visit, Mrs. Bonar, dressed in a white doctor's coat with only a kerchief on her head, was training a younger woman to take over from her. Some of the younger women didn't wear head scarves. I never did learn if the project was stopped by the repressive government that took over. Were these women forced to remain at home?

By this time on my long journey, I had reached a saturation point. But I wanted to finish my travels and start editing the film footage and sort out all the photos, so I decided to soldier on, as planned, to Nigeria, where I encountered a series of late and canceled flights. I did manage to film and photograph research on a special sorghum and millet mill and test kitchen in Maiduguri, a city in the northeast; then I flew south to the International Institute of Tropical Agriculture in Ibadan, where I took sequences on plant breeding experiments to prevent cassava being infected by a blight disease, and the making of more nutritious food products with cassava flour (tapioca), known locally as *gari*.

From Nigeria, I flew to Senegal, where I found myself driving northward along rural roads with Pap, the driver who had crashed IDRC's Range Rover with Bob Stanley and me, only six months earlier. The vehicle had been restored and Pap had not been fired. Thankfully, Pap had learned to slow down on washboard gravel roads. We were laughing about our previous misadventure, me communicating with him in my basic French, when suddenly Pap halted the vehicle, looking this way and that, and muttering under his breath. We were lost in the Sahel. But this new challenge led us to the site of Fulani tribesmen at a well with a massive congregation of their cattle and goats—a spectacular sight to film.

Fulani tribesmen with their herds —Photo by Neill McKee/IDRC

We finally arrived at Mbidi Forestry Station to cover rangeland reforestation research, using various species of trees, which would hold the soil in place and increase rainfall—attempts at developing a more humid micro-climate in an increasingly parched landscape. I also filmed and photographed the harvesting of gum arabic from *Acacia senegal* trees—a valuable sap used as a stabilizer in foods and soft drinks, as well as an ingredient in traditional printing, paints, glues, cosmetics, and other industrial applications.

Not to be outdone by such a practical conclusion to my extensive travels, the workers at Mbidi organized a more entertaining ending, when I had a chance to film a tribal dance, complete with prancing camels. Afterwards, we feasted on goat legs roasted over a fire, and then I fell asleep on a simple mat in the open air, while gazing up at a majestic display of stars over the Sahel.

My travels were over, for the present. By the time I reached Ottawa, according to the trip reports I wrote and kept all these years, I had visited 77 project sites in 26 countries, and had survived 104 takeoffs and landings, plus one car crash. Clyde wrote the script for my first IDRC film and we decided to give it the title, *Stretching the Earth*.[6] He also wrote an article for our magazine on my travels during the past 10 months, which he titled *Stretching the Filmmaker*.

Healthy Filmmaking at Home and Hearth

I recall the remainder of 1976 and most of 1977 as a wonderful period for me and my family. We gave our upstairs tenant notice, took over all of our old house, and I finally had time to make some improvements on weekends. The upstairs kitchen served as Derek's bedroom, furnished with a handy much-needed sink for infant care. Our backyard with its tall cedar hedge became our private park and picnic place, where Derek could practice his walking skills. With warmer weather, Beth made inroads in the community, meeting other women with their young children in parks, gradually forming a playgroup, which gathered in a nearby community center, where they met on rainy days and in the winter. This was exactly the kind of home she had been seeking. She wanted nothing more than to settle down here for the rest of her life. She applied for and became a Canadian citizen in October 1976, in a ceremony with a judge and a Royal Canadian unmounted policeman—so Canadian, eh?

Beth had gladly left the United States in 1970, shortly after the Kent State University massacre, when Ohio National Guardsmen killed four and wounded nine unarmed students as they protested America's involvement in the Vietnam War, and its expansion into Cambodia and Laos. She was overjoyed at becoming a Canadian, and so quickly.

We also reconnected with former Malaysia CUSO volunteers, now making a living by working for international

Beth becoming a Canadian –Photo by Neill McKee

development organizations in Ottawa. Peter and Barbara Hoffman, whom we worked and sometimes stayed with during my second Malaysian sojourn, had bought a house about 10 minutes from us by car, and were juggling jobs and raising their two children, Janne and Chris. With such people nearby and new friends, I figured Beth would never be left completely alone while I was away.

I recruited Hélène, a spunky young French-Canadian woman, who quickly learned the ropes and got down to work running the photo library and projecting films and slide shows for visitors in our beautiful little theater. This allowed me to spend more time at the studio, cranking out films. Besides our global 22-minute film, *Stretching the Earth*, with the help of my colleagues, we produced several regional briefing films: *Common Task*[1] for Latin America, *Continent in the Making*[2] for Africa, and *Asia: The Search for Solutions*.[3] We also made French and Spanish language versions for use in Canada, West Africa, and Latin America. I continued to hire the services of my editor friend Sally MacDonald, when needed.

I was keen on fully utilizing the footage I had taken on rural health systems in Panama, Venezuela, Thailand, Bangladesh, and Iran during my marathon travels. But the Health Science Division decided we should include an initiative in Canada as well, which wasn't funded by IDRC. In February 1977, during our usual deep freeze in Ottawa, I flew to Regina, Saskatchewan, into an even colder arctic chill, to do a sequence for the film. At Regina airport, I rented a car to drive to Qu'Appelle Valley, 30 miles (48 km) to the north. As I entered the Piapot Indian Reserve, now called Piapot First Nation, I looked down on a small group of buildings in the wilderness and wondered, *What could the Cree people be doing here "Now that the Buffalo's Gone*," as Buffy Sainte-Marie sings. In 1941, she had been born into poverty on this reserve before being adopted by Albert and Winifred Sainte-Marie of Massachusetts.

When the Cree leaders and the Government of Canada started the new health system here in 1964, they were wise enough to understand health is not just an isolated part of someone's life. They wanted to develop a broad educational approach, which covered everything, from how and where people placed houses and found a source for clean water, to the quality of their daily foods. I interviewed and filmed Eugenie Lavalie, an elderly health worker who had joined the system shortly after it began. She had recently retired but had trained a younger woman, Violet Piapot, to take over. I filmed Violet weighing children and keeping health records on each child in the community, visiting the local primary school to give health talks, and assisting the supervisory nurse from Fort Qu'Appelle with immunizations.

In my interview with Eugenie, she talked about the holistic approach she took to health care, involving the community in each step. Reflecting on her years of service, she said, "I used to go by seasons: accidents in the winter, and in the spring it was X-rays for TB, and stuff like that, and clean-up. In July, it was gardens and in August judging of the gardens—everything pertaining to health is what I worked on."

When I returned to Ottawa, I completed the editing and production of a film we titled *Rural Health Workers*,[4] using the Saskatchewan footage, along with that from the five similar projects I had visited. Through this work, I came to understand the importance of expanding the delivery of basic health services to millions of people in places where few doctors will go. IDRC funded pilot projects, which were at the forefront of this movement.

This wasn't my first IDRC film on health. One of the first assignments I had been given, after I joined IDRC, was to edit a lengthy film made by a university in Thailand. It involved training traditional village midwives in modern sanitary low-risk methods of delivery and newborn care. We titled this 15-minute production *Pâa-noi, The Village Midwife*.[5]

Later, I received a similar request. The Health Sciences Division tasked me with re-edited two long anthropological films on traditional psychiatric medicine in Zaire (now called the Democratic Republic of the Congo). One was on rural traditional healers and the other documented an urban healing group. My job was to make them into a single shorter production.

The urban film focused on communal rituals, which helped rural-urban migrants, especially women, adjust to life in Kinshasa, the capital city. Psychiatric ailments were blamed on spirits. The urban film caught my eye as the

HEALTHY FILMMAKING AT HOME AND HEARTH

most exotic, involving plastering women with ochre cream, black and white lines, and the wearing of knotted bracelets and bells. I retained some of the traditional dances to drum music, which ran through the original production. Patients in therapy were never cut off from their families and carried on with regular duties, like shopping in markets and cooking. Those who wanted to become healers, themselves, had to perfect their dancing, mimicking the movement of larvae, which they also had to swallow as these creatures crept across palm leaves.

The rural film documented a traditional hospital at a village called Mbindo-Lala, in the south-central part of the country. It was run by a couple—a woman by the name of Congo and a man named Enzongo. They had not been able to conceive a child, after they married, and they searched for cures from western medicine, to no avail. Finally, they visited a traditional healer, who identified the spirit that was blocking their fertility. They learned the healing craft, themselves, and established this village hospital 25 years earlier. Patients came from near and far with family members and lived normal lives while undergoing treatment. In the village there were altars for forest spirits, river spirits, and most importantly, ancestor spirits, to help people reconnect with family members, from whom they had been separated due to conflict or tragedy.

I found the testimony of a teenage student by the name of Ndanda compelling and kept it in the film. He suffered from headaches and sleeplessness. He visited regular hospitals and they tested and treated him for parasites, with no improvement. Finally, he came to live in the village hospital and was treated with some of their 100 herbal recipes. In the interview, he claimed his problem turned out to be the jealousy of other students, which was conjured through water spirits. I retained the sequence of him lying on the ground and being covered with palm leaves to reconcile his relationship with these jealous students. But he's not ready. The leaves start to shake and he finally jumps up and runs into the river. There are other scenes of patients who are ready, but they must first perform a special dance in front of the whole community before they are declared cured and leave the village with their families.

The healers appear to read information in a mirror while talking to patients, but are really digging for the causes of their trauma. This seemed no different than western psychotherapy to me—just let people talk through their problems. Western medicine brought by missionaries had failed these people. Performing these rituals amongst the community and family members provided an avenue for healing. We titled this 25-minute film *A Message from African Healers*.[6] It emphasized the psychosocial part of healing, so often ignored by western medicine.

While editing, I managed to retain most of the background sounds from the sound track of the original film. But the sound in one dramatic scene of a dark woman was damaged. I showed the sequence to Beth and asked her if she could reproduce the sound of this African woman suddenly jumping up from a bench, shouting in great distress, while flailing her arms and legs for half a minute. We recorded this in our basement and I matched the sound in the editing room. Beth's frantic screams were convincing.

Our friend Barbara Hoffman, who had previously done radio announcements with her smooth and mellow voice, narrated the film. One evening we showed the finished film to the Hoffmans and when it came to the scene of that agitated woman, I said, "That's Beth screaming!" and all the adults laughed.

A few days later, Barbara's young son Chris commented to his mother, "I didn't know Beth used to be black."

Besides films on health, I received a more challenging request from the Information Science Division. They wanted me to make a film on the worldwide agriculture information system, which IDRC supported. In May 1977, I traveled to Costa Rica, Colombia, and Venezuela for this purpose. Jaime Rojas of our Bogota office assisted me. Fortunately, my division had just purchased a synchronized camera and sound system for me, one of several filming packages first acquired by the Canadian Broadcasting Corporation (CBC) for use in covering the 1976 Summer Olympics, in Montreal. Here was my chance to try out my Éclair 16mm camera and high-quality compact Stellavox tape recorder.

To enliven the film, I opened and closed with an end user of the information, a subsistence farmer in rural Colombia plowing fields with his cattle and talking to an extension agent. My new filming technology brought the scene alive. The four parts of an agricultural information system: researcher, planner, extension agent, and end user, were emphasized in our 14-minute film. In *Thought For Food*[7] I outlined that these four linked participants are the basis for success in agriculture. In fact, that's true for any development discipline, including health and social sciences.

For this film, I employed basic animation to demonstrate agriculture information dissemination between the subnational, national, regional, and global levels—all while seeking to avoid duplication of efforts. Without animation and the inclusion of the farmer, my film would have been

A farmer ploughing his fields —Photo by Neill McKee/IDRC

The author with his new filming equipment
—Photo by Jaime Rojas/IDRC

totally boring—only meetings, printing presses, documents, libraries, and rooms of those now ancient computers with magnetic tapes running and spitting out paper records.

I arrived home from Latin America in the first week of June, and just in time, for our daughter, Ruth, was about to pop into the world. I write "pop" because Beth's water broke at home and I had to frantically find a babysitter and rush her to the hospital. She was wheeled up to the delivery area while moaning through contractions. There was no way to use those breathing exercises this time, for I peeked under the covers and shouted to the nurses, "Hey, I see the baby's head coming out!"

The hospital staff ran over to take a look and immediately wheeled Beth into the delivery room. It only took one or two pushes and Ruth popped out, screaming about such an abrupt and unceremonious entry into this world. Our doctor, who liked all things natural, didn't make it to the birth, but he showed up about an hour later, carrying his motorcycle helmet. He said it would be okay to leave in the morning, after Ruth received some standard medication. Beth hated hospital routines and food, so, we took our new baby home before noon.

Ruth Alma McKee was baptized at the end of June by Beth's Lutheran minister, Pastor Rath. I found this man to be somewhat traditional and authoritarian, so I only attended church at Christmas and Easter, and never took communion. I don't know what names he called me, but I privately called him "the Wrath of God." He didn't want me involved in Ruth's baptismal service.

Ruth a few months later –Photo by Neill McKee

Inspired by the birth of our daughter, I took out the back wall of our westward-facing kitchen and installed a sliding glass door. Outside I built a deck high above the ground and stairs down to the thick green grass. On the deck's railing I fixed a steering wheel so Derek, almost two by then, could drive the whole deck as far as his imagination could take him, and Ruth also, when she was ready to fly.

We frequently visited a favorite place on the Ottawa River for picnics with my editor friend, Sally. She would pack an old picnic basket with crackers, cheese, and other goodies, including a bottle of wine. We would drive to a spot near a large willow tree with low branches, which the kids could climb, as they got older. The Ottawa River is about a third of a mile (500 meters) wide at this point, with dangerous rapids, so we didn't swim. Looking upriver to the northwest, we viewed long-lasting orange sunsets, and to the east, we could see the foaming water as it rushed towards cliffs, with Canada's parliament buildings perched on top.

HEALTHY FILMMAKING AT HOME AND HEARTH

This stretch of the river had hosted much of the history of our country—Huron, Algonquin, and Iroquois tribes, who during 1613 to 1615 guided Samuel de Champlain, the first French explorer to penetrate the interior; followed by young Frenchmen—*coureurs de bois* and *voyageurs*—many of whom married native maidens and trapped and traded, while mapping the continent. Then came Scots and Irish traders, farmers, miners, and lumbermen, who floated long timber rafts downstream to sawmills. Sally had read all the history and loved to refer to it in our conversations. We breathed in the fresh air and her stories, as we sipped wine and watched the children romp around us, hopefully avoiding all the Canada goose droppings. Picnics with Sally became a delightful part of our children's experience of growing up in Ottawa, and memories Beth and I will never forget.

Our picnic spot and willow tree bedside the Ottawa River
—Photo by Neill McKee

That summer I also returned to my own childhood by doing some fishing in a small boat with Robert Yap, the Malaysian immigrant, whom we had helped settle in Canada, along with his family. We caught a few pike and bass—a meager reward for a long day's effort. An even worse outcome was the excruciating back pain I felt when I stepped out of the boat. I had experienced a back injury while working in my dad's factory in my teens, and another from my first parachute jump during my university days, but had escaped any acute reoccurrence until that fishing trip. I had been jogging most mornings to keep in shape, but without doing proper warm-ups. I believe my new injury was also an outcome of all my travels, which entailed slogging heavy filming equipment around the globe.

Our meager catch soon to be made into Chinese fish ball soup
–Photo by Beth McKee

I was glad not to have to travel again right way. Although only 31 at the time, my back felt like that of a 60-year-old.

I tried proper exercises and laid off jogging for a while. Eventually, I took classes in body awareness through proper movement—the Feldenkrais technique. I also found a medical doctor who carried out chiropractic manipulation and prolotherapy—injecting a special solution into the ligaments up and down my spine to strengthen them. My back recovered, but I had to be careful to only sit on chairs with proper back support and I began to carry a lumbar cushion with me wherever I went.

The other therapy that saved me was Transcendental Meditation (TM). My younger brother Philip had taken it up and even traveled to Spain to study at Maharishi Mahesh Yogi's TM institute. In 1968, the Beatles had visited this Maharishi in India for spiritual replenishment, and by doing so, they helped spread TM worldwide. Philip taught me the basic method and gave me my secret *mantra*—a sound I repeated in my head for 20 minutes, two times a day, while breathing deeply, sometimes falling asleep, which was okay according to Philip. Eventually, I learned how to do this just about anywhere, even in noisy airports. Learning TM helped me survive the busy years to come.

After spending a period of healthy recuperation in Canada with my growing family (except for that brief trip to Central and South America), it was time to take my lumbar cushion and *mantra* and leave home and hearth once more.

10. Getting an Education on Education

Growing up in the early 1950s during the post-war baby boom, I sat in crowded classrooms drilling on the alphabet, copying letters and numbers from the blackboard into small brown notebooks, cutting colored paper, and pasting it in designs prescribed by the teacher. I graduated to doing arithmetic on blackboards and reading storybooks with simple images, while daydreaming about playing cowboys and Indians, hiking in the woods, fishing, and catching rabbits in traps. I don't think my teachers knew who I was or what was going on in my mind.

In February 1978, I found myself in a very different primary school in the Naga Valley on Cebu Island, Philippines—probably one I would have done much better in, as a child. I saw no crowded classrooms. Children were divided into small groups, helping each other work through learning modules. Older pupils facilitated small groups of younger ones in open learning kiosks with thatched roofs, while the teacher moved from group to group—observing, answering questions, making corrections, and sometimes taking a pupil aside to work with him or her alone.

These schools buzzed with excitement as my new sync sound camera rolled, while an American filmmaker based in Hong Kong, Frank Green, recorded the sound. We followed the on-the-spot direction of Don Simpson, IDRC's Associate Director of Social Sciences for Education, and Rosetta Mante, the director of the project. It was run by the Southeast Asian Ministers of Education Organization's

Regional Center for Educational Innovation and Technology (SEAMEO-INNOTECH). Filipinos, I found, love long names and acronyms. They called it "Project IMPACT," which stood for "Instructional Management by Parents, Community, and Teachers." Rosetta and her team had dreamed up the project with Don and Pedro Flores of IDRC's Singapore Office. They believed cost-effective innovations in primary education could be found to overcome the problems, which blocked progress.

What problems? With exploding populations in most developing countries, there were many obstacles to children's enrollment and retention in school. For one thing, there were not enough classrooms and teachers, while training teachers and paying their salaries soaked up 80 percent of education budgets. I had seen it myself when I was a volunteer teacher in Sabah, Malaysia, only 600 miles (965 km) from Cebu. As mentioned in Chapter 1, when I was sent there, I knew little about education because I was never trained as a teacher. I had to learn on the job and, after leaving Borneo, I took up filmmaking instead of teaching as a profession. One reason was I always found schools too structured, routine, and boring. But the schools I captured on film in Cebu appeared exciting and vibrant—something very different.

We filmed meetings in Manila and in the project's headquarters in Cebu City, as well as the process of producing illustrated color-coded modules adapted from the national curriculum. They were reproduced using inexpensive typed-up templates run through ink-based copiers—no expensive printing at all. These step-by-step learning modules were easy to revise and for the children to work through in Community Learning Centers, as they were called instead of schools. Over 1,000 pupils were enrolled in five centers in the Naga Valley, a lush tropical location, which provided a picturesque background for our film.

If children had to drop out of school for a period—as many did for the harvest season, caring for farm animals, helping to babysit younger siblings, or working in family businesses—when they returned, they could be tested for recall and fitted into the appropriate module for their level, instead of being required to return to, and perhaps struggle in a fixed grade.

Traditional educators might look at these centers and shake their heads. To them, the learning environment would look chaotic with no walls between classrooms and children scattered all around the schoolyard. But beneath the apparent chaos lay a system, in which pupils signed individual contracts for learning objectives, and teachers weren't faced with a mass of children, not knowing what was going on inside their heads. Pupils could

Various activities in Project Impact's Naga Valley community learning centers
—Photos by Clyde Sanger and F. Marte/IDRC

be shifted to different groups and configurations, and older pupils learned leadership skills as peer group leaders. The system involved a lot of reading assignments and far less rote learning than traditional primary education.

Radio lessons were beamed in from project headquarters to reinforce learning. We also captured a scene of a pupil practicing by reading a module to her mother at home. Literate parents were encouraged to become part of the system.

Involvement of families, communities, community leaders, and local educational officials was paramount for the success of Project Impact, and we filmed meetings of all this. We also captured sequences of a local carpenter teaching basic skills, and students working with a tailor in his shop. Now, why didn't that happen when I was a kid? We had such a variety of businesses and industries in my hometown to demonstrate, as well as farms all around us. I don't think I would have daydreamed so much.

A Filipino boy wondering how the girls got so smart
–Photo by Clyde Sanger/IDRC

GETTING AN EDUCATION ON EDUCATION

From the Philippines, we flew to Jakarta, Indonesia, and then onto the city of Solo to film a similar educational experiment in a rural area. There were differences, of course, so flexibility was needed; but both systems employed the modular approach to pupils' progress and peer group learning. Also, both included lots of physical exercises and cultural education such as music and dancing. In fact, I used a sequence of a graceful group of Indonesian girls dancing to traditional gong music for the end sequence of our film.

Preliminary results of the project demonstrated a 30 to 50 percent savings in imparting primary education to pupils. One of the greatest fears about this experiment came from some traditional teachers who suspected they might be replaced in such a radically different system. This did not happen, for eventually many more teachers were trained and classrooms built. Elements of Project Impact spread to other countries such as Malaysia, Bangladesh, and Jamaica.

A 1981 evaluation report of Project Impact[1] revealed that:

> The graduates of the Impact schools were equipped with the needed knowledge, skills, and attitudes for further schooling, and that they compare favorably with graduates of conventional schools as shown by evaluation of their performance or achievement, self-concept, and attitude. Likewise, Impact leavers compare favorably with non-Impact leavers in their post-school experiences. The learning modes in the Impact system enabled learners to gain as much knowledge and as many skills and positive attitudes as are gained by those who are under the direction of professionally trained teachers. The

Impact modules met the objectives of basic education as well as professional classroom teachers. The Impact learning system, which is more economic than the conventional school system, is just as efficient as the conventional system and the fear of the parents about the inefficiency of programmed teaching and of the modules is not supported by the achievement and the outcomes of this evaluation.

My brief exposure to this educational innovation widened my horizons. Bit by bit, I was gaining knowledge into new ways of thinking about world development. My job was like attending a "university of the world." But the best thing about making this film was working with Don Simpson. He was one of the only associate directors in IDRC who wanted to stick with me through the whole filmmaking process. His attitude was that he was learning as much about filmmaking as I was about education. He even helped to lug around my heavy equipment when required. And in the evenings, over dinner and drinks, we had in-depth talks about education and development, as well as a lot of laughs.

When we wrapped up the filming and returned to Canada, I started the final creative process. By this time, I had graduated to using a Steenbeck editing table, then the latest thing for filmmakers. It was easy to while away the hours at Crawley Films. Don joined me in seeing our rough footage once I synchronized all the sound, and later returned to approve the "rough cut" and to write the narration. For Don, the dissemination of results of development research was just as important as the interventions themselves. Visibility brings attention and discussion, and possibly more resources

GETTING AN EDUCATION ON EDUCATION

from other sources. IDRC's job was to think up big ideas that have consequences and possible impact, not just to contribute to the publication of more academic papers to further careers. We titled our film *Project Impact: the Overview*,[2] and we also made another more instructional film for implementors titled *Project Impact: the System*,[3] in which we detailed the elements of the innovation in the Philippines.

I had first come to know Don in my CUSO filmmaking days. In the early 1970s, he was running an international resource center at the University of Western Ontario (UWO), in London, Ontario, linking that institution by computer with resources at the University of California's system—not easy to do in the 60s and 70s. He incorporated my films into orientations for CUSO volunteers before they left for their overseas posts.

Don started as a high school teacher but completed his doctorate in history, writing a dissertation on the African Canadian population of Southern Ontario, which later was published as a book, *Under the North Star: Black Communities in Upper Canada before Confederation*.[4] In this book, he detailed the life and times of many people who came to Canada to escape slavery in the U.S., as well as how some returned to fight in the Civil War. Many remained in the U.S. after slavery was abolished, but others returned to Canada to become community leaders. Due to Don's interest in people who struggle in the face of discrimination and hardship, he developed a deep love for Africa. He helped set up the NGO, Crossroads Africa, and was the first CUSO regional director in West Africa, based in Ghana. After leaving IDRC, he became the Director of International Business at the Ivey Business School, at UWO.

There were periods when we were not connected, but we kept meeting up in various places. One such meeting occurred in 1991, when he was director of an innovative program at a management center in Banff, Alberta. Then we lost contact until one day in 2002, when I was walking through Union Station in Washington, D.C., I saw a familiar face sitting in the station's central hall restaurant. There he was, with all his papers spread out on the table. From that time, we kept in touch more frequently, and I followed his many activities and transitions. Even as I write this book, he continues to work on collaborative initiatives with the many people in his extensive network involved in finding solutions to complex problems, which include diverse stakeholders. I had the pleasure of working with him once more during the last assignment of my career.

Through making those films on Project Impact, I was educated about education and innovation, while Don Simpson's request for my services led to many more invitations to make films on specific IDRC projects.

The author and son with Don Simpson at Banff, Alberta, 1991
–Photo by Ruth McKee

Making Films on Food for Africa

The rest of 1978 and 1979 were busy periods for me. The Agriculture, Food, and Nutrition Division (AFNS) asked me to do a film on cowpeas, often referred to as "black-eyed peas" in North America, where that variety is most popular. Andrew Ker was the IDRC researcher and project officer who pushed me to make this film, and he had the full support of his director, Joseph Hulse, who we secretly called "Joe Pulse" because of his love for legume research. (For non-agronomists, a pulse is the edible seed from any legume plant.)

Actually, cowpeas are beans, not peas. The cowpea (*Vigna unguiculata*) was domesticated in Sahelian Africa around 3,000 to 4,000 years ago and remains an important food in the semi-arid regions of Africa and Asia. It was brought to the Americas by Portuguese explorers and settlers. The plant does well with few inputs, such as fertilizer, because its root nodules are able to fix nitrogen from the air. This makes it a valuable crop for subsistence farmers who may not have enough manure and cannot afford chemical fertilizers. Other crops, for instance sorghum and millet, also benefit from the nitrogen produced from this natural fertilization process, when they are intercropped with cowpeas. After harvesting the beans, the rest of the nitrogen-rich plant is a valuable food for animals. In some areas, people also cook and eat the green parts. The whole plant is an ideal food, providing protein, starch, minerals, and fiber.

Filming the cowpea story took me to Upper Volta (now called Burkina Faso), in West Africa, as well as back to the International Institute of Tropical Agriculture (IITA) in Ibadan, Nigeria. We covered all aspects of research: breeding new species that are insect and disease resistant, field trials with farmers, and intercropping. When we finished the film, we titled it *Pods of Protein: The International Cowpea Improvement Program.*[1] It was technical and instructive, aimed at budding agriculture researchers and extension workers.

There's not much more to write about in the making of a film on cowpeas, but that's not so when it comes to my further experience with the way things work in Nigeria. I traveled east by road from Ibadan to Lokoja on the Niger River, with a British team member whose name I didn't record, but I believe it was Jack Owen. On arrival in Lokoja late in the evening, we went to a large government-owned hotel where Jack asked for two rooms for us and one for our driver.

The Nigerian man behind the counter had been dozing and we woke him up, as he replied automatically, "We don't have rooms."

Jack continued, "Well, do you have one room for us and one for our driver?"

"We don't have driver's rooms."

"Do you have one room for all of us?"

"We don't have any rooms in the hotel for you."

"What about the large annex I see over there? You must have room there."

"They are occupied."

"But there are hardly any vehicles parked at the hotel. Are you sure there aren't any free for us?"

"No. We don't have rooms."

MAKING FILMS ON FOOD FOR AFRICA

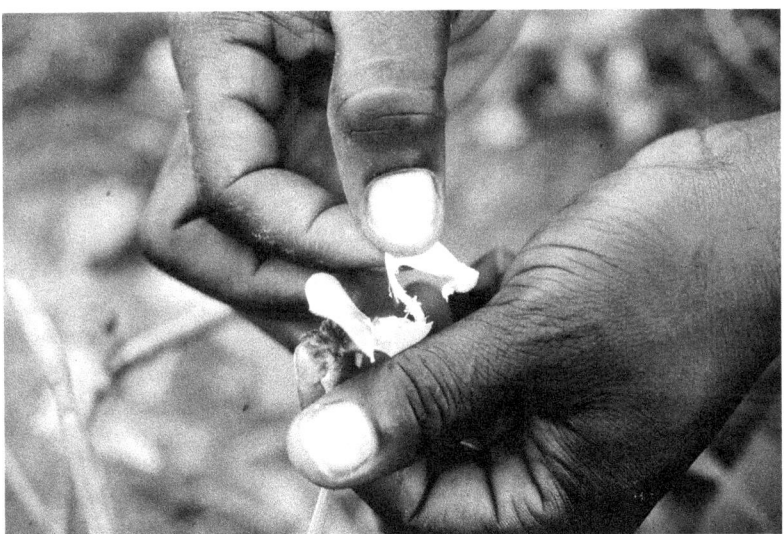

Researcher cross-breeding cowpea varieties at IITA
—Photos by Neill McKee/IDRC

Jack looked at him blankly, while I stayed silent. He knew the culture better than I did. He continued this line of inquiry for some time, never losing his cool. After about 10 minutes, he motioned to me to step back from the counter to discuss our strategy. In a hushed tone, Jack said to me, "This will take a while longer." He took his wallet from his pocket and asked me to do the same. He pulled out a wad of Nigerian Naira (one Naira then worth 60 cents U.S.). We walked back to the counter where he started again, "Do you have one room for us and one for our driver?"

The man looked at the money, and said, "We don't have any clean rooms. The cleaners have not come."

Jack replied, "Well, can we see a room? It's late and we aren't fussy."

The man finally offered, "There's one room that is possible but someone is sleeping there."

"So, it's rented?"

"It's occupied."

"Can we see it?"

Finally, the man told an old attendant to take us to the room. There he banged on the door and woke up the occupant. The sleepy man gathered his things and left, and the attendant went to fetch clean sheets and towels—real service. It was too late for dinner in the hotel and decent restaurants would be hard to find, Jack told me, so we had to go to bed hungry. Fortunately, the room had mosquito nets.

While the attendant was gone, we discussed the matter. It was apparent that relatives of the hotel staff were occupying rooms without payment. Our inducement of flashing cold hard cash was the only thing that could break the barrier. We went back to the counter and paid while the old man went to find a suitable room for our driver. I thought, *Hopefully, he won't have to sleep with someone's relatives.*

The staff of IITA, including the Nigerians I worked with, were pleasant and accommodating. There were many

MAKING FILMS ON FOOD FOR AFRICA

enjoyable moments during our travels, but this experience overshadowed them all, and I became pretty good at acting it out for colleagues and friends when I got home. It took another decade before Nigeria began to privatize hotels and other state-owned enterprises. This was my third trip to this troublesome country and I figured, three strikes and you're out.

It's not enough to grow and harvest beans and grain. I knew a little about this from my CUSO filming days in Ghana, and I received a full education in post-harvest technology when I was asked by IDRC's expert in the area, Bob Forrest, to make a film on it in Kenya. There, I had a completely different experience with government-run operations. I worked with a team of Kenyans in the Crop Storage Section of the Training and Extension Service, Ministry of Agriculture. They supplied a qualified sound technician, David Malungu, and I quickly briefed him on my sound equipment. The leader of the team was James Kwanzu, a seasoned extension officer, and Christopher Warui, an entomologist, wrote the script with me. We traveled for three weeks from the coast to the highlands, the Rift Valley to Lake Victoria, as well as to the drier lands further north. This was the first time I had seen the full glory of Kenya and experienced Kenyan culture, hospitality, and teamwork—a rich experience I shall never forget.

When a non-African looks upon a traditional Kenyan village, he or she will notice some larger round houses (*rondavels*) and a lot of small ones. At least at the time, some of the smaller ones may have been for second or possibly third wives, but many were grain storage bins. For most Kenyans, the grain is maize—called "corn" in North America. If you tell a typical Kenyan this grain originated in Mexico, where it was first domesticated and cultivated by Amerindians, you'll get an expression of disbelief. Most Kenyans, as well as many other eastern and southern Africans, do not feel they have eaten properly until they've had their daily allotment of maize meal, cooked for breakfast as porridge, and for other meals as *ugali*, a drier form, which you mash with your hand, mixing in some braised collard greens called *sukuma wiki*, and beans if you have them, or meat for special occasions. Other traditional grains and starches such as sorghum and cassava, can be substituted to make *ugali*, but if they are given a choice, most Kenyans will choose maize.

In our film, we focused on maize storage, from the subsistence farmer to large government reserves, and temporary storage silos used before export. We made the film instructional and slow-paced, so the Swahili version could be used to educate rural audiences through the Extension Service's mobile cinemas. The team worked together to translate the English script to Swahili, and I recorded James doing the narration before I left the country—a most efficient operation.

During this trip, I learned about the millions of dollars of food wasted in Kenya each year, due to poor storage methods, and the ways the extension team was teaching farmers to prevent this loss, such as: proper drying methods before storage; raising the small storage bins off the ground with poles; installing metal guards on the poles to block invasion by hungry rats and mice; keeping the ground around bins bare and clean to deter insect damage; and preventing the development of mold by making proper ventilation holes, and rainproofing roofs and sides.

MAKING FILMS ON FOOD FOR AFRICA

Christopher Warui, entomologist, inspecting quality of maize in a village storage bin —Photo by Neill McKee/IDRC

On location with my Kenyan crew —Photo by one of our crew

I also filmed entertaining sequences, like a woman singing her head off while harvesting maize, and many more scenes demonstrating the natural beauty of the country. I don't think I wholly appreciated Africa before this trip. In the evenings, I joined my Kenyan colleagues in eating *ugali* with *sukuma wiki* and cowpeas, but I have to admit it got a little boring. I never grew partial to African food after my years in Asia.

When I returned to Ottawa and completed the film we titled it *When the Harvest is Over*.[2] The Swahili version was used by the Extension Service team for years and viewed by thousands of farmers in evening discussion sessions, helping to improve their lives, and educating agriculture extension workers and managers on improving their systems.

With my "certificate" in proper grain storage, I proceeded to learn about the next stage of African post-harvest technology. A few months later, I flew to Johannesburg with one of our science writers, Rowan Shirkie, where we rented a car and drove through the northern farmlands of South Africa, still firmly held in the hands of white South Africans—the racist apartheid system continued in that country. As we headed northwest, the countryside became drier with more thorn trees, rather than the lush land held by the whites. Given our political opinions on the matter, we felt like spies.

We entered Botswana near the town of Lobatse and drove on until we reached Kanye, a medium-size African town made up of tin-roofed rectangular houses and thatched roof *rondavels*. It was surrounded by dry farmland with fields of sorghum and millet—indigenous African crops, rather than maize. These African plants do well in this drier climate. The problem is their grains are covered with a hard hull, which has to be soaked in water to make it easier to remove. The traditional dehulling process for sorghum often

MAKING FILMS ON FOOD FOR AFRICA

involved two or three women working together, rhythmically pounding their pestles into a single mortar, while singing to relieve themselves of the monotony and backbreaking labor needed to feed their families.

After dehulling, they had to let the rough flour dry in the sun and then winnow it several times to separate the yellow and bitter-tasting hull from the desired white kernels of sorghum. Then, the rough flour was pounded once more to make it fine—just the right texture for cooking as porridge or drier dishes. It would take a woman an hour to process just one kilogram (2.2 lbs.) of flour, and some of the moisture remained in it, making it spoil if it wasn't used immediately.

To avoid these tedious tasks, some women had started buying imported maize meal from stores—a big expense for them. This was a good reason for developing a new technology to dehull sorghum and millet.

African women pounding sorghum with a tradition mortar and pestle
—Photo by Neill McKee/IDRC

The project was centered at Kanye's Rural Industries Innovation Centre (RIIC). By the time of our visit, the RIIC team had already made substantial progress on the development of a machine that could dehull sorghum and millet without losing much of the good nutrients inside. The team had scaled down a larger Canadian-designed version of a grain dehuller, used by the Botswana Agriculture Marketing Board. The larger model was successfully operating to satisfy urban markets such as the capital, Gaborone, but was doing little to stimulate wider rural grain production. The RIIC team had made improvements to the rotating grinding stones used in the machine, which was driven by a small diesel engine. It could also dehull maize and cowpeas.

RIIC's mini-dehuller –Photo by Neill McKee/IDRC

I filmed a line of customers waiting for service outside the mill—a good sign—and interviewed a woman by the name of Mrs. Msese. She brought 44 pounds (20 kg) of sorghum grain to the mill to be processed—a very satisfied customer because a half-day's work had been done in just a few minutes. She didn't have to carry the heavy grain to the mill or return home with the flour sack on her back, for RIIC engaged local drivers. One of them had a cart made from an old car, pulled by donkeys, which was rented for a small fee. What could be more appropriate than this technology?

Kanye's version of appropriate, low-cost transport
–Photo by Neill McKee/IDRC

So, did this pilot project in Kanye have any impact? I found a year 2000 report online by ICRISAT, the International Crops Research Institute for the Semi-Arid Tropics,[3] which made me smile. Its summary reported:

> By 1982, 17 sorghum mills, each including at least one dehuller and hammermill, had been established. RIIC supplied the machines and offered

a training course in machinery maintenance to entrepreneurs buying the machines, and to operators hired to run and maintain the equipment. Twenty new mills were established in 1990, and 33 mills were established between 1991 and 1995. Between 1996 and 1998, another 75 dehullers and hammermills were installed. New mills were being established virtually every month. Almost all these mills sought to produce sorghum meal for the retail market. The industry for the production of sorghum meal had become highly competitive.

The majority of these mills now buy grain for processing and sale through local retail shops and supermarkets. The status of sorghum has changed from being a food security crop largely consumed in the rural areas, to become a commercial crop competing in the urban food market. The development and expansion of the industry was due largely to the ready availability of suitable processing technology, provision of capital grants for commercial investment, and consistent access to high-quality grain.

In truth, much of the sorghum now consumed in Botswana is grown in South Africa. I suppose that's okay, for apartheid ended in 1994 when Nelson Mandela came to power with a democratically elected government. Since the time of my visit, Botswana has become a relatively rich African country due to the discovery and mining of diamonds, starting in 1982. That has led to the over-reliance on diamonds in the economy and increasing poverty for many, mainly due to inequalities in wealth distribution. I prefer the "technological gem" IDRC helped to develop in Kanye. True and impactful development has to take place from the bottom up and must focus on improving the lives of women, especially. We titled our short film *An End to Pounding*[4]—a title that would resonate well with African women.

A big surprise for me, in Kanye, was to meet Richard Carothers at RIIC. He is the man I dubbed "Tanga Man" in the CUSO film I made on him in 1971 (see Chapter 2). He was solving various problems in appropriate technology, and gave some advice to the crew working on the dehuller, although it was not his focus. He had adapted to the culture—living humbly in a thatched roof hut and was learning Setswana language—his usual style of operation.

Following the release of *Tanga Man*, Richard kept popping up in my life out of nowhere. First, we met up again in the early 1970s when I was in Ottawa, editing films. Then, in 1976, on that East African filming and photography trip with Clyde Sanger, I bumped into him at a gas station in Dar-es-Salaam, Tanzania. He was fueling a motorcycle he had borrowed while on a vacation from Canada. I couldn't believe my eyes. Now we met again in rural Botswana and spent the evenings reminiscing and talking about his work and life in Kanye. After that, I met him by chance in an Ottawa restaurant, when I was on leave from one of my overseas postings. Today, Richard owns his own plane and takes me for rides when I meet him in Canada. A lifelong friend with a similar experience and outlook on life to mine—one of the best results of my African journeys.

MY UNIVERSITY OF THE WORLD

Richard Carothers and his airplane –Photos by Neill McKee

Documenting Oysters in Mangrove Swamps and Seas

In late January of 1979, Beth and I took a break in Jamaica, leaving Derek and Ruth with neighborhood friends whose children were their playmates. We perched ourselves in a small hotel on a hill overlooking the Caribbean Sea at Port Antonio, a town on the northeast coast of the island. We read books, ate, walked, made love, and slept. This was Beth's first real break from motherhood and she missed the kids, so believe it or not, we returned a day earlier than planned—a dedicated mother. She had even arranged for postcards to be dropped in our friends' post box every day, each one with a different letter spelling out their names—a dedicated teacher.

A much needed break from motherhood —Photo by Neill McKee

I had arrived in Jamaica a week before Beth to film some sequences on an IDRC experiment in oyster culture. William Herbert ("Bert") Allsopp, Associate Director for Fisheries and Aquaculture in the AFNS Division, asked me to do films on his projects. He was a distinguished Afro-Guyanese man born in British Guyana. He spoke with an impeccable British accent, having received much of his education in Britain, like many more educated Guyanese of his generation. Bert Allsopp and project officer Brian Davy were solid advocates for popularizing their science of fisheries and aquaculture.

I had visited the Sierra Leone oyster culture project in 1976, when it was just getting started, and returned to do more filming, for it was more advanced than the one in Jamaica. I was welcomed by Abu Bakar Kamara, Project Leader, whom I interviewed on an oyster farming raft in a mangrove swamp—anything to liven up the subject, for oysters just sit there—no movement for the camera or sound to record.

I also interviewed one of the team's biologists, Cho Wellesley Cole, whom I found to be an attractive and articulate young woman. When I met her, she told me, "I'm Canadian too."

I asked, "What do you mean? Your accent is more British than Canadian."

She smiled, "My ancestors came from Nova Scotia in 1792."

"Really?"

"Yes, they were slaves in the American colonies, and they escaped to Nova Scotia to be on the British side at the time of the Revolution. They were among over 1,000 of those who decided to return to Africa. We're called 'Creoles' here, and we helped to found the first permanent ex-slave colony in West Africa."

DOCUMENTING OYSTERS IN MANGROVE SWAMPS AND SEAS

Abu Bakar Kamara, Project Leader, demonstrating his pride and joy —Photo by Neill McKee/IDRC

That made sense. Sierra Leone was colonized in 1787 by freed slaves from England, as well as Nova Scotia, and others who arrived from Jamaica in 1800. The territory became a British crown colony in 1808. I shouldn't have been amazed that Cho knew her history so well. The Creoles had become some of the most educated people in the country.

The capital of Sierra Leone, Freetown, is located on the Freetown Estuary, consisting of 100 miles (161 km) of coastal

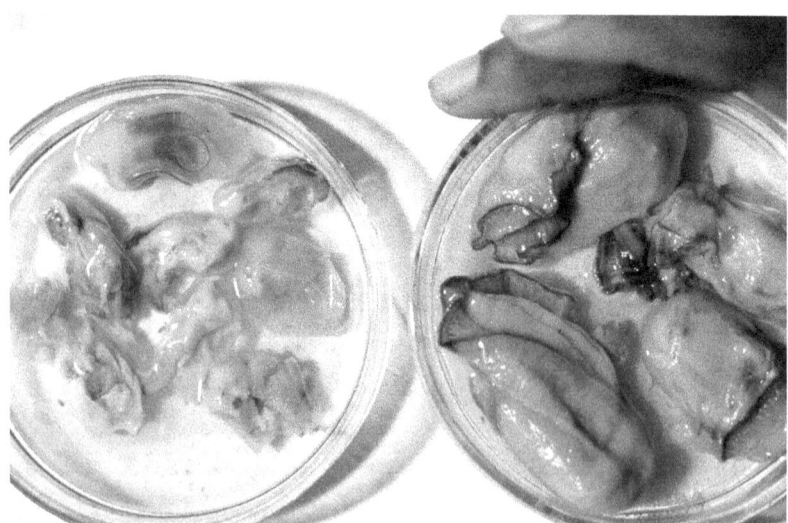

Cho demonstrating the difference in size between natural and cultured oysters —Photos by Neill McKee/IDRC

DOCUMENTING OYSTERS IN MANGROVE SWAMPS AND SEAS

mangrove forest, a natural habitat for oysters, which lodge on mangrove roots. Since fish supply is seasonal in this part of West Africa's coast, oysters had become an important source of protein for the coastal population. But the problem with relying on the natural growth of mangrove oysters is they spend half of their life out of water at low tide, and therefore only grow to a small size. Another problem with harvesting them directly from mangrove roots is that people in small canoes use large African knives known as "pangas" to cut the roots and bring the oysters home to shuck. Continual cutting damages the mangrove trees. An improved method of growing and harvesting oysters was needed.

In Sierra Leone, the experiment involved culturing oysters on strings hanging from bamboo rafts, which floated on oil drums. This new system allowed them to be submerged in water all the time, with the result that they grew three times larger in less than half the time. Two oysters three inches (8 cm) in length can provide enough flesh to satisfy an adult's daily protein needs—all nine essential amino acids plus many vitamins and minerals.

After capturing a good amount of excellent footage, I left Freetown on a flight to Lagos, Nigeria, to catch another flight to Nairobi, on the eastern side of Africa—a 10-hour trip of 5,668 miles (3,522 km). I feared the stop in Lagos, worrying my luggage, including my exposed oyster culture footage, would be lost. Sure enough, when I arrived in Nairobi, the suitcase containing my precious footage, unused film stock, and my lights for interior shots were nowhere to be seen. I remained at the airport, waiting for it to appear, and then insisted on going through the hole where the luggage came out, to take a ride on a small vehicle to the offramp of the jet I had arrived on, to see if it might be there. (This was before international terrorism had reached its peak, so I could get away with such antics.) But I had no luck. The Kenyan airport staff were accommodating but probably amused by my behavior. There was nothing more I could do. This demonstrates how precarious international filmmaking was before the days of instant playback on high-quality digital video equipment.

The next morning, I had to catch a flight through Johannesburg, South Africa, to Swaziland (now called Eswatini) to film an agriculture project. I stopped in Johannesburg to buy new filmstock and rent a set of portable lights. To make a long story short, on returning to Nairobi airport about a week later, I walked into the luggage area and spotted my missing suitcase sitting in a corner with other lost luggage. Luck returned to me—my oyster culture sequences were saved.

Filming oysters took me to other locations during 1979, including a shoreline near Nanaimo, British Columbia, on Vancouver Island, where I filmed and interviewed Daniel Quayle, one of the world's experts on molluscan biology and bivalve culture. He became a technical advisor for my film. He had been the Director of Fisheries for the Province of British Columbia (1956-57) but didn't like bureaucracy much, so he retreated to the Pacific Biological Station at Nanaimo, where he was located for most of his career. I didn't know at the time, but when writing this book, I found out he'd been a pilot in World War II and had been shot down over Germany, spending a year and a half as a prisoner of war.[1] I now understand why this tall and gentle soul loved the quiet shores of British Columbia and its peaceful oysters. But at the time I met him, he remained adventuresome in retirement, flying off to the tropics on consultancies for IDRC and other agencies, after a long and successful career.

Dan Qualye choosing fresh oysters –Photo by Neill McKee/IDRC

Dan had a great sense of humor. He picked up and shucked a large fresh oyster from the shore full of the creatures, offering it to me and saying, "Here you go."

I said, "What do you want me to do with it?"

"Eat it."

"Just swallow it?"

"Sure, but chew it first," Dan replied.

I said, "You go first."

He ate it and quickly shucked another, offering it to me. It went down with difficulty. I almost threw up. I must admit, I have never liked oysters on the half shell, no matter how fresh they are. Dan agreed that my preference for cooked oysters was safer because in the tropics they are more than likely to contain all sorts of contaminants, which could lead to severe diarrhea and even death, especially if they are raised and harvested near human settlements. So, I stuck to cooked oysters throughout my travels.

Next, I flew to Tokyo, Japan, where I met up with Frank Green, the filmmaker I had hired as a soundman for Project Impact (see Chapter 10). We made our way by train to Hiroshima, where oysters have been farmed for at least 400 years and where I could film large-scale operations, although not in tropical waters. Through Bert Allsopp, we made contact with another world expert, Dr. K. Y. Arakawa, who arranged for us to be taken around, filming from a boat on the Inland Sea—a vast expanse of saltwater sheltered from the winds, currents, and high tides of the Pacific. Here, during the summer, they use old oyster shells hung on racks to collect the spat. The spat, or "seed," are minute oysters, which attach themselves to any hard surface. Then they are separated and hung on long lines from bamboo rafts, in deep water, to let the oysters grow for two years before they are harvested, using boats with mechanical winches to raise the heavy strings. We filmed men chopping off the bottom stoppers on the strings, allowing the whole line of oysters to quickly tumble onto the collection ships' decks. I learned that one raft usually carries 600 strings, producing an average of 360,000 oysters, from which three tons of oyster flesh is harvested.

DOCUMENTING OYSTERS IN MANGROVE SWAMPS AND SEAS

Harvesting of cultured oysters on Hiroshima Bay, Japan
—Photo by Frank Green/IDRC

We filmed thousands of oysters pouring off boats on conveyor belts, going through mechanized washers, and then to lines of Japanese women shuckers. The women were experts at this task, using traditional tools and methods, which allow each one of them to shuck up to 3,000 oysters per day. There were over 600 family businesses like this in the area. We included Japan in the film to show the potential of oyster farming. Could the same be replicated in tropical waters in societies with much different cultures?

This visit gave us a chance to see the Hiroshima Peace Park and Museum, ground zero for the atomic bomb dropped by the United States Armed Forces, on August 6, 1945. It led to the death of 140,000 people. After staring at graphic photos on the horror of that day and its aftermath, we sat on a bench in the park and meditated, marveling how the people of Hiroshima, so productive in many endeavors like oyster farming, had risen out of the ashes.

Next, Frank and I flew south through Hong Kong to my old stomping grounds, Sabah, Malaysia, to film another IDRC experiment in oyster culture. The project leader, Lim Aun Luh, a Chinese Malaysian, had devised a complicated system of collecting spat on coconut shells or on asbestos-cement strips placed in racks. Then, after five weeks, they moved the trays to growing areas in deeper water. After a period, the larger oysters were cut off the culch and placed in trays for further growth. In only a year in this climate, an oyster could reach marketable size. But to me, the process seemed to entail too many steps to be done economically, at scale.

Our time in Sabah was worthwhile, for we learned about and filmed problems that can occur with tropical oyster

Cleaning oysters in trays at low tide in Sabah, Malaysia
−Photo by Frank Green/IDRC

farming, including biofouling—the buildup of seaweed, barnacles, and other growth on oyster shells. These problems occur when oysters are submerged continuously. We also filmed attacks by predators such as crabs and small snails, called oyster drills, which can kill off stationary oysters, especially those sitting in trays. In addition, there was competition for space from Sabah's timber extraction industry—loose floating logs could do much damage to trays. Also, expanding coastal human settlements meant possible fecal contamination. Oysters are efficient water filters and they collect and hold dangerous bacteria, as Dan Qualye had warned me.

When I returned to Canada and edited the film, I ended it with a sequence of a Chinese Malaysian family happily eating fried oysters and rice with chopsticks, set to traditional clanging Chinese music as the credits rolled. We titled the film *Oyster Farming in the Tropics*.[2]

I searched for signs of success in Sierra Leone and Malaysia today, but could not find anything resulting from IDRC's support, which was brought to scale. Perhaps my doubts on the complicated steps involved in the Sabah experiment were right. In 1991, Sierra Leone descended into 25 years of civil war, military coups, and political unrest, causing the deaths of thousands of people and the displacement of over two million. On top of that, the Ebola virus struck the country in 2014, and by the time it was contained in 2016, it had infected more than 14,000 Sierra Leoneans and killed almost 4,000, damaging the country's economy.

I did find some evidence of a private sector oyster farming project partially supported by British foreign aid.[3] Today, oysters remain a favorite dish among the coastal people of Sierra Leone, so as the country moves forward more peacefully, perhaps the findings of IDRC's work there are being put to use.

What about the trials in Jamaica? In my internet investigation, I was surprised by what had happened since 1979. I found a video report online about a successful start-up: *Oyster Farming in Green Island* by the Green Island Friendly Fisherfolk[4] on the northwest coast of the country. Due to overfishing and climate change—warming water temperatures, storm surges, and rising water levels—fish catches in the area had decreased. In 2017, the Jamaican Government's climate change adaptation fund came to the rescue with assistance in financing, technical and business training, plus marketing plans for the community. I read a newspaper report[5] on how such activity was expanding and that experimental oyster farming was taking place in Kingston Harbor.[6] The object was to expand the practice substantially and thus restore the quality of the coastal waters, using the natural filtering system of oysters.

So, the lesson here is we have to be patient with oysters, for oysters have always been patient with humans. Anthrozoologists estimate oysters first appeared in the Triassic period over 200 million years ago, when dinosaurs ruled the Earth. Maybe oysters can be used to help clean up the mess we have made of the planet—or maybe they are just patiently waiting for our disappearance to clean up after us and live for another 200 million years, along with more respectful Earth mates.

13. Filming Fish from the Earth's Vast Oceans

During the same period, I had been asked to produce another overview film on IDRC for its 10th Anniversary celebration in 1980. By then, Dr. Hopper had left to become the Vice President for South Asia at the World Bank, and Ivan Head had taken over as President. He had been a legal scholar and foreign policy advisor to Prime Minister Pierre Trudeau. Mr. Head's appointment was seen as a move to ensure IDRC would retain its annual grant from the Parliament of Canada, during more conservative-leaning times. He thought a new film would help. So, I had to get back on the road again to cover more recent developments. The shooting script we wrote required stops to do sequences on projects such as:

- research on the effects of industrial development on women working in factories in Malaysia;
- a study on breastfeeding and birth spacing in the Yucatan Peninsula of Mexico;
- a pilot project on sanitation technology and hygiene education for indigenous people in Guatemala;
- cropping systems and fish marketing research in Sri Lanka; and
- shelterbelt research and an agriculture information system in Tunisia.

MY UNIVERSITY OF THE WORLD

In addition, I returned to Alexandria, Egypt, to film a fascinating study on the use of damsissa (*Ambrosia maritima*), a naturally occurring plant with promising molluscicide effects to control snails, which live and reproduce in the canals and ponds of the Nile Valley. These snails host parasitic flatworms (blood flukes) of the genus *Schistosoma*, which cause the debilitating disease of schistosomiasis (bilharzia) in people who come into contact with the water in those canals and ponds. On this visit, I also had an opportunity to take a few shots of the pyramids and a display in a museum in Cairo on damsissa being used for the same purpose in ancient Egypt. As I gazed at these artifacts, I wondered, *Does our quest for knowledge just go in circles?*

My stop in Alexandria also gave me a chance to take a few shots along the seafront of this famous city, the setting of Lawrence Durrell's novels, *The Alexandria Quartet*.[1]

Fisherman fighting winter wind, Alexandria, Egypt
—Photo by Neill McKee/IDRC

FILMING FISH FROM THE EARTH'S VAST OCEANS

It was winter and the waves of the Mediterranean crashed against the shore that day. Here is a place where Western thought had crashed into, and perhaps been absorbed by, Eastern mysticism and religion for over two thousand years. I thought of the ideas behind Durrell's writing, the convergence of East and West, and about all I had seen during my journeys in the past few years on land and sea—a moment of reflection while being splashed by cold Mediterranean water.

During this period, I also experienced warmer waters of the South Pacific. Clyde Sanger, who had moved to the Commonwealth Secretariat in London, asked IDRC if they would allow me to make a film on their projects around the world. This added even more travel and work to my agenda, for no extra monetary compensation. But Clyde was responsible for bringing me into IDRC and giving me this wonderful job. He also told me my film would likely be shown at the Commonwealth Heads of Government Meeting in Lusaka, in 1979, and that Queen Elizabeth would be there. So, how could I refuse? Clyde later reported our film *Making Ends Meet: An Account of the Commonwealth Fund for Technical Co-operation (CFTC)*[2] was indeed shown there. He even invited Margaret Thatcher to take a front seat, but she refused to budge from the back row, saying, "I will stay where I am." Later, I read that she was rather cool about the idea of this club of black and brown men. The Queen didn't attend the showing, but I like to think she was given a private screening.

For the Commonwealth, I had to travel as far as Fiji and Western Samoa to film African, Indian, and Caribbean professors teaching university students various subjects such as development management and pest control on coconut palms. To me, this was the Commonwealth at its best—true south-to-south exchange. But the project that sticks in my memory, concerns the United Nations Convention on the Law of the Sea, which was formulated between 1973 and 1982. It finally came into force in 1994, establishing the legal framework for all coastal marine and maritime activities. Since that time, each country with ocean shores has assumed jurisdiction over the 200 nautical miles (370 kilometers) of water, seabed, and air space off its coast.

For this film, I traveled to the Solomon Islands, a nation that was soon to gain sovereignty over an area of sea 50 times larger than its landmass. My work entailed filming surveillance of the ocean by a number of means: mapping, patrol boats and planes, as well as radio communications. I also did an interview with a British consultant who was setting up the legal and taxation framework needed to implement the Law of the Seas program.

Tuna fishermen heading out to sea, Solomon Islands
–Photo by Neill McKee/IDRC

I had the pleasure of joining the Solomon islander crew on a tuna fishing vessel. I filmed them throwing a trail of bait behind the boat to catch the attention of schools of tuna, which would follow and strike all at once. The fishermen had only to throw in their lines armed with barbless hooks, whipping the huge fish onto the deck, one after another, some almost hitting me. I was told to stand back but wanted to film close to the action.

During this period, I was also asked to make more films for IDRC's fisheries and aquaculture section. I traveled to Guyana, a country on the northeast coast of South America. Its population originated as slaves from Africa or indentured laborers from Indian, and also included some people of Chinese and European descent, as well as indigenous tribes in the interior.

I had visited Guyana on my first filming trip for IDRC, in 1975. At that time, I caught a ride on a small shrimp trawler, the "Arasuka No. 2," a Japanese-owned vessel. As it plied through the Atlantic Ocean on the continental shelf off the coast, I wasn't prepared for the rolling waves of the open sea. My stomach also rolled and I had to lie down on the bottom bunk bed assigned to me and make quick dashes to the ship's washroom to puke, until there was nothing left in my stomach. As I lay there, one of the crew members made sure I continued to drink water, but otherwise they just left me alone. In mid-afternoon, I heard a shift in the ship's gears as it slowed down, and then the sound of winches. I pushed myself to get up and see what was happening, cameras in hand. I was just in time, for the crew was pulling in the nets.

True to what I had read before traveling, the shrimp that the nets had dragged off the ocean's bottom only accounted for about 15 percent of the catch. The crew had the job of separating the shrimp and packing it below deck in cold storage, while using shovels to throw all the dead by-catch back into the water, where it fed sea birds swirling around our boat and sharks trailing us—"garbage men of the sea." Some small sharks were also caught in the nets and were tossed overboard too.

I managed to get all the shots I needed to graphically demonstrate this waste. This was only one trawler out of about 200 operating from Georgetown, the capital of Guyana. If you added up all the discarded fish, it amounted to about 200,000 tons of edible protein thrown overboard each year. Shrimp thrive in coastal tropical waters around the world, and, at the time, shrimp trawlers threw away between 16 and 21 million tons of so-called "trash fish" annually—a staggering figure almost equal to the amount of aquatic protein then being consumed annually by people in developing countries.

Starting in 1975, new government regulations required Guyana-based trawlers to keep at least the last day's by-catch instead of discarding it. I had been lucky to catch a ride on this trawler. It had returned to shore to pull in a disabled trawler and only needed to return to sea for two days to fill up its hold. Normally these vessels stayed out for three to four weeks, bringing in valuable shrimp, mainly for export, and throwing away by-catch.

Guyanese fishermen saving by-catch –Photo by Neill McKee/IDRC

Fortunately, on my return to Guyana in 1980, I had the earlier footage and didn't need to go out to sea again. Besides, I found much progress to film in the pilot fish processing plant. By then, the government had banned all fish imports. IDRC had brought in experts from the Canadian Federal Fisheries Laboratory to help the Guyana State Corporation acquire equipment and train people on new processing techniques. The fish factory now employed at least 100 people, but still couldn't meet the demand from local or export markets. By this time, trawlers were required to bring in two tons of by-catch per trip. The plant could only process 10 percent of that, and had to sell the rest to local fish traders and hawkers.

I rolled my camera and filmed all I could see: the processing of salt fish, a Caribbean favorite; fresh frozen fish fillets cut from sea trout and other larger species; fresh frozen dressed fish; minced fish; fish paste for a sandwich spread;

shark flesh marketed as "white flake," shark fin to make that famous Chinese soup; and even fish jam, pickled fish, and fish sausage. While filming, I had to take a few breaks to go outside and breathe fresh air because fish plants naturally reek of dead fish.

I also managed to take shots of employees teaching people new fish recipes at an exhibition, hawkers selling by-catch in the Georgetown market, and dried salt fish being loaded onto boats for transport upriver to the protein-starved interior population. I filmed an interview with Fred A. Peterkin, Project Coordinator, an Afro-Guyanese man who spoke with a British accent, just like Bert Allsopp, the head of IDRC's fisheries and aquaculture section. Fred said his dream was to develop a system of refrigerated collection tanks on trawlers, and the offloading of by-catch onto collector vessels at sea, thereby vastly decreasing the amount of wasted protein from shrimp trawling operations.

Did Fred Peterkin's dream ever come true? When writing this chapter, I searched for evidence and could find no such collection systems. The wastage of much of this valuable source of protein continues around the world according to a 1994 Food and Agriculture Organization (FAO) report[3] and a 2017 report by Oceana Canada.[4] But I did find that Guyana has become a major private sector fisheries center,[5] a fish processing and exporting center for the Caribbean Region, and is exporting fish products to the U.S.[6] This is positive but not exactly what IDRC had intended when it helped to set up that government-owned fish processing plant in Georgetown. Pilot projects can have many unpredictable outcomes. However, I did find evidence of another positive result: Guyanese now consume more fish per capita than any other people in the region.[7]

FILMING FISH FROM THE EARTH'S VAST OCEANS

We titled our 13-minute film *Fish By-Catch: Bonus from the Sea*[8] and it won *Le Prix Gestion des Resources Naturales* (the prize for natural resources management) at the 9th International Scientific and Technical Film Festival, Brussels, 1982. As I recall, this was my first film award.

My fondest fish filming memories are on trips to the Philippines, where I visited the research site of the Southeast Asian Fisheries Development Center (SEAFDEC) near Iloilo, on Panay Island. There, I captured the story of the milkfish (*Chanos chanos*), the most important aquaculture species in the country. It's a silvery marine fish that is the only living member of the family *Chanidae*, which dates back to the Cretaceous Period (145.5 to 65.5 million years ago). It is believed milkfish aquaculture began around 1200 C.E. in the Philippines and spread to Indonesia, Taiwan, and the South Pacific. In 1521, during his stay in these beautiful islands, Ferdinand Magellan, a Portuguese explorer, recorded milkfish ponds in the last few pages of his diary. He was killed on Mactan Island by natives who resisted his aggressive Christian evangelizing, but his crew escaped with his diary to continue the first recorded circumnavigation of the globe.

IDRC-funded milkfish research began in the early 1970s, and by 1974 a Filipino-Canadian team had succeeded in inducing artificial spawning of an adult milkfish by using hormonal injections and fertilization of its eggs with milkfish sperm. This was important because supply of fish fry was always limited and the full lifecycle of the milkfish in the wild remained a mystery.

MY UNIVERSITY OF THE WORLD

Harvesting milkfish at SEAFDEC, Panay, Philippines
—Photo by Neill McKee/IDRC

I had to return several times and hired Frank Green and others to cover all angles of this project. We filmed induced spawning of captured adult milkfish, but also took scenes of villagers with large fine nets mounted on floating bamboo frames, plowing through the shallow water near the shore at dawn, scooping up these minute fish fry—almost transparent except for their eyes—and transferring them to containers onshore. Some of the fry that escaped the villagers' nets would head back into the sea and return as adults, six or seven years later, to spawn and produce more fry.

At the time, this traditional operation of capturing wild milkfish fry provided seasonal employment for over 200,000 coastal people during April and May each year, but fewer than half of the fry survived the capture, transfer, and distribution process, while many more that did reach fish ponds never made it to marketable size, due to poor rearing methods. This whole process was a tremendous waste of natural resources in a country where 50 percent of the population suffered from protein deficiency.

The research IDRC supported at SEAFDEC was quite technical. I took various film sequences on improving pond culture with the right bottom soil chemistry to induce the growth of zooplankton, on which milkfish feed, and to determine the best methods of ensuring fry survival. But I added some artistic touches and music sequences to maintain audience interest. On my last visit, I recreated a sequence on the success of August 1980, when the project achieved natural spawning of a four-year-old fish in captivity—a huge breakthrough. I commissioned artwork to demonstrate the intention of setting up milkfish hatcheries and nurseries onshore, in combination with floating cages offshore, where milkfish would grow to sexual maturity.

SEAFDEC arranged an army helicopter so I could take aerial shots. I flew with a pilot nicknamed "the General" and his five-man crew in a huge military craft with open doors, two machine guns at the ready. Fortunately, we did not have to fly over the interior of Panay Island, where the

New People's Army, the armed wing of the Communist Party, was operating. I filmed some of the vast stretches of milkfish ponds on Panay Island's shores, as well as floating cages, and mangrove forests along the coastline. The General was cooperative. With our headset communication system, I directed him to fly low and slow to reduce vibrations, and he even held the helicopter stationary when I asked him to.

Milkfish pens at SEAFDEC –Photo by Neill McKee/IDRC

SEAFDEC also hired an underwater cameraman to film milkfish in their off-shore floating cages, where studies in maturation and spawning were taking place. I was surprised to see a whole film crew arrive from Manila: the cameraman, a coordinator, an assistant, and a representative of the man who owned the camera, along with his two wives.

The milkfish, known locally as *bangus,* is the national fish of the Philippines. The main object of the project was to learn the best methods of more intensive milkfish aquaculture rather than expanding areas of pond production, which would only destroy more coastal mangroves—the breeding grounds for many fish and shellfish species. To show the potential of the industry, SEAFDEC hired a helicopter to fly me over some of the 37,000 acres (15,000 hectares) of milkfish pens in Laguna de Bay, a large freshwater lake near Manila.

Milkfish pens in Laguna de Bay, Philippines –Photo by Neill McKee/IDRC

I also took shots of *bangus* in markets and restaurants serving a wide variety of *bangus* dishes. I loved the taste of this fresh seafood and the spirit of the people I ate with after we completed those sequences—camaraderie and satisfied bellies. Our celebration at the restaurant when we finished the mission was needed because it took us many days to get security clearance for me to fly over this area, since it was near some military installations. I had to complete a 10-page application, which included much of my personal history and even the names of my neighbors in

Ottawa. Finally, when permission was granted, the document read "Mr. McKnee" to film "Manila Bay." The fact they had made a spelling mistake on my name and wrote the wrong bay didn't seem to matter. I love Filipinos for their relative informality and ability to get around rules.

Was all this research successful? When writing this book, I googled "milkfish breeding and farming in the Philippines" and a flood of information appeared. Milkfish aquaculture production expanded from about 110,000 tons (99,790 metric tons) annually,[9] when the IDRC project began, to over 400,000 metric tons per year by 2019.[10] This was mainly due to the vast increase in fry production in hatcheries—over 860,000 by 2019 with a goal of 1.5 billion by 2024.[11] This increase was mainly due to the country's Bangus Fry Sufficiency Program, which benefited by IDRC-supported SEAFDEC research.[12]

Furthermore, the Department of Agriculture planned to establish 299 community-based hatcheries across the country. I also read SEAFDEC was completing a new broodstock facility and hatchery with thermal manipulation technology to ensure the water remains at the right temperature for year-round spawning, and the organization continues other studies such as the effects of climate change on the industry.[13]

When I finally finished the film titled *The Mysterious Milkfish: Increasing Yield Through Research*,[14] I invited Canada's popular science television host David Suzuki to the studio and sent him sequences of the film for use on his program, *The Nature of Things*, seen on the nation-wide Canadian Broadcasting Corporation (CBC). Also in 1983, *The Mysterious Milkfish* was given an Honorable Mention at the 26th San Francisco International Film Festival.

By then, I had also received an "honorable mention" at the showing of our new IDRC overview film, *Choices: The Role of Science and Technology for Development*,[15] on the occasion of IDRC's 10th Anniversary dinner. It was held at the National Arts Centre in Ottawa, and Prime Minister Trudeau was the guest of honor. After the showing, I had a chance to take a bow and briefly talk to him, reminding him of our first meeting at the garden party in New Delhi, in January 1971 (see Chapter 1). I don't think he recalled our previous encounter but, being a good politician, he didn't say anything that would show memory lapse.

I met Pierre Trudeau once more at a judo studio in Ottawa in the mid-80s, then a single father following his divorce from Margaret. He was attending the judo lessons of his young sons, Justin and Alexandre (Sacha), as I was for my children, Derek and Ruth. I reminded him of the film show and he fondly remembered it, but I didn't complain to him about what our kids had told me: Justin and Sacha were using the offensive tactic of spitting on them to win their matches. I can only hope that Justin, who went on to become the 23rd Prime Minister of Canada, eventually learned how to refine his fighting techniques, adhering to proper rules of competition.

Meanwhile on the Homefront

Despite my busy travel schedule during those years of filming and photographing the worldwide programs of IDRC, I always made it home for our children's birthdays. Beth put a good deal of energy into these celebrations, baking and icing cakes in colors and shapes ordered by Derek and Ruth—a clown's head, a butterfly, a fat cat, a dinosaur, a Raggedy Ann doll, Canada's coat of arms, a world map split into quarters forming Bartholomew's Regional Projection, and sometimes individual cupcakes decorated by the children to their tastes. My job was to photograph and sometimes film these occasions, as well as to supervise the use of my own backyard creations: a climbing frame, a shallow pool, and a set of swings.

From the family album—Birthday parties galore!
—Photos by Neill McKee

Beth also grew as an artistic calligrapher—not one who was satisfied with filling out certificates and diplomas with names of people she had never met. She got her start in oriental calligraphy, which is an art, and helped to found the Calligraphy Society of Ottawa, which grew into a large group of colleagues and close friends. Some of them had the objective of advancing occidental calligraphy from a craft into an art—embellishing beautifully written poetic words with complementary designs.

In the early 1980s, we had a carpenter insulate the third-floor attic of our old house, cover the wooden floor with tough indoor-outdoor carpet, and install a large window to improve the light in Beth's new studio. Beth painted the walls and ceiling at the other end—a magical scene with a large tree and green hills—and had our children paint flowers around the bottom. They and their friends were allowed to place our old stiff sofa cushions on the stairwell leading down to the second floor, and take turns sliding all the way down. The walls of the stairs were painted light-gray and acted as a free space for the kids' graffiti—the only walls they were allowed to draw on. We put our children into French immersion preschool, kindergarten, and elementary school—determined they become bilingual in our bilingual country—and Beth babysat other people's children after school, using the magical attic as a play area in cold or wet weather, and a great place for rainy-day birthday parties.

On the issue of religion, Beth finally gave up on the Lutheran Church and convinced me to go with her and the kids to a downtown Anglican church. She had heard a former Lutheran minister from Germany was the assistant rector there. I can clearly remember that early summer Sunday in 1981. The sun radiated through stained-glass windows as the rector took us through the rather formal proceedings, compared to what I had known during my

MEANWHILE ON THE HOMEFRONT

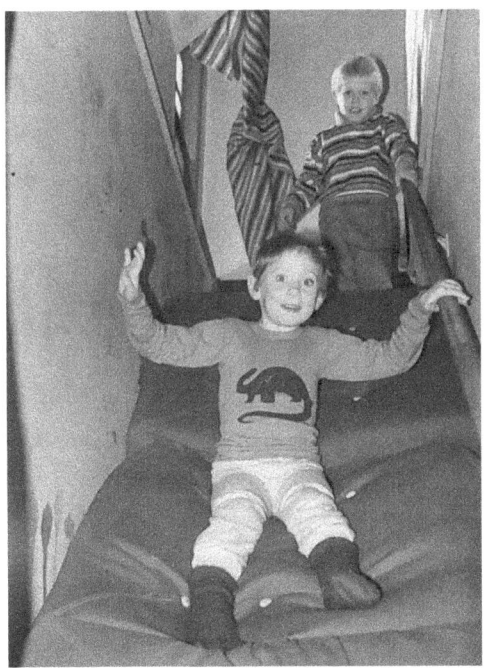

Mayhem in the magic attic –Photos by Neill McKee

plain Methodist-United Church upbringing. There was a lot of bobbing up and down, which I followed, and kneeling, which I avoided, but I sang the hymns—many familiar from my childhood. The first attention-grabbing part was the sermon. The rector had just returned from a conference in the United States, where Ronald Reagan and his so-called "Moral Majority" had recently taken over. The rector railed against such conservativism and fundamentalism in any religion, including the recent Islamic Revolution in Iran. The message made me wake up and pay attention. Here was a clergyman not afraid to speak his mind on social and political issues—making his church relevant in the world.

However, the best part of the service followed, when the assistant rector, Reverend Paul Busing, prayed. He was slow and quietly powerful in his German-accented delivery. His prayer was like a meditation on correcting the ills of the world without the usual platitudes and Bible references. At the end, Beth and I looked at each other and smiled in wonder. It's not that I suddenly reverted to Christianity, it was the fact this brand of religion had a lot in common with my own philosophy.

Beth had found her "father figure" in this church, whom she admitted she needed. We learned he had studied under Dietrich Bonhoeffer in Germany, during the 1930s. Father Paul, as we called him, had escaped Germany with his half-Jewish wife, Erika, as Hitler and the Nazis took over. I had read some of Bonhoeffer's writings in senior high school and university and was enthralled that I now knew someone who had studied under that famous man who, in 1945, was executed for his part in a plot to assassinate Hitler.

Father Paul preached to Lutheran congregations in England for a few years, and then he and Erika emigrated to Canada. For a period, he stuck to Lutheranism in small churches in the Ottawa Valley, but gradually grew weary of what he called "the tyranny of the congregation"—meaning the control each congregation had over how things should be done. He switched to the Anglican Church, in which the clergy have more say due to its ecclesiastical structure.

We soon struck up a friendship with Father Paul and Erika, and a small group of parishioners formed a reading group that met once a month in our house to discuss books with religious or spiritual themes, usually ending up by hashing over social and political issues. The group built their meeting dates around my travels, as much as possible. So, here I was in an enlightened Christian community where all my doubts about organized religion were accepted. Father Paul was a man who would also openly express his own doubts.

Beth had found the spiritual community where Derek and Ruth could get their grounding in the Bible. That was important to her, and our children loved it. I agreed it's hard to really understand Western history and literature without such background. Our kids joined the junior choir, which was run by the church's musical director, a gay man whose partner also attended the church. When I was home, I'd usually attend church with them and then we'd go to a Chinese restaurant for *dim sum* on the way home—a great family ritual.

My film editor friend and teacher, Sally McDonald, also became part of a family ritual by coming over to our place almost every Saturday morning for pancakes. I was in charge of making them, hollering "PANCAKES!" to the kids playing upstairs, when they were ready. Sally lived in a small apartment down the street and had become an honorary aunt, often treating the kids to small gifts when she visited.

During the years 1979-82, I was busy with travel, covering many projects, so I hired Sally as my editor for *Fish By-Catch* and *The Mysterious Milkfish*. She was always interested in detailed discussion and asked technical questions on every project I filmed. I suppose that came from her technical education as an engineer, but she also loved to engage in just about any social, political, or historical topic. She'd get on the nerves of some of the other employees at Crawley's, especially men, for her incessant questions and challenges in conversations. But I found such discussions interesting for they led me to new lines of thought.

When Sally wasn't working, she took university-level courses in geology and would often take off camping in her canoe to explore the Canadian Shield—a large area of exposed igneous rock, which forms the ancient geologic core of North America, stretching north from the Great Lakes to the Arctic Ocean. She usually traveled by herself through the rivers of the southern part of this wild forested land, picking rock samples and carefully numbering them. I'm sure she kept a detailed record of the location and type for each rock. When discussing her trips she described the colors of the sky, rocks, and forests as grayish blue-green—her favorite hues. One summer she joined a party to journey by canoe down the Mackenzie River to the Arctic Ocean. For her, this was like entering heaven.

In early 1982, I sent her to Southeast Asia to do a film script on post-harvest technology. I met her in Kuala Lumpur, while on another assignment, and she seemed fine. But in Bangkok, she experienced a pain in her gut and loss of

MEANWHILE ON THE HOMEFRONT

The author with Sally in Kuala Lumpur, Malaysia
—Photo by Neill McKee/IDRC

appetite. When I met her back in Ottawa, I encouraged her to see a doctor, thinking it was something she contracted in the tropics. But Sally was old-school—preferring not to complain or discuss her health issues with others. Health was a private matter. As the weeks went by, she continued to deny there was a major problem. I could see she was losing weight and kept bringing up the issue with her, as did her friend, Judy Crawley, wife of the owner of the studio. Finally, she saw her doctor, who referred her to an oncologist. Tests proved she had pancreatic cancer. I knew this diagnosis was probably a death sentence then, and anyone's chances of survival remain slim, even today.

Sally deteriorated quickly and I had to finish the editing of our milkfish film. To this day, I associate the music I edited into the soundtrack with Sally's demise. I can't recall much of the period except being called by Judy to replace her at Sally's hospital bedside the evening she died. It was then I realized most deaths we see in the movies are "Hollywood deaths." I sat with Sally for a couple of hours. Despite the morphine she had been given, she periodically went into spasms of pain as the cancer cells attacked her brain. Her skeletal head and torso would rise off the bed in such a gruesome way, eyes wide open, teeth grimacing. Finally, I said and motioned, "Hey Sally, it's time to give up."

A few minutes later she departed, and I just sat there with tears in my eyes before calling the nurse. Then Judy returned to comfort me. Before that dark night, I had no direct experience with human death, or what the poet Dylan Thomas might have meant in his poem *Do Not Go Gentle Into That Good Night* by calling on us to "Rage, rage against the dying of the light."

Although Sally came from Protestant Scots-Canadian background, she was never religious. So, we held a wake for her, without a body, in our house, inviting her other friends and studio colleagues. There were no prayers, just a few short speeches. As I recall, her brother followed her wish of cremation and scattered her ashes over the Bay of Quinte

MEANWHILE ON THE HOMEFRONT

on the shores of Lake Ontario, where she was born—United Empire Loyalist country.

We helped Sally's brother clean out her apartment—layers of paraphernalia she had collected through the years. We knew she was a hoarder but had not expected the extent of this obsession. We gladly accepted a set of green crystal tall-stemmed wine glasses, which appeared never to have been used. We also selected part of her rock collection, which we planted in our garden. Some of those special rocks traveled the globe with us, as we moved from place to place during the following years. Some had special numbers, which eventually wore off, but not our memories of Aunt Sally.

A few years later, Beth became inspired by those memories and wrote a poem about Sally, creating a piece of grayish blue-green calligraphed artwork, which hangs on our wall to this day.

Poem for Sally by Elizabeth McKee

Poem for Sally

This is a poem for Sarah (Sally) MacDonald, rock hunter and child extraordinaire whose body ceased to function when she was sixty three years young but whose heart wouldn't stop beating until two days later.

And for all the other perpetual travelers and seekers after truth who were not able to finish their quests. This is for all the Scots who found the rocks and all the others who could not leave them unturned. This is a poem for Sally.

This is a poem for all the immigrants who tried to tame the land and failed and loved it anyway: who found a place where both wild and tame could co-exist—respectfully though not always comfortably: who wanted peace and justice and the unAmerican way, and for their children who are trying to keep it that way.

This is a poem about a man of Scottish ancestry who grew up in the shadow of the Precambrian Shield and met Sally who searched for rocks in wild places and a woman who came from no fixed address who took the rocks that Sally had tamed and planted them in her garden with the wild flowers which she could not tame. Although she tried.

This is a poem about tame people who were touched by the wild soul of a monumental lady who do not wish to have their children lose her legacy—her love and awe of the land and her undying need to go into wild places and discover just one more secret—uncover one more rock.

And this is a poem for these children who search for wild rocks in tame places because they have never ventured out to where the wild rocks are: and the parents who have never taken them there.

This is a plea for wild places and wild rocks that they will always remain wild and free and discoverable because this is a poem for Sally.

Poem and calligraphy by Elizabeth McKee © 1986

Harnessing the Monsoons in Sri Lanka

Sri Lanka, formerly called Ceylon from the Portuguese name, *Ceilão*, is shaped like a teardrop falling from the southeast coast of India. Some have described its shape as a pearl, but to me its long history of invasion and colonization, conflict and wars, favors the teardrop interpretation. I'm lucky to have spent time on this beautiful island in a period of relative calm. I finally had a chance to visit in February 1980, while shooting the IDRC overview film *Choices*. I was accompanied by Paul McConnell, the Executive Assistant of IDRC's President, Ivan Head, who told him, "If you really want to learn what our organization does, travel with McKee." I agreed to take Paul along if he would help me carry equipment and act as my soundman, when required.

We visited and filmed several Sri Lankan projects, but the one I recall the most was on Cropping Systems. Simply defined, it was a movement at the time, throughout Asia, led by IDRC and the International Rice Research Institute (IRRI) in the Philippines, to adapt new varieties of rice to the systems already established by small farmers, rather than imposing innovations on them. Using these new varieties in completely new systems would be beyond their capacity, in terms of labor requirements and other inputs such as irrigation and expensive chemical fertilizers.

On arrival in Colombo, a driver from Sri Lanka's Department of Agricultural Research took us to their office in Kandy, a city in the highlands that was once the seat of the last Sinhalese kingdoms before European invasions began. The Sinhalese arrived on the island as Indo-Aryan settlers from northern India's Ganges Plain, in the late 6th century B.C.E. It is believed they introduced Buddhism in the mid-3rd century B.C.E. Kandy, at an elevation of 1,640 feet (500 meters) above sea level, was a cooler climate than the sweltering coast for the Sinhalese kings and then the Europeans—Portuguese, Dutch, and British—who ruled the island from 1619 to 1948. It's also near Sri Lanka's famous tea estates—another colonial legacy.

But we were not destined to stay in this lush landscape. We soon traveled north and downhill to a hot dry region full of scrub bush, poisonous snakes, and dotted with impoverished villages. Sri Lankans call most of this northern territory the "dry zone." This land was the original domain of ancient kingdoms of Sri Lanka, where Sinhalese and Tamil rulers built impressive cities, palaces, and temples—some ruins of which can still be seen today at Anuradhapura. As early as 300 B.C.E., Sinhalese kings ordered the building of sophisticated irrigation schemes,[1] including underground canals, to feed this otherwise dry land with waters from the Mahaweli River and other rivers flowing from the rainy highlands.

For centuries, ancient engineers also directed the construction of thousands of smaller reservoirs, which Sri Lankans call "tanks"—some in a cascading chain linked to the main canals, and other so-called "minor tanks" on higher ground, where they are rainfed. These minor tanks allow crops to be grown in areas outside the reach of the large irrigation schemes. Much of the vision and leadership for achieving this work goes to the Sinhalese ruler, Parakramabahu I, who reigned over the northern Kingdom of Polonnaruwa between 1153 and 1186 C.E. Due to the nourishment of all these canals and tanks, Sri Lanka was once an exporter of rice to much of the rest of Asia.

These marvelous irrigation systems began to crumble with the invasions by Tamil kings and their armies from southern India. Other historians have speculated the *Anopheles* mosquito, and the malaria it brought, were mostly responsible for the Sinhalese population's gradual move into the highlands and the southwest coast of the island—areas with plenty of rainfall. At the time of our visit, the government, with international support, was in the process of rebuilding the ancient canals and large reservoirs, while realizing much of the higher areas of the dry zone would always lie outside the reach of irrigation water.

Paul and I learned a good deal of this detail when we arrived at the research station of Maha Illuppallama, where we met Dr. Walter Fernando, Director of Agriculture Research. He was a pipe-smoking man with a weather-beaten face. I supposed him to be in his late 50s or early 60s. He came from the Burgher community, a small Eurasian ethnic group who descend from Portuguese, Dutch, British, and other European men who settled in Ceylon and had children with native women. In Fernando's case, I figured it was Portuguese ancestors who had been attracted to beautiful Sinhalese women.

Dr. Fernando was slow-talking and pensive, so it was easy to take notes for the script. We got to know him in the evenings at the Circuit Bungalow during our short visit, as we shared his favorite food and drink: roasted wild boar washed down with *arrack*—a distilled alcoholic beverage usually made from the fermented sap of coconut flowers. The *arrack* helped him embellish his stories on Sri

Lanka's agricultural history and his thoughts on what he and his team were achieving in their research at the village of Walagumbahuwa. He asked me to make a more detailed film for wide use throughout the country using the Department of Agriculture's mobile cinemas. I only required a short sequence for the general film I was making at the time, but as we talked into the evenings, I grew inspired by the possibility of returning to cover all aspects of the project. I had been communicating with IRRI about a cropping systems film, and this project seemed to fit the bill.

Model of Walagumbahuwa showing its tank, rice fields, uplands, and village —Photo by Neill McKee/IDRC

I returned to Sri Lanka, in mid-January 1981, with Claude Dupuis, my new audiovisual unit assistant. He helped with lugging the equipment and I trained him to be my soundman

and to take photos, when needed. At Colombo airport, we were met by Dr. Upesena, Cropping Systems Coordinator, who took us to Kandy, where we filmed population scenes in the city center before departing for the research station at Maha Illuppallama to meet Mr. Samarakoon, the local coordinator of activities at the village of Walagumbahuwa. By this time, these names were rolling off my tongue like an old Sri Lankan hand.

For the next week, from sunup to sundown, we filmed many technical scenes such as weeding, spraying, fertilizing, harvesting, winnowing, and threshing rice. We also filmed and photographed work on higher ground, known as the *chena* in Sinhalese, where upland crops such as chickpeas, cowpeas, soybeans, and chilies were grown. We took sequences of rice breeding experiments at the research station, and shots in another area where villagers were already adopting the new cropping systems methods.

When Dr. Fernando arrived, we recreated and filmed one of their organizational meetings, which had taken place when the project started in 1976. We also arranged filming of the annual harvest festival ceremony on the tank bund—an embankment holding back the water. This necessitated the collection of rice and coconuts from all the villagers, a process that took most of the day. At 4:00 pm, 18 portions of a rice-coconut porridge were served to honor Aiyannar, who, according to legend, was the engineer responsible for constructing their tank more than 1,500 years ago. Afterwards, another five portions were served to the "divines," as the village's religious leader chanted a Buddhist prayer over the offerings, holding his arms out toward the tank water. Then, about two hundred villagers, both adults and children, lined up to receive their portions of the communal rice meal—a beautiful scene that I knew would become our film's finale.

My companion, Claude, proved to be a winner with Sri Lankans. He was a handsome and affable young fellow who attracted a large following of children wherever we went in the village. He roped them into carting the equipment around, which they did with pleasure. Claude ate everything I ate, including Sri Lanka's famous breakfast, string hoppers (*idiyappam*), a chili-laden noodle dish, which starts your day by blowing your head off. Following my example, he even began to wear a *sarong* at the end of each day—a loose, wrap-around piece of cloth. It took Claude a little while to adapt to the idea of wearing a "skirt." He was pretty macho, priding himself on building his muscles by weightlifting.

When we returned to Kandy, I had to satisfy Claude by going to the Queen's Hotel, where Bo Derek and Richard Harris were staying while filming *Tarzan the Ape Man* (1981). Harris had left, but we managed to find Bo at dinner with some of the crew. Their film was one of the most ridiculous ever made. It involves Tarzan, played by a white muscleman, lusting after Bo's perfect body, while Richard Harris threatens to kill him. Tarzan doesn't speak one word throughout the whole movie—only yells while thumping his chest, as any respectable ape should do. Claude found a nearby table, where we could get the best view of Bo. To me, she seemed like an expressionless statue, but for Claude, this was possibly the highpoint of the trip.

The highpoint for me happened when we rented a helicopter to get aerial shots of Walagumbahuwa and the dry zone, the ruins of ancient kingdoms, and the completed Mahaweli irrigation scheme, as well as other irrigation works still under construction. The pilot removed the door of the craft and strapped me in with an extra belt, so I could put one foot on the step and lean out at an angle to get the best shots. I sped up the camera and opened up the aperture of the lens to make the shots smoother. Claude took photos from the rear seat, as best he could, but handed his camera to me to take unobstructed shots on second passes.

To do this film properly, I needed footage during the dry season and I arranged to hire a well-known Sri Lankan cinematographer, Willie Blake, who agreed to travel to Walagumbahuwa in August to film activities in the *chena*. The cultivation of crops on this drier upland requires special care, including allowing the land to remain fallow for a few years after growing crops, and then slashing and burning the bush before replanting. The problem for Willie was there was an abnormally brief period between monsoon

Slash and burn agriculture –Photo by Neill McKee/IDRC

rains that year, and he had to douse the bush with kerosene to film the burning part. This man knew the best tricks of cinematography.

Claude and I returned to Sri Lanka on October 13, 1981, and were met again at Colombo Airport by Dr. Upesena. An essential part of our mission this time was to film the monsoons, so we were a bit concerned to learn the rains had not arrived. To the contrary, Dr. Upesena assured us the monsoons would come on the 15th! The northern half of Sri Lanka is usually blessed with the northeast monsoon, the *Maha*, blowing off the Bay of Bengal from October until December, and the lighter *Yala*, the southwest monsoon during May and June.

We needed to show the *Maha* arriving in October and filling up a village tank to demonstrate the complete cycle: 1) as the rains begin, planting new varieties of quick maturing rice on the lands below the village tank, while it fills up; 2) harvesting the rice crop in January and holding the ceremony we had already filmed on our previous visit; 3) planting a second rice crop in March, using tank water in addition to the lighter *Yala* rains, starting in May, to bring the rice to maturity; 4) preparing the *chena* by slashing and burning the scrub brush, and after the second rice harvest, allowing the padi lands below the tank to lie fallow, as cattle and water buffalo graze on the grass that grows there, while at the same time fertilizing the soil with their dung; and finally, 5) starting the cycle over on the padi lands during October, when the *Maha* begins again, and at the same time, the *chena* and home gardens are planted with upland crops such as chili, beans, vegetables, and castor, which, along with the rice, will be ready for harvest in January.

Using buffalo to plough rice fields –Photo by Neill McKee/IDRC

Upland crops of chili and castor –Photo by Neill McKee/IDRC

Drying harvested chili –Photo by Neill McKee/IDRC

With Dr. Upesena, we headed toward the project area to cover scenes that were not possible before. But October 15th came and went, and the rains did not arrive, as he had decreed they would—and we kidded him about that. So, instead we drove to Kandy to film wet rice planting, tea plantations, and a fertilizer factory, all the time bouncing around on rough roads in our Agriculture Department jeep, which had little in the way of shock absorbers. Added to that, buses came flying at our vehicle even as cattle, elephants, dogs, and water buffalo suddenly appeared in front of us out of nowhere.

We returned to the project area on October 20th. While passing a village tank occupied by a few water buffalo, the delayed *Maha* suddenly arrived. I jumped into action while Dr. Upesena organized people to hold umbrellas over me and my camera. The drenched and contented beasts in the water gave texture to the scene of the tank starting to fill up again.

Filming the coming of the *Maha* monsoon
—Photo by Claude Dupuis/IDRC

The new cropping system had doubled the income of many farmers in Walagumbahuwa. We demonstrated this by starring Mr. Ranaide in a number of the sequences. He had recently purchased a small tiller-tractor for cultivating his land, and that of others for a fee. He could also use the tractor to transport his tools and harvests in a small cart. We filmed interviews between him and research assistants, who gathered comments and statistics from all the villagers on the effects of the experiment.

Mr. Ranaide and son on their new tractor
–Photo by Claude Dupuis/IDRC

During our visits to Sri Lanka, I clearly saw the ingenious concept behind IDRC's policy of funding local researchers to do their own thing, and only bringing in external technical guidance when needed. These researchers demonstrated patience, not imposing anything on the farmers. Instead, they used demonstration plots, discussion groups, and consensus meetings, as well as in-depth interviews to try to understand the farmers' points of view. They had employed a "total systems" approach, going beyond their biases and areas of specialization. They were beginning to apply the "Walagumbahuwa Concept" to other areas. The potential was excellent because there were an estimated 500 minor tank villages with a total of 250,000 acres (101,171 hectares) throughout the island nation that could benefit from adopting this system.

By contrast, I had a chance to visit a nearby project funded and run by the Canadian Government's aid agency, CIDA, which had been operating for three years. This involved Canadian agriculturalists—some with experience in dryland farming in Western Canada. They came with expertise in water management, agriculture engineering, animal husbandry, and weed control. They employed a local team of agriculture specialists and assistants based at the Mahailluppallama Research Station, but the Canadian experts lived in Kandy, 100 miles (161 km) away, where their families were housed and children schooled. I was told by their local staff they only visited the project site a couple of days a week. They had a fleet of cars and trucks, whereas their Sri Lankan staff didn't even have enough motorcycles to do their work.

The local staff I met complained about communication between them and their highly paid Canadian bosses. I wondered what these Canadian experts had to offer the dryland farmers of Sri Lanka. I talked to some of them and found them to be cynical, only waiting out their contract periods. Instead of looking at the total system, they were attempting to introduce changes based on their specific areas of expertise. Their methods, by all indications, were failing. One frank Sri Lankan official I met summed it up like this: "If we could only have the money and resources these CIDA fellows are eating up, we could achieve a lot more."

On the last day of filming at Walagumbahuwa, our model farmer, Mr. Ranaide, invited us to tea at his small thatched-roof house—a real honor. That evening, we recorded a few local musicians for the film's soundtrack, and then we drank *arrack* and beer with the project staff who had helped us so much. The next morning, the combination of *arrack* and beer proved to be near-fatal, compounded by Dr. Upesena's insistence we try some toddy as a hangover aide: fermented coconut flower sap—fortunately not distilled like *arrack*.

Villagers and staff gather for a final goodbye photo at Walagum-bahuwa, Dr. Upesena on the far left —Photo by Claude Dupuis/IDRC

We had to leave the research station by 9:00 am because, we were told, by 1:00 pm the two-lane highway to Kandy would be the "Queen's Road." It so happened that our visit coincided with Queen Elizabeth II's tour of Sri Lanka. As we drove south, road crews were making last-minute repairs and local people were decorating their towns and villages with bamboo structures cloaked in Union Jacks, Sri Lankan flags, and banners displaying the words "Long Live the Queen" and "Long Live the President." We laughed when we passed through one town where we saw people in the process of raising a banner, half in Sinhalese and half in English, welcoming "Queen Elizabeth and Duck Edinburgh." We drove into Kandy, greeted by throngs of people waiting for the royal procession, which wouldn't arrive for five hours. We waved at the crowd as we passed, imitating the Queen's usual stilted handwave, and got some puzzled reactions.

There was much reverence for the Queen because, from independence in 1948 until 1972, the British monarch remained the head of state of the Dominion of Ceylon and the Queen was represented by a ceremonial Governor-General, who by 1954 became a Ceylonese national. This was the same arrangement still maintained today by Canada, Australia, New Zealand, and a number of former British colonies that take the attitude "If it ain't broke, don't fix it." But it's not the attitude of many French-Canadians, like Claude, who couldn't believe what he saw on the road that day. He said, "This is crazy! Why would these people have so much reverence for a former colonial ruler?" At the time, Quebec's separation from English Canada was still a hot topic.

Before going to our hotel, we paid a visit to Dr. Fernando at his office. Our discussion was brief because the cropping systems project was the last thing on his mind. As guardian of Kandy's Botanical Gardens, the next day he was to meet the Queen and show her around. But we did manage to discuss his plan to distribute the Sinhalese and Tamil versions of our film through 25 mobile cinema vans in the 25 divisions of Sri Lanka.

That evening, Kandy was decorated with lights for a *perahara*—a colorful parade of elephants and dancers with torches. We were told security would be tight and we had no permission to film. But Claude and I waited in the hotel until 8:00 pm and then, carrying our imposing equipment, marched through the crowd to a lighted spot beside a government film crew. We announced ourselves as "friends of Willie Blake," the famous cinematographer I had hired to cover the dry season. No further explanation was needed. Willie's name was our passport. We waited there, across from the Queen's Hotel, where we had observed Bo Derek a few months earlier, to see Her Majesty pass by and wave her white gloved hand at us. I need not describe the difference in enthusiasm expressed by Claude between the two encounters.

We had little purpose for occupying this spot—there being no place in our film for a royal blessing of cropping systems. Claude recorded some useful background music, while elephant trunks sniffed my zoom lens and Claude's long boom microphone, and torches passed precariously over our heads. There wasn't much room between the elephants' feet and the rather volatile crowd. We were told there were rumors of riots in the air. Thankfully, the crowd was somewhat subdued by the late arrival of the Queen and a light rain.

The next day, we took Dr. Upesena and his family to an early lunch to express our gratitude for his good guidance, and then headed to Colombo by road. Fortunately, there was little traffic, for the Queen and her entourage were taking the slow train downhill to Colombo. We rushed to the airport but found it was already closed for the arrival of the Queen. Three hours later, we finally took off, thinking of what all the rupees spent on the red-carpet arrangements and machine-gun security could have done for the people of Walagumbahuwa and other tank villages in the dry zone.

Harnessing the Monsoons: Improved Cropping Systems in Asia[2] eventually became the title of our film. I returned in early May 1982 for the Sri Lankan premiere, attended by my Sri Lankan friends, including Dr. Fernando, who had become the overall Director of Agriculture. On that trip, I helped with producing a Sinhalese version. Reports reached me that our film was used throughout the country for some years, and the English version was also widely screened by IRRI and other partner organizations in Asia, to disseminate the concept of cropping systems. Our film was useful in educating students and project personnel around the world on the meaning of a full-systems approach to agricultural development in the tropics. It won the prize of Best Audiovisual in an annual contest run by the Information Services Institute, Ottawa. I also wrote an article titled *The Return of Aiyannar* on the Walagumbahuwa concept for Asia 2000, a start-up magazine based in Hong Kong. I enjoyed this new writing sideline.

Thinking back to that day in October 1981, when Claude and I left Colombo airport surrounded by machine guns, they were probably present because riots had begun that year between the majority Sinhalese and minority Tamils. At the time, we had no idea an armed conflict was breaking out between the Tamil Tigers and the Sinhalese-dominated government—a civil war that unfortunately lasted until 2009. Fortunately, the central drylands, where we filmed, and the southern drylands, never became main war zones.

While writing this chapter, I googled "cropping systems in minor tanks, Sri Lanka." I was happy to see a website demonstrating how the work has continued,[3] with technical papers on the best mix of crops and optimum use of water, as well as a video that include interviews with villagers who know about the 1,500-year history of the large and small irrigation tanks in their country,[4] including the need to sustain these systems, which, to this day, continue to feed millions.

For the present, at least, the machine guns have been put away, and Sri Lankans move forward with innovations in crop and water management in the dry zone of their tear-shaped island.

Clean Water and Sanitation for the Developing World

In the ancient world, the citizens of China, India, Peru, Persia, and parts of the Roman Empire, developed clean water supplies and sewage disposal methods in some of their cities. These systems did not spread widely, nor did they last, as the ruins of such innovations remind us today.[1] Lessons were lost to future human settlements. In fact, one time in the 1980s on a stop in London, I went into a museum to see a replica of a well dug into an old pit latrine. It had provided drinking and household water for a London neighborhood until the mid-1850s. Such wells were covered to prevent dirt and garbage from falling in, and the water was usually drawn using handpumps. Despite these precautions, cholera broke out in London in 1831, 1848-49, and 1853-54, killing thousands. At the time, most people thought cholera was spread through the air until a doctor by the name of John Snow reasoned if it was spread by air, it should cause lung diseases, whereas the main symptoms were gastrointestinal—severe diarrhea and vomiting, often resulting in death.[2]

Through the scientific methods of observation and collection of statistics on cholera cases in one London neighborhood, Dr. Snow pinpointed how these cases mainly occurred by drinking unboiled water from a particular well on Broad Street, which was surrounded by pools of polluted water. It took a few years for him to convince others, through further research, that when human and animal feces were dumped into cesspools on the ground around wells, the pollution could seep into well water.[3]

On February 2, 1983, I found myself in Kibera, a squatter settlement in Nairobi, Kenya, with my colleague Fibi Munene, a Kenyan journalist recently hired by our Communications Division to act as our Eastern and Southern Africa representative. She had a great sense of humor but didn't laugh or even smile at what she saw in her city: thousands of insects feeding and breeding in trash heaps and stagnant water pools; long lines of people waiting their turn to get treated city water from a few taps; people defecating in the open because of run-down filthy latrines; black streams of water full of the bacteria, viruses, and parasites—all of this contributing to the spread of cholera, typhoid, and dysentery. In the developing world at the time, acute diarrhea caused by these diseases was killing five million children under five years of age, annually. Repeated attacks led to severe malnutrition, a condition that caused the death of millions more.

In our walk through Kibera slum, we had to keep our mouths shut and watch where we stepped. Fibi had never entered Kibera before and was horrified at what she saw—the result of thousands of rural-urban migrants pouring into the city over the past 20 years, with little or no planning, resources, or regulation for their illegal but tolerated occupation of the land. There were five other squatter settlements in the city and we visited two of them, always accompanied by a police guard arranged by Fibi for our safety. Fibi's low-keyed approach really helped us get the

CLEAN WATER AND SANITATION FOR THE DEVELOPING WORLD

Street in a Nairobi slum —Photo by Neill McKee/IDRC

shots I needed. One time a rock was raised at me by an angry youth, although not thrown, fortunately. I hated taking shots that would appear insulting and exploitative. But I had an idea on how I would use them sensitively.

These were the first scenes I captured for an educational film I was asked to make on water, sanitation, and hygiene, working closely with Donald Sharp, an American immigrant to Canada and public health expert in IDRC's Health Sciences Division. This film was different from my other IDRC productions in that, rather than covering scientific research or a pilot project, the purpose was to widely disseminate well-known ways of preventing the deaths of thousands of people in developing countries. The narration of our finished film started with these words:

> Human life and human progress depend on water—water which is both servant and master. For the majority of women in rural areas of the

developing world, water is their master. Much time and energy are used in its daily pursuit. Children too must join the unending task. The goal of the 80s is to bring a safe and adequate water supply and sanitary facilities to as many people as possible, throughout the world.

Kenyan girl collecting water —Photo by Neill McKee/IDRC

CLEAN WATER AND SANITATION FOR THE DEVELOPING WORLD

The United Nations had declared the 1980s to be the International Decade on Drinking Water and Sanitation because, by the end of the previous decade, nearly two-thirds of the population of the developing world had no access to safe drinking water and even a larger portion lacked the means for hygienic human feces disposal.

After Kenya, I flew to Sri Lanka. On February 6, I filmed similar scenes in a Colombo slum, this time accompanied by representatives of the Sarvodaya Movement, an NGO working for development and social justice in the poorest sectors of the population. Here, I was joined by my assistant, Claude Dupuis, and Bill Clarke, an artist from Crawley Films. Bill was shocked at what he saw. I wanted him to get a taste of this reality because I had hired him to design animated film sequences of the fecal-oral routes of infection. I knew using live action of defecation would be too disgusting for most people to watch, and it could stigmatize particular national or ethnic groups as "dirty people." Animated figures, on the other hand, could be drawn in a more neutral manner as "somewhere in the tropics."

Crowded community water tap, Colombo –Photo by Neill McKee/IDRC

Next, Sarvodaya personnel took us 170 miles (274 km) south on a winding narrow coastal highway, with buses flying by in the opposite direction, while bullock carts, motorcycles, and pedestrians suddenly appearing on the road in front of us. Like elsewhere in South Asia, Sri Lankan drivers get where they are going by blaring their horns, playing chicken with on-coming vehicles, and applying their brakes or swerving at the last second. Claude and I were used to this chaos from earlier visits, but Bill was rattled. When we arrived at the town of Matara, at the very southern tip of the island, we checked into a decent guest house, which charged the equivalent of only U.S. $4.00 per person per night, and then we plunged into the Indian Ocean. That, and a gin and tonic or two, cooled Bill's nerves.

Just outside Matara, we filmed the installation of an innovative water pump fabricated in Sri Lanka by Sarvodaya. Don Sharp was spearheading an experiment with pumps made locally, using plastic components, as described later in this chapter. Before returning to Colombo, we also filmed a preschool at the Sarvodaya center—children from low-income families being taught the basics of household hygiene. We had to get across the message that clean water supplies and well-built latrines would do little if people didn't understand the fecal-oral route of disease. At Matara, Bill also had a chance to try out his initial drawings on Sarvodaya field staff.

On February 10th, we flew to Bangkok, Thailand, and the next day linked up and discussed progress with Don Sharp, accompanied by Lee Kam Wing from our Singapore office. We took a boat tour through the *klongs* of that famous city, not to film its golden-roof temples, but the slums where thousands of people regularly dumped household waste, feces, urine, and offal directly into the water. Then we went to visit PDA—the Population and Community Development Association of Thailand, where we met Mechai Viravaidya, its leader. He's a famous Thai personality who had popularized family planning in unorthodox ways, including blowing up condoms as balloons at public gatherings. Mechai's communications head, Tanaporn Praditwong, reviewed our animation storyboard and finalized a detailed schedule for us.

On February 13th, we drove in a van to the northeast of the country, accompanied by two delightful PDA hostesses. For the next four days, when stopping for lunch or dining in the evening at local restaurants, they ensured we never repeated a dish. This was Thai hospitality at its best.

In rural areas near Khon Kaen, we took useful footage of people drawing household water from open polluted wells, and the construction of water tanks for a rainwater roof catchment project. The northeast of Thailand is its driest area, so storing water in the rainy season is vital. My problem was PDA had added their own video crew and a visiting consultant to our tour. When Don and Kam Wing arrived, it seemed there were more visitors than villagers. I actually had to look out for extraneous bodies wandering into frame. I had prided myself in getting good shots and sequences with a minimal crew: myself, a soundman, and—when needed—a technical guide who could also act as interpreter. This crowd was frustrating; so the next day, with one PDA staff member, Claude and I escaped the large group to get some useful sequences of poor household hygiene practices, communities building latrines, a health worker addressing a village, and school children being taught hygiene lessons.

Bill had gathered enough background and feedback to finish his artwork, so he returned to Canada, while Claude, Kam Wing, and I flew to the Philippines. During February 20 to 27, we were hosted by Cecilia "Caby" Verzosa of PATH—Program for Appropriate Technology in Health. Caby had to obtain official permission for us to film because the BBC had recently broadcast a TV program on poverty and corruption in the Philippines under President Marcos. She had to assure the authorities we would not take any footage that portrayed the Philippines negatively. Apparently, Caby was trusted, for no government minder was assigned to accompany us.

Caby, Kam Wing, and some of Caby's crew with the author
—Photo by Claude Dupuis/IDRC

We did get excellent sequences of clinics and community action programs run by women—the main facilitators of social change in the country. One morning, we drove to Malabon, a fishing port near Manila where we could film urban squalor. We boarded a small boat and soon found ourselves on a dark creek, thick with floating human and animal feces. Caby held a handkerchief over her nose. We filmed desperately poor people living along this sewer. *Great shots*, I thought. But then our boat's propeller hit something hard while we were passing under a bridge, and we had to get down beside a latrine and pig pen, carefully avoiding the mushier-looking "mud."

By this time on our trip, Claude and I had learned how to keep our lips sealed, our eyes to the ground, and never to take an uncalculated step. We all climbed out of the sewer, took some deeper breaths, and caught a jeepney taxi back to our hotel for showers. Caby had a degree in communication, so she knew we needed general footage with impact. She had delivered. But like Fibi Munene in Nairobi, I don't think she was prepared for seeing, up close, the extent of the problems rural-urban migrants faced when they sought new lives and means of making a living in overcrowded cities.

On February 27th, Claude and I flew to Bangkok to catch a connecting flight to Dhaka, Bangladesh, our last location for this film. We had to take a fully packed Bangladesh Biman flight—a precarious carrier at the time—and we felt even more apprehension when boarding because some of the Bangladeshi passengers on board were wearing crash helmets (purchased in Bangkok for use on motor-cycles). In spite of the odds stacked against helmetless passengers, we arrived safely in Dhaka at midnight. But one bag containing vital camera parts and all of my exposed film from the Philippines was missing. (I have included the details that follow to give the reader a taste of the problems I sometimes encountered as an itinerant filmmaker in those days.)

I insisted on inspecting the airport and the cargo section, to no avail. Next, I had to transfer my long equipment list, including the missing items, onto their official customs forms. Everyone was following the rules exactly because General Muhammed Ershad had taken over in a coup in 1982, and had declared martial law.

After a two-hour process, the customs authorities politely impounded everything but our clothes. Then an airline employee came running with a telex, gleefully announcing our missing case would arrive in the morning on a Thai Airlines flight. As on previous visits, I found Bangladeshis to be accommodating and as welcoming as possible.

The next day, our host agency's representative connected me with a man from the Ministry of Information and I headed back to the airport with him. After 45 minutes, he obtained permission from the martial law authorities for us to enter the customs area, where he had to go through 10 separate steps. I was amused by the sight of the man from the Ministry bobbing in and out of offices to chase down various officials for signatures. The officials had to search through Dickensian-sized ledger books, transferring descriptions, numbers, and dates from one antiquated form to another. This brought back memories of the absurdist existential plays I had studied at university. Nevertheless, in a couple of hours, we managed to get my equipment out.

With the missing items returned, I was finally able to focus on my assignment. It is believed cholera originated in the swampy Sundarban forests of what is now southeast Bangladesh, previously part of Bengal, India. The British East India Company had started to exploit the area in the early 1800s, releasing the bacterium *Vibrio cholera*. Our host agency was the International Centre for Research in

CLEAN WATER AND SANITATION FOR THE DEVELOPING WORLD

Diarrheal Diseases, Bangladesh (ICDDR,B), which originated with the founding of the Cholera Research Laboratory and Hospital in 1960. Among its many achievements, this institution had played a key role in the development, testing, and use of oral rehydration solution (ORS), a simple treatment estimated to have saved tens of millions of lives, worldwide.

I had met Dr. Mujibur Rahman, Deputy Director of ICDDR,B in 1976, when he accompanied me while I was filming *Rural Health Workers* (see Chapter 8). Don Sharp had lined up a meeting between Bill Clark and Dr. Rahman in London, and now he was keen on getting our film produced. He especially loved the idea of using animation to show fecal-oral contamination.

On March 2nd, we flew south to Cox's Bazaar on the Bay of Bengal, and then proceeded down a bumpy single-lane road to Teknaf, the most southern and possibly the most isolated district of Bangladesh, then with a population of 90,000. Besides Dr. Rahman, we were accompanied by the local research coordinator, an anthropologist, a field research officer, and a female health educator. At first I thought there were too many people involved, as in Thailand, but we went over the shot-list in the evening and by the morning they had divided up their duties; then each team member headed off in a different direction to make filming arrangements.

For the next two days, all Claude and I had to do was follow them around to take the scenes they had set up: both good and bad hygiene in households, latrines, and pumps, and a hygiene education lesson at a Koranic school. The involvement of the health educator was instrumental, for women in Teknaf lived in *purdah*—separate rooms or behind curtains, or dressed in enveloping black *burkas*, to stay out of the sight of men, especially strangers. The health educator somehow gained permission for us to film women doing their daily work in a few households.

Left to right, Dr. Rahman and staff member with villager
–Photo by Neill McKee/IDRC

In Teknaf, we stayed in a run-down guesthouse without electricity or running water. Fortunately, it had mosquito nets because, at the time, Teknaf was one of the world's hotspots for cerebral malaria. Also on the plus side, March was the Bengali spring, with cool nights. During our second evening, I recorded an interview with Dr. Rahman to gather background for the film script and a magazine interview on ORS. He was so articulate, insightful, and helpful that I decided, then and there, he should be credited as a technical advisor on our film, along with Don Sharp.

As our group sat around and talked by candlelight, I could see a full moon and the mountains of Burma (now renamed Myanmar) silhouetted across the Naf River. Even in the 1970s and 1980s, the now-famous Rohingya Muslim people crossed the river daily, without passports, to see their cousins in Bangladesh, or to buy and trade goods. There really was no border.

On March 5th, we returned to Cox's Bazaar to catch a night train to Dhaka, our only option. The next day we recuperated in the morning and then went over the animation storyboard with the ICDDR,B team for a final time. We saved the worst for our last morning in Bangladesh—filming in the Cholera Hospital: diarrhea victims hollering in agony from acute dehydration, some who had come too late and were near death; others on the road to recovery; and complicated cases of malnourished children with diarrhea. For these victims, the agent of sickness and death was *Shigella* dysentery, not cholera. Those recovering were the lucky few who lived near enough to make it to the hospital in time for proper treatment.

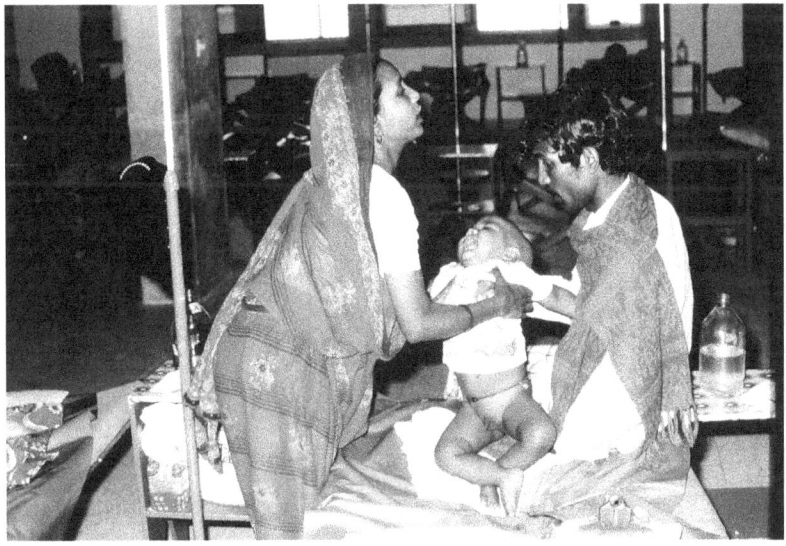

Shigella dysentery patient with parents –Photo by Neill McKee/IDRC

I used the live action negative and somewhat disgusting footage, which audiences would not want to watch while eating lunch, in the opening of the film, and in some later parts for reinforcing messages. By carefully editing shots between differing countries, I avoided stigmatizing any one nationality or ethnic group. I also used live action to show Asians and Africans doing things right, the need for community involvement, and the important role women play at every level in delivering safe water, sanitation, and hygiene.

According to the feedback we received, however, the key to our film's success was the careful creation of seven animated film sequences on the fecal-oral route of diseases and how to prevent it. This included scenes of animals and humans defecating in a river, with their pollution represented by a glowing gray-white substance carrying bacteria, viruses, and parasites—all flowing downstream to a young girl scooping up the polluted water in a jug. She takes it home and pours it into a larger water vessel, which is then used by the family for drinking, washing, and cooking.

The same gray-white substance demonstrated the danger of using water from open contaminated wells. It also showed the main points of contamination within households; for example, a mother not washing her hands thoroughly after cleaning a baby's bottom, and then preparing food for the family.

Through the magic of animation, people who never had been taught disease theory could see how fecal contamination happened, and how the gray-white substance could be eliminated by taking a number of safety measures: building low-cost safe latrines, only drawing water from safely covered wells with reliable handpumps, installing drainage systems around wells, preparing a separate place where people could bathe and wash their clothes, and by eliminating household infection points. We received feedback that our main messages were understood by illiterate audiences, even without voice-over narration in their languages.

Before Claude and I left Bangladesh, we met with Ken Gibbs, a United Nations Children's Fund (UNICEF) water and sanitation engineer. Gibbs had already reviewed the shooting script and trusted Dr. Rahman's opinion. He told us he would use the film to train 700 mid-to-lower-level water supply engineers who had inadequate education on sanitation and hygiene. He also offered to fund the Bangla language version of the film. This was a fortuitous meeting for, after I finished the film, it was used all over Bangladesh in mobile cinemas for health education, and it led me to do much

Frames from animation showing fecal-oral route of disease

more work with UNICEF on other language versions around the world.

During the post-production process, I took a copy to Geneva to meet Dr. Rahman with Dr. Michael Merson, the Director of the World Health Organization's Diarrhoeal Diseases Control Programme. He and his team loved it, and that helped to put our 23-minute film on the world stage. We titled our final production *Prescription for Health*,[4] and in June 1985, it won the World Health Organization Special Prize for best primary health care film at the 11th International Festival of Red Cross and Health Films.

In 1985, I also worked once more with Don Sharp and his team to make a film on handpumps made of plastic, as briefly mentioned above. More specifically, some of the main internal components were made of polyvinyl chloride (PVC) and polyethylene. Research on this had first begun at the University of Waterloo, a few miles from my hometown in Ontario. In the surrounding countryside, as a child, I had seen old rusty handpumps on farms, some with broken handles, so I was quite familiar with the technology. Even in the 1980s, most handpumps were manufactured in Europe or North America and their designs had hardly evolved. These pumps were suitable for use on single-family farms, but not for continuous use by 200 or more people a day in African or Asian villages.

Don Sharp and I visited the Faculty of Engineering at the University of Malaya, Kuala Lumpur, Malaysia, to film Dr. Goh Sing Yau and his team in action, manufacturing their version of the Waterloo handpump. We filmed the changes they made to the Waterloo design, and endurance testing in their lab. They had already produced many units for field testing

Assembling PVC piston valve and completed pumps, University of Malaya
—Photos by Neill McKee/IDRC

in rural areas, and the next day we filmed handpump installation and maintenance by Ministry of Health personnel in a village called Kuala Pilah, a short drive from Kuala Lumpur.

We also filmed testing of the pump in Thailand, but more memorable to me was a return to Sarvodaya in Sri Lanka. Arriving at Colombo airport, Don and I were easily waved through customs with all my equipment when we said, "We're visiting Dr. Ariyaratne of Sarvodaya." We then proceeded to Sarvodaya headquarters to meet him. As the leader of his movement, Dr. Ariyaratne had become a famous personality, known for his good works throughout the island nation and around the world. Through his Buddhist ideals of selflessness and compassion, he had come to be known as "Sri Lanka's Gandhi."[5] Unlike many of his countrymen, he practiced principles of non-violence and bottom-up development. He involved millions of villagers in improving their lives through shared labor, galvanizing them to build over 5,000 preschools, as well as thousands of community health centers, libraries, cottage industries, and village banks. The Sarvodaya Movement also initiated the construction of thousands of wells and latrines, while promoting biodiversity and solar energy, as well as rehabilitation and peace.

The next day, we traveled with a Sarvodaya media crew, climbing up the winding road to Kandy and then headed east to a small town called Padiyatalawa. The town bordered land occupied by the Liberation Tigers of Tamil Eelam, otherwise known as the Tamil Tigers, who continued their war against the government, trying to establish a separate state. But Dr. Ariyaratne told us we would be fine in a Sarvodaya vehicle. Regardless, it was a little unnerving when another vehicle was sent ahead of us to determine if it was safe to continue.

Arriving in Padiyatalawa, we immediately began to film the Women in the Handpump Technology Project, which was jointly sponsored by IDRC and CIDA. I filmed a group of young women dressed in smart blue shirts and pants, making PVC pumps in a workshop: running lathes, drilling, welding, grinding, assembling, and installing them in villages. Some women had set up small workshops for basic pump repairs and they were allowed to make extra income by repairing farm tools and household items for villagers.

These young women, who had an average education of Grade 10, were allowed to join the project so long as they signed a pledge not to get married for two years. This had the dual benefit of decreasing wasteful attrition of the work force, and also delaying child birth in the area, thereby increasing women's chances of attaining higher education and having safer births, when and if they married. This was one of the poorest areas I had seen in Sri Lanka, and I knew improving the role and status of women was a key to change.

Earlier, the Sri Lankan Government, with support from UNICEF, had come through the area with an expensive

Sri Lankan women manufacturing and installing the Sarvodaya handpump – Photos by Neill McKee/IDRC drilling rig and peppered it with Indian-made pumps; however, most of their metal parts had corroded and people found the water metallic tasting, so they were only using the wells for washing and bathing. Sarvodaya took a different approach. They built their own drilling rig at a fraction of the cost of a commercial one. Also, they consulted villagers on their preferred places for well and pump installations, and once installed, they instructed them on proper use and maintenance.

Sarvodaya made changes to the University of Malaya design, based on the quality of materials available. Both PVC and brass were used, with leather piston rings, since locally manufactured PVC pipe was too rough and would cause PVC rings to wear out rapidly. Due to these modifications, the project seemed to be successful. People liked the taste of the water from their new wells. Before our project, there had been little or no involvement of local people—by then a familiar story to me.

Don had commitments elsewhere, so I flew by myself to Addis Ababa, Ethiopia, our final filming location. The country remained in the hands of President Mengistu Mariam and his Derg, the socialist-military *junta* backed by the Soviet Union, as mentioned in Chapter 8. Ethiopia had recently suffered from two years of famine, during which an estimated million people died, partly due to forced resettlement. The northern Tigrayan armed rebels were on the rise. I mused with irony, *What a great time to return to this country!*

I was met at Addis Ababa airport by Professor Asegeb Mammo, the project leader at the University of Addis Ababa, and Alex Redekopp of IDRC's Health Science Division in Ottawa, who had arrived a couple of days earlier to monitor the project and ensure all arrangements had been made for our filming. Right away, we boarded a Canadian-built DHC-6 Twin Otter plane bound for the Bale Region, in the far south of the country. By 4:00 pm on the same day, I was filming a handpump training session at 10,000 feet (3,048 meters) above sea level. Prof. Mammo had tried to line up a soundman, but failed, so Alex had to learn how to run my sound equipment on the spot.

The water pump training session involved village men, and women in bright flowing dresses. I think they wore their best clothes for the occasion. The pumps, which had been installed earlier, were being heavily used by the villagers, most of whom had been relocated by the government to this isolated settlement.

It was a good thing to show another example of adaptations made to the original Waterloo design in a completely different cultural setting. The stationary foot valves were first made of PVC, but the PVC produced in Ethiopia was found to be of such poor quality that the piston valves, which move up and down, wore out quickly, and had to be replaced by valves made of brass castings with leather rings. In addition, it was found any above-ground exposed PVC components would not last, for they would soon be chewed up by hyenas. Apparently they took them to be bones.

Returning to Addis Ababa, we filmed manufacturing in the university's workshop, including the casting of brass pistons in a small foundry. I got the bright idea of filming

Ethiopian women learning the basics of handpump maintenance
—Photo by Neill McKee/IDRC

ancient-style Ethiopian Orthodox Church crosses, which were made of brass and sold in local markets. We had just about finished the sequence when we were arrested by the People's Militia, bearing AK-47s. It took some time to explain what we were up to, despite Dr. Mammo's letter of permission to film. The head soldier of the unit went off to consult his superior, while we waited. Fortunately, the local chief was an intelligent fellow and we were released. Although I am not a believer, for a few moments I held on tightly to my newly purchased cross—a dramatic ending to another filming trip.

Eventually, with funding from CIDA, the University of Malaya became the center for a worldwide network for PVC handpump development and testing. Today, many varieties of PVC pumps are made locally and their handles are bobbing up and down all over the developing world. When we finished our film, we gave it the title *A Handle on Health*.[6]

The 1980s International Decade on Drinking Water and Sanitation brought clean water to 1.2 billion people and sanitation systems to 770 million, but that decade was only the beginning of concerted action. I also found an even more impressive statistic. Between 1980 and 2015, annual childhood diarrhea deaths declined from five million to one million, while the population of the world nearly doubled.[7]

Yes, human life and human progress depend on water, and IDRC's research, pilot projects, and our two films had become part of a successful international movement in human health and development.

Finding Solutions for *Campesinos* in South America

I landed in Bogota, Colombia, on April 23, 1984, with a bang. Our Eastern Airline DC-10 blew one tire on hitting the runway and another while taxiing in. It was fully loaded and it took a couple of hours for two small vans to carry 20 people at a time to the airport terminal. Another two hours passed by before my equipment cleared customs, even with the help of my IDRC Communications Division colleague Stella Feferbaum.

She also brought along Heriberto Garcia, a Colombian filmmaker who would act as my soundman and interpreter for the next month, as we made our way southward through the Andes Mountains. Since he had never traveled south of Colombia, he was looking forward to exploring his home continent with me. Heriberto became a wonderful partner in filmmaking. He had a great sense of humor and was fluent in English, so could easily translate my directions: "Friend, don't walk so unnaturally!" "Please don't stare at the camera." On top of that, he loved discussing things and asking questions.

I was not a complete novice to South America. In 1975, I had filmed in Colombia, Venezuela, and Guyana (see Chapter 8). Then, in March of 1981, I had taken two still cameras and a tape recorder and flown to Santiago, Chile. From there I traveled south by train for 600 miles (900 km) to an area where Mapuche indigenous people were struggling

Heriberto Garcia interviewing a pig –Photo by Neill McKee/IDRC

to survive in the cold foothills of the southern Andes. Next, I journeyed north through Chile, Peru, and Colombia. I visited, in all, 15 IDRC research projects on education, health, agriculture, and fisheries, traveling by myself with little ability in Spanish. Fortunately, I always found English-speaking personnel at our project sites. It was a pleasure to meet so many smart and motivated people; and, for a change, it was a relief to travel without lugging around all my heavy equipment.

On that trip, I managed to take about 2,000 images and the interviews I taped with project leaders served as background for four articles, which I later authored or coauthored for *IDRC Reports*, our quarterly magazine. I also received many requests from project leaders to return and make full films featuring their work.

This return mission, in 1984, was for the purpose of shooting a film requested by Tony Tillett, Associate Director for Science and Technology Policy in our Social Sciences Division. Tony gave me some background on the countries I was to cover:

> "Extreme land tenure inequality has been a constant feature of Central and South America since the conquest by the Spanish, over 400 years ago, and it had a major impact on indigenous communities and increasingly commercial smallholders. Although there were calls for major land reform and more equal distribution and ownership, this was only significant in three countries: Mexico in the 1930s; Bolivia in 1952; and Peru under the military regime in the 1970s. The Cuban revolution did not redistribute land, but claimed it for the state. In other countries, during the 1960s and 1970s, there were some land reform initiatives but not on the major scale of those noted above."

Tony also told me the projects I visited and filmed made up a network of small attempts to revalidate indigenous agricultural practices, human rights, and increase knowledge about rural markets and appropriate technology.

In the morning, Stella briefed me, saying the situation in Colombia had deteriorated over the last three years. Leftwing guerrilla groups and rightwing paramilitary organizations were involved in drug trafficking, extortion, and kidnapping to finance their activities. The drug trafficking had begun in the 1960s by U.S. mafia, but it had been taken over by competing Colombian groups with links to U.S. criminal operations, and innocent people were getting caught in the crossfire. From the time I entered Colombia until I left a week later, I was always on edge. I felt like a target with all my equipment and *gringo* looks.

Next, Stella, Heriberto, and I took off for Cali, a city to the southwest in the tropical Cauca Valley—a land described in the 18th century by Simon Bolivar, the Venezuelan-born liberator from Spanish colonization, as "an earthly paradise." It's close to the Pacific Ocean and lies at an altitude of 3,337 feet (1,014 meters), compared to Bogota's altitude of 8,660 feet (2,640 meters). It was good to breathe properly and feel warm again, but I had to be prepared for many altitudinal fluctuations on this trip.

From Cali, we made our way through the countryside to the campus of La Fundación para la Aplicación y Enseñanza de la Ciencia (FUNDAEC), which is translated as "the Foundation for the Application and Teaching of Science." (South Americans love using acronyms because their institutions often have long names.) FUNDAEC is an NGO founded in 1974 by Farzam Arbab, an Iranian physics professor of the Baha'i faith. It involves impoverished rural communities in action research in agriculture, community organization, and new income-generation initiatives. I found that South American's educated class usually called the rural poor "peasants," when discussing their problems in English, but the word sounds so medieval and pejorative to the modern native English ear. The expression "small farmers" also sounds limiting, so I will use the Spanish word, *campesinos*.

In much of South America, these people are of mixed indigenous and European blood, but in the Cauca Valley we filmed many Spanish-speaking descendants of African slaves. They had lost their small parcels of land due to expropriation or competition from large privately owned *haciendas*—sugar plantations and other agribusinesses such as enormous cattle ranches. Some of the rural poor worked in these enterprises, but with mechanization, many were losing their jobs and migrating to cities to live in poverty, while others clung to small plots for survival. They had the desperate choice of either rural or urban hunger and ill-health.

We interviewed the Executive Director, Gustavo Correa, a highly articulate man, and during the next four days we filmed male and female students of both African and mixed Hispanic descent in classes, and in the field, while they studied agriculture extension work or learned new ways to earn a living. We also filmed experiments in appropriate technology, a model farm, as well as small businesses and micro-industries such as metal works, cement products production, grain milling, and bakeries—all resulting from FUNDAEC's outreach to the community. The instructors taught students by using the institution's own textbooks, course curricula, and methodology. There were three levels of trainees: promoters, technicians, and "engineers of rural well-being." FUNDAEC personnel referred to their institution as a "rural university" but only the engineers were educated up to the tertiary level. The graduates served as bridges between the world of modern science and technology and the *campesinos'* traditional methods. The object was to institutionalize the process of development within rural communities themselves, not impose answers from outside.

Classes and field instruction at FUNDAEC
—Photos by Neill McKee/IDRC

Our time at FUNDAEC was rewarding and I took a lot of film footage, not knowing what I would find in other countries during the trip. The organization seemed to be idealistic and

A bakery started with support from FUNDAEC –Photo by Neill McKee/IDRC

somewhat socialistic, fighting the trends of 20th century capitalism. The words they used to describe the purpose, objectives, and strategies, appeared to have an overly intellectual tone, which contrasted with their practical activities. That philosophy, I knew, came from the tradition of education started by Paulo Freire in Brazil, as stated in his famous book *Pedagogy of the Oppressed*,[1] which I read before my first long trip through South America. But I wondered if this was all rhetoric and whether FUNDAEC would be able to continue, due to the violent armed struggle going on in Colombia at the time.

While writing this chapter, I punched in "FUNDAEC"[2] on my computer and found the organization alive and well today. Obviously, this institution must have had some success through its 46 years of operation, despite the drug wars in the area. Otherwise, donors and Cauca Valley residents would have given up on it. I read the language on its website, which was just as flowery as ever, if not more so. That's the Latin America way, as exemplified by what they said about their logo:

> FUNDAEC's emblem is a symbol of movement, interrelation, harmony and strength. All these lines intertwined with each other, resemble the development processes of a town. Each process alone as a thread of a loop is not very strong, but when it is joined with the others, the force that this union produces is clearly seen. These well-managed processes become a vital force capable of driving the continuous improvement of a community, small or large.

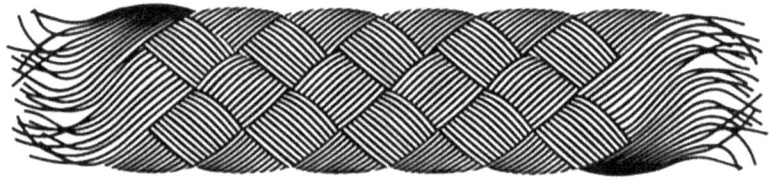

FUNDAEC logo

From Cali, we flew back to Bogota, where Stella ended her trip, while Heriberto and I boarded a flight for Quito, the capital of Ecuador—altitude 9,350 feet (2,850 meters). In Ecuador, we visited the Centro Andino do Accíon Popular (CAAP),[3] the "Andean Center for Popular Action" in English. I had to smile when I read online what they do today (possibly a computerized English translation):

Each thematic space called program, implements and is made up of specific projects that involve research-training activities and organization of action as components, which aim to recognize, debate and incorporate knowledge, resources and local initiatives, towards the recognition and revitalization of processes. Building alternatives from society, from its practices, skills and initiatives, considering its diversity and heterogeneity, is recognized and incorporated as an operational concept. This defines, as a substrate, the CAAP methodology, concurrent with its central objective, and therefore its actions and intervention modalities. Each action of intervention and technological generation also implies, as intrinsic components, specific punctual investigations.

Hmm...okay, but what did they do in 1984? Believe it or not, these activists were more practical than that description, and we got down to work right away—fortunately with an expert guide by the name of Lenny Field, a British agriculture economist. This solved my problem of trying to understand what CAAP's work was all about. I found that Spanish conversations flow very quickly, with lots of acronyms and buzz words. Also, many words in Spanish have quite different meanings from what sounds like the same word in English. (We call these false cognates or "false friends.")

At the time, CAAP's main objective in Ecuador was to save ancient Andean agricultural crops and patterns from the onslaught of agribusiness. The IDRC-sponsored research had just begun, but for two days we filmed large *haciendas* and multinational companies such as a Nestles' baby food plant, a noodle factory, and pyrethrum plantations grown for the production of insecticide. We also interviewed farmers and took sequences of crop trials on their fields, eroded

CAAP researcher interviewing a farmer —Photo by Neill McKee/IDRC

soils, mountain scenes, and Heriberto and I couldn't leave Ecuador without having one of CAAP's staff members snap a photo of us at the equator.

Standing at latitude 0.00, a line, from which, Ecuador derives its name
–Photo by CAAP staff member

On May 4th, we flew from Quito to Lima, Peru on the Pacific coast. Our stay in this warm metropolitan center, teeming with activities, allowed me to catch my breath in more oxygenated air. I had gotten to know and love this vibrant place on my 1981 trip, but this time my stay was brief. The next morning, Heriberto and I hired a taxi to take us to Huancayo. Within minutes we were climbing steeply up a winding highway into the Andes. When we reached the highest point, at exactly 15,899 feet (4,843 meters), we got out to take the obligatory photo. I tried to walk around but my whole body felt like lead, whereas Heriberto and the taxi driver were used to high altitudes. Fortunately, the ride downhill to the Mantaro Valley brought me back to life, although the City of Hauncayo is still relatively high, at 10,730 feet (3,271 meters).

In 1981, I had visited Grupo Talpuy (Talpuy Group), an association of ethnologists and artists, and told them that, one way or another, I would return someday to make a film on them and their work. The local language, Huanca, is a dialect of Quechua, which is spoken throughout much of the high Andes. In Huanca, *talpuy* means "to sow." I was impressed with Maria Angelica Salas and her German husband, Herman Tillmann, two social anthropologists. They insisted I call them "Maruja" and "Timmi." It was the beginning of over 40 years of collaboration and friendship.

Heriberto and I were invited to stay with them in their wooden house, constructed in native Huanca style, with a large balcony running along the front, normally for storage and domestic work. On the first night, Timmi and I stood there sipping the famous Peruvian drink, pisco sour, while I asked him about the fires I could see burning on the other side of the valley.

"Timmi, those flames seem to be in the shape of a hammer and sickle."

"Yes, Sendero Luminoso."

"Shining Path, the Maoist guerilla group?"

"Yes, we will film over there in the hills tomorrow."

"Are you kidding?"

"They know our group and they are watching us. But at this point, they don't know what to do with us."

The Shining Path was an arm of the Communist Party of Peru. Their objective was to overthrow the government through guerrilla warfare, replacing it with a dictatorship of the proletariat, bringing about a cultural revolution. Fifty percent of the fighters were women. Grupo Talpuy was in no way aligned with these insurrectionists, but was respected by the Huanca people for its work. A few times after we talked to local people, Timmi told me which person he suspected belonged to Shining Path.

I learned some of the history of settlement in Mantaro Valley. It goes back to 500 B.C.E. and their culture flourished until around 1530 C.E. At first, they were herders; however, about 1000 C.E. they turned to maize cultivation. For centuries, they fought off domination by the Incas but were finally defeated in the mid-1400s. When the Spanish explorer Pizarro and his men arrived in 1526, the Huanca joined them to defeat the Incas. In fact, Pizarro's success was largely due to the Huanca and other native groups who despised their Inca overlords.

Before Grupo Talpuy was created, the official Peruvian agriculture extension service had tried for 30 years to disseminate and implement models and methods of improvements, which had been attempted worldwide. These had failed in Peru. What interested me most about the work of Grupo Talpuy was their communication approach through a popular magazine called *Minka*, which means "the cooperative way" in Quechua and its local dialect, Huanca. The magazine was used to reclaim and diffuse useful traditional culture and technologies, which were rapidly being lost. I found it interesting that most of the estimated 200,000 Huanca in the valley could speak and read Spanish—a good advantage for using a magazine as a main means of disseminating ideas.

Grupo Talpuy had found their first few issues of *Minka* were too full of "technological recipes," which held little meaning for their readers: illustrations such as plans for houses that

Mantaro Valley farmers using appropriate technology –Photo by Neill McKee/IDRC

were not within their tradition, and fragmented messages in cartoon style. They consulted the people through qualitative research and began to partner with local artists, who used traditional artistic designs to communicate stories. For instance, the Huanca had a long tradition of carving stories on gourds and doing paintings of house building and fiestas, which were central to their culture. These were disseminated via *Minka*.

We spent our days in the valley filming traditional technology: housing construction, spinning and weaving wool, sewing and embroidering, wood carving and engraving gourds. Another example of reviving traditional technology was the *chaquitacalla* or *chaka*, a narrow shovel with a special place to put your foot while shoving down into the soil. Many people had forgotten about this useful tool used for centuries by their ancestors.

Huanca artistic creations
–Photos by Neill McKee/ IDRC

Minka was attempting to bring it back. We also took sequences of Grupo Talpuy members interviewing *campesinos* on their complicated agricultural practices on the slopes of the Mantaro Valley. The Talpuy researchers found that families would spend the evening hours reading and discussing each issue covered in *Minka*.

Due to mounting armed conflict between the rebels, the Peruvian Army, and local police, Timmi and Maruja found it too difficult and dangerous to work in the Huancayo Valley, so they moved to Germany, with their two children, shortly

Maria Angelica Salas talking to a Huanca farmer on the utility of the *chaka*
—Photo by Neill McKee/IDRC

after I filmed them. The team they left behind continued to publish *Minka* until 1996, when funding ran out. But out of Minka came the Coordination Commission of Andean Technology (CCTA) in Peru, and a group of activists named Proyecto Andino de Tecnologías Campesinas (PRATEC)[4] (Andean Program for Peasant Technology), a program aimed at the reaffirmation of Andean cultures.

After a week, Heriberto and I returned by taxi to Lima to fly to Cusco, where we would do more filming facilitated by the Inter-American Institute of Cooperation on Agriculture (IICA). This included spectacular shots of people harvesting maize on valley floors, shepherds minding flocks of llama and alpaca on high plateaus, and scenes in between—an intricate system of agriculture managed by *campesinos* on small terraced plots: grains, vegetables, fruits, tubers—more than 60 domesticated crops, which, when grown together, support soil fertility, repel insects, and deliver the best nutritional value for each crop.

The highlands of Peru, Bolivia, and Ecuador are known as the original home of the potato. Over the centuries, the *campesinos* of these lands have bred numerous varieties in different sizes, shapes, and colors, which grow well at various temperatures and altitudes, up and down the slopes. Some contain natural insecticide and thus repel pests. Their bitter taste has to be washed out by placing them, for some time, in fast-flowing streams before being cooked and eaten. Some bitter varieties grow above 13,000 feet (4,000 meters) and are planted for the production of *chuño*—frozen, washed, and dehydrated potatoes, which can be stored for many years.

Maize, pastureland, and potatoes galore! –Photos by Neill McKee/IDRC

The Spanish brought the potato to Europe, where many farmers practiced monocropping of a few larger and fast-growing varieties, leading to disasters such as the Irish potato blight and famine, which caused my own maternal ancestors to emigrate to Canada. If only the Spanish had sailed home with the wisdom of Andean *campesinos*, along with potatoes.

In addition, we filmed experiments in cropping and intercropping varieties of *quinoa*, a high-protein Andean grain, which, at the time, was pejoratively considered "Indian food" and was in danger of being abandoned as the older farmers died off. (Probably no one knew, at the time, that 40 years later, it would be available in just about every upscale grocery store in North America and Europe—part of the health food movement. Unfortunately, this "*quinoa* craze" has driven up prices so high that now most of the harvested grain is exported from Andean countries. Many local people can no longer afford it and have to rely on less nutritious grains.)

An old woman proudly displays her *quinoa* plot
–Photo by Neill McKee/IDRC

Next, Heriberto and I flew southeast to Asunción, Paraguay, a city at a mere 322 feet (98 meters) above sea level. It's a

FINDING SOLUTIONS FOR CAMPESINOS IN SOUTH AMERICA

landlocked country between Argentina, Brazil, and Bolivia, where the majority of people are *mestizos*—a mixture of Guaraní natives and the Spanish who invaded the land during 1524-1537. When we arrived, most Paraguayans were celebrating a two-day May Day holiday. Despite this, the director, Domingo Rivarola of CPES, the Centro Paraguayo de Estudios Sociológicos[5] (Center for Sociological Studies, Paraguay), took us on a long trip through the southeast of the country toward the border with Argentina, where poor *campesinos* were attempting to make a living by hacking away at the forest to clear small plots for farming. These were people of few resources, juxtaposed against large soybean farms owned by German, Japanese, and Brazilian settlers. We spent a night in a cold cabin in the forest. The owners must have built it in the summer and forgot to install a fireplace or stove. It was May and approaching winter in the southern hemisphere.

A settler clearing a small plot to farm in southern Paraguay
–Photo by Neill McKee/IDRC

Brickmaking in rural Paraguay –Photo by Neill McKee/IDRC

CPES's research had just begun, but we managed to film many relevant scenes on their attempts to improve the lives of *campesinos*: small-scale maize and soya farms, brick production, a factory making soap out of coconut, another producing syrup from sugar cane, and a small enterprise producing pottery and other crafts. We also filmed interviews between *campesinos* and CPES researchers, and took shots of large cattle-raising *haciendas*. By this time, the South American story was familiar to me—the never-ending struggle between vested interests and people of little means.

The role of CPES entailed doing studies and trying to influence government policy through publications and seminars. That was undoubtedly a tough sell, for, at the time of our visit, the country was run by the right-wing dictator Alfredo Stroessner and his Colorado Party. He

FINDING SOLUTIONS FOR CAMPESINOS IN SOUTH AMERICA

remained in power until 1989, when he was overthrown in a military coup. After civilian rule was restored in the early 1990s, except for a brief period, the Colorado Party has continued to rule over the country, ensuring the rich get richer and the poor stay poor.

Our final southward flight took us back over the Andes once more; this time to Santiago, Chile, to meet and film the Grupo de Investiogaciones Agrarias (GIA),[6] another band of social scientists and agronomists trying to find answers for the *campesinos*. That was a tall order. In 1981, I had written this paragraph in one of my articles about the country's many superlatives and fluctuations:

> Chile is a land of superlatives: the world's narrowest country with the longest coastline and the driest desert. A local tourist brochure I read boasted of the world's highest lake, the most concentrated solar intensity and the ocean's biggest oysters. At the time of my visit, the country had probably experienced the world's greatest fluctuations in social and agrarian policy: 1960—the Catholic Church had begun to turn over some lands to *campesinos;* 1968—the Agrarian Reform Law was passed but only enacted in a minor way; 1970—major agrarian reform began, and by mid-1973, 5,906 large farms had been expropriated—a total of 24.7 million acres (10 million hectares); and

then in September of the same year, Allende was overthrown by General Pinochet in an American CIA-backed coup; in 1974—agrarian reform was reversed, and by mid-1977 a third of the expropriated land returned to the original owners, another third auctioned off, and the remaining least productive land parceled out to *campesinos*.

GIA's director Jaime Crispi and his staff gave us a good rundown on the situation in the country before we headed 124 miles (200 km) southwest with Lizardo Pina and Joachim Benavente, who had efficiently lined up scenes for us to film: *campesinos* working on seed-bed preparation, apiculture, raising pigs, charcoal production, fish farming, and a small-scale greenhouse. GIA had built a technical program centered on different low-cost technologies, which *campesinos* could adopt.

The next day, two other GIA staff members, Miguel Diaz, a veterinarian, and Marc Nederlof, a Dutch agriculture student, accompanied us on a 10-hour train trip south. Four days of steady rain miraculously ended to allow us to film sequences of GIA staff working with the Mapuche native people in the cold wet hills east of Temuco. The harvest was over, so there was little activity to film on the land. I recall walking with our filming equipment for over an hour through mud—a thick cold mud, which defines Mapuche land for much of the year. In the rainy season, the land is transformed into a quagmire, and the *campesinos* huddle in their isolated shacks for some semblance of warmth.

FINDING SOLUTIONS FOR CAMPESINOS IN SOUTH AMERICA

A Mapuche home in the Andes foothills –Photo by Neill McKee/IDRC

In their language, *mapu* means "of the land," and *che* means "people"—an ironic meaning, for Mapuche have little land. The terrain was familiar to me, for as I mentioned in the opening of this chapter, in 1981, I had traveled even farther south by train from Santiago. Reaching Osorno, I had been taken around by another Dutch student, Jani Brower, who was doing her master's thesis research with a Chilean educational group, which was funded by IDRC. The group was focusing on communication between parents and children in Mapuche communities. I learned a good deal about the land and its people. This excerpt from my article reflected that:

> This is a land of little comfort, marked by a history of conflicts—border squabbles with Argentina and class struggle; fights between those in favor of and those opposing land reform during President

Salvador Allende's time in the early 1970s; then after the coup that overthrew him, the Mapuche began to fight among themselves and they became badly disorganized. Unemployment was high in the region and *chicha*, a crude local alcohol drink, was the release mechanism. But alcoholism is only a symptom of much greater social illness. The gulf between the "haves" and the "have nots" was so wide you couldn't see one side from the other—just like the terrain, almost permanently shrouded in mist.

During the Pinochet era, he introduced a law, declaring there were "no indigenous people in Chile, only Chileans," despite the fact Mapuche make up 10 percent of the population—that's over a million people today. I was impressed with their resilience against great odds.

A Mapuche family -Photo by Neill McKee/IDRC

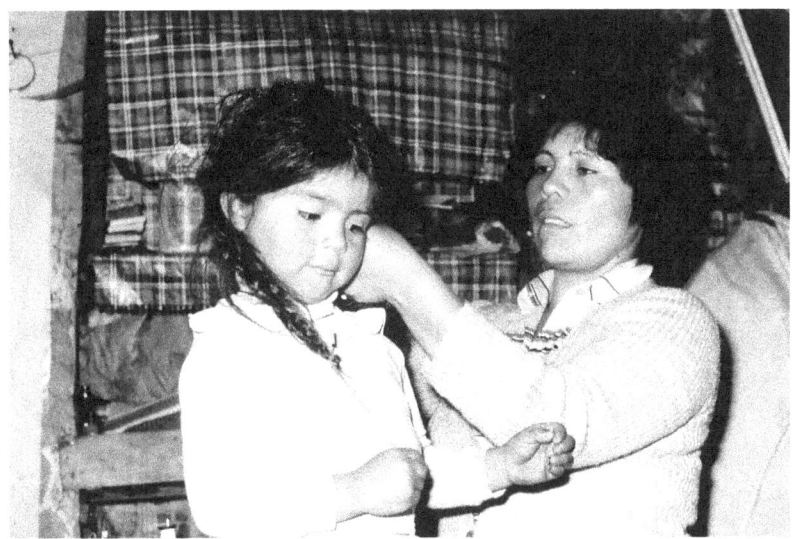

Mapuche mother and child —Photo by Neill McKee/IDRC

Today, Chile is one of the most prosperous nations in South America, but like the rest of the continent, and most of the world for that matter, it's plagued by wide income disparity. Mapuche still face difficulties in getting jobs and receiving equal pay. But in 1993, the government passed the Indigenous Act, which theoretically provides for protection and development of indigenous groups in Chile. No land transfers can take place without their consent, and a state authority with Mapuche representation was established to oversee the enactment of the law. I read Chile has been defined as a multiethnic society for the first time in the nation's history.[7] But we shouldn't be over-optimistic, for the same article goes on to say:

> Chile has a high pressure to develop fast according to the neo-liberal model. Large-scale development projects, which were initiated during the

Pinochet era, go on today. There are roads being built through Mapuche areas, the forest is being felled at fast speed and big power plants are being constructed in the rivers. When it comes to these large-scale projects, the Mapuche still feel infringed on their historical and cultural rights.

It is difficult to pinpoint causation in economic and social development, but somehow, while reviewing my trip reports, the articles I had written, and the film I shot with Heriberto Garcia during those 30 days in 1984, there's some evidence this IDRC-supported research in South America had positive effects. When completing this chapter, I asked Tony Tillett what he thought. He replied:

"Each of these projects had begun separately and was based on a community/communal methodology to social change. Some were in their second phase; some had just begun. They were not a scientific approach to agriculture production, although this was an important element in many of them, but were based on community perceptions about how change should occur, reflecting on 'traditional' knowledge. The value of the network was that each organization brought a different approach to local issues. Thus, CPES in Paraguay, used modern survey and observational techniques; CAAP in Ecuador brought the power of a broad indigenous organization; FUNDAEC in Colombia focused on structured approaches to learning, so that the individual community

FINDING SOLUTIONS FOR CAMPESINOS IN SOUTH AMERICA

extension worker would go through a series of stages to become a "rural engineer;" and Grupo Talpuy in Peru, with its publication *Minka*, added a capacity to communicate both activities and results."

The organizations I visited and filmed had been ready with the facts and strategies needed to make a difference for South America's *campesinos*, as political conditions improved. In English we titled the film *Footholds*[8] to indicate climbing mountains is difficult work, but I prefer the Spanish title, *Paso a Paso*—step by step. That version received an Honorable Mention at the 2nd *Festival de cine del desarrollo* (Festival of films on development), Colombia, in 1985. Not bad for a gringo!

18. Filming Multipurpose Trees Around the World

On August 1, 1984, I traveled through West Africa with my colleague Jean-Marc Fleury, to film trees and the lack of them. He is a science writer who acted as my interpreter, soundman, and guide, for he had come to know the region well. At the time, he was based at our regional office in Dakar, Senegal, the country where, in 1976, during my first year at IDRC, I had survived our vehicle rolling over at dusk in a rural area (see Chapter 8).

I had been tasked with making a series of short films for IDRC's forestry experts: Gilles Lessard, Derek Webb, Cherla Sastry, and Karim Oka. Jean-Marc and I started with scenes of desertification around Ouallam, 56 miles (90 km) north of Niamey, the capital of Niger, a former French colony in the Sahel—that dry band of land stretching across Africa south of the Sahara. Here, all forms of life were precarious because the rains had failed for years. The few trees I could see were dying. We filmed crops withering, goats eating the last vestiges of leaves, and cattle carcasses lying all around. The desert was advancing southward. At the time, few people were talking about human-induced climate change on a global scale, but we were witnessing it first-hand.

Niger had been colonized between 1900 and 1960. The French imposed a European export model on the entire Sahel region, totally changing the landscape, institutions, and practices of agriculture and forestry. This succeeded during wetter

Drought, famine, and firewood exploitation in the Sahel
—Photos by Neill McKee and Jean-Marc Fleury/IDRC

periods in generating wealth for the colonizers and a few local elites, but such exploitation increased the vulnerability of most people—especially during episodes of drought—leading to frequent famines for millions of rural farmers and pastoralists.

The principal factor, according to the information available, was the expanding population's insatiable demand for firewood, the only affordable source of energy for most Africans, at the time. Electricity was only available in cities and larger towns, and petroleum products were too expensive. Solar cookers had not yet been adapted to African cuisine, and energy efficient stoves were only being used experimentally. So, firewood comprised 90 percent of their energy requirements, and open fires have more than a cooking function. Gathering around a fire at night to tell stories and celebrate life is a cherished ritual in Africa, just as in North America, at least when on vacation or camping—never mind that most of the energy produced goes up in smoke.

FILMING MULTIPURPOSE TREES AROUND THE WORLD

Returning south toward Niamey on the same day, we took shots of women and children hauling small loads of firewood on their heads, and men with larger loads on bicycles, on camels, in trucks, and on boats while transporting it across rivers. We also captured sequences of wood burning practices: bakeries, breweries, brick kilns, fish smoking, and traditional barbeques at restaurants and in home compounds.

After making arrangements, Jean-Marc and I drove to Zinder, 590 miles (950 km) to the east. Flight schedules had all changed and we predicted the old Land Rover with driver we had rented would not make it. Fortunately, the Canadian Embassy lent us a driver and a vehicle with an official Government of Canada logo on its doors. With this imposing emblem and the *ordre de mission* Jean-Marc had arranged, we made our way through about 20 police checkpoints to Zinder.

There, in the evening, we met Hamari Zada, Director of Forestry for the region. He had a whole program lined up for us. He told us how the area to the north of Zinder had also been devastated by a long drought, and he would take us there the next day. We agreed, but I wondered why we had come all this way to film more of what we had already captured on film near Niamey. While traveling, we asked him to stop so I could take a shot of a row of dead cattle. But he refused, saying we could take them on the way back. I knew by experience it would be too dark by the time we returned. Despite this incident, the day was not a total waste, for we did capture a camel caravan heading north toward the Sahara, a scene used in the opening of our film.

Camel heading north in Niger —Photo by Jean-Marc Fleury/IDRC

The next morning, August 7th, we traveled southeast of Zinder into a very different Africa. I sped up my camera to take a steady moving shot of a green land of crops dotted with trees. We drove to the small town of Matamèye, where IDRC had been carrying out an important experiment in community forestry for a decade—growing village woodlots that had involved the villagers from the beginning. It was not an easy process: ethnic affiliations, grazing rights, and complicated land ownership patterns had to be taken into account. The project's researchers had spent time learning about the ancient relationship between trees, crops, people, and their animals in this region.

Before this intervention, the people had received opposing advice from agriculture extension workers and foresters. The former wanted them to clear land for crops, and the latter advised conserving trees. Now, the two worked together with the villagers to plant native acacia trees and fast-growing neem trees from India. These were being intercropped with cereals such as sorghum and millet. Older *Acacia albida* trees (also known as *Faidherbia albida*), dotted the land around Matamèye, their roots holding the soil firm. These leguminous trees also have the ability to fixate nitrogen from the air on their roots and produce nitrogen-rich pods and leaves to further fertilize the soil, as well as provide shade and fodder for animals.

Millet fertilized by a leguminous tree –Photo by Neill McKee/IDRC

We filmed meetings with villagers and small tree nurseries run by farmers, each producing hundreds of seedlings each year. Previously, the villagers considered planting trees to be the government's business. But after being taught the correct methods, they took responsibility for planting, and caring for the seedlings by building simple barriers to keep hungry animals away.

We took a sequence of children in school being taught the importance of trees. We also filmed villagers cutting some of their woodlot trees for firewood and building materials, and pruning second growth to allow new shoots to grow more rapidly. They were drawn together to reap the benefits. The whole scene inspired me. This experiment was really working!

MY UNIVERSITY OF THE WORLD

Villager watering seedlings in his mini-nursery
—Photo by Neill McKee/IDRC

Harvesting wood from a village woodlot
—Photo by Jean-Marc Fleury/IDRC

When we returned to Niamey, we filmed "The Day of the Tree," including the President of Niger and his entourage, the diplomatic core, and a large crowd who had been rallied for the purpose. A brass band played, followed by speeches and formalities, then everyone, including the President, walked to a field to the beat of African drums to plant trees. An impressive show, but I wondered how many of the seedlings would survive, and whether this political commitment would have any impact beyond Niamey. I didn't take any shots of the President's face, for I knew that could date our film. African presidents continued to be frequently overthrown in coups by their military.

Despite our skepticism about the "The Day of the Tree," before we left Niger, Jean-Marc and I were told the IDRC-supported Matamèye experiment had already become a model for similar projects elsewhere in the country, for example at Maradi. This sounded hopeful, so we decided to title the English version of our 18-minute film *Trees of Hope*[1] and *Les arbres de l'espoir* for the French version. Our film went on to win a special prize at Ekofilm '86, the 13th International Festival of Films and Television Programs on the Environment; and also in the same year, the Red Ribbon Award for Environment and Ecology at the American Film & Video Festival.

So, what happened to all this experimental work and our toil and sweat while capturing it on film in temperatures of 110 degrees Fahrenheit (43°C)? When writing about these memories, I searched on the Internet and found, to my surprise, our efforts had not been wiped out by climate change. In 2018, The Guardian newspaper, U.K., published an article titled *The Great African Regreening: Millions of 'magical' new trees bring renewal*.[2] The article emphasized that "This is not a grand UN-funded project aiming to offset climate change. Small-scale farmers have achieved it because of what the trees can do for crop yields and other aspects of farming life."

Not satisfied with what could be "newspaper hype," I looked further and found a series of scientific articles on what had happened since our relatively small intervention in the 70s and 80s. Many other agencies had entered the scene. One 2011 article titled *Rebuilding resilience in the Sahel: Regreening in the Maradi and Zinder regions of Niger*[3] stated the following:

> The societies and ecosystems of the Nigerien Sahel appeared increasingly vulnerable to climatic and economic uncertainty in the late twentieth century. Severe episodes of drought and famine drove massive livestock losses and human migration and mortality. Soil erosion and tree loss reduced a woodland to a scrub steppe and fed a myth of the Sahara Desert relentlessly advancing southward. Over the past two decades this myth has been shattered by the dramatic reforestation of more than 5 million hectares in the Maradi and Zinder Regions of Niger. No single actor, policy, or practice appears behind this successful regreening of the Sahel. Multiple actors, institutions and processes operated at different levels, times, and scales to initiate and sustain this reforestation trend….and any reversals toward de-forestation or reforestation were preceded by institutional changes in governance, livelihoods, and eventually in the biophysical environment.

When I read this, I thought, *Need I search more?* This article spelled out the intended role of IDRC—supporting on-the-ground research and pilot projects by developing country teams, to be adopted and disseminated widely by other donors and national players.

Returning to our travels in 1984, Jean-Marc and I continued our Sahelian tour by heading east to Senegal on a "milk run" Air Afrique flight, to start shooting another film on multipurpose trees. We also wanted to cover more on solar energy experiments, the making of charcoal, and energy-efficient charcoal stoves. IDRC had helped to develop one called the "Jiko stove." In fact, Jean-Marc had one at home in Dakar where, on my visit, he asked his maid, a tall and lean Senegalese woman by the name of Thérèse, to cook the famous Senegalese *Thieboudiènne*—a fish and rice dish—in his Jiko, instructing her to use only a fraction of the firewood she would normally use. But our instructions didn't make sense to Thérèse and she burned the dish so badly Jean-Marc had to throw it out. Yes, this technology was still in the experimental stages, indeed!

I was happy to return to the Mbidi forestry station, where, in 1976, I had filmed the last sequence of my first round of filming for IDRC (see Chapter 8). There, I found much progress with the gum arabic tree (known scientifically as *Acacia senegal*). The plantation was now much more advanced. The *Acacia senegal* trees had grown and they had generated a local industry.

MY UNIVERSITY OF THE WORLD

Gum Arabic harvested from *Acacia senegal*
–Photos by Jean-Marc Fleury/IDRC

FILMING MULTIPURPOSE TREES AROUND THE WORLD

Besides the benefit of its nitrogen fixing qualities, this tree's wood is used for firewood and making charcoal, as well as utensils, poles, and fence posts. Furthermore, its bark and roots provide fiber for making strong ropes and fishing nets, while its foliage provides valuable fodder for sheep, goats, and camels. Its flowers produce nectar for bees in honey production. Today, if you google *Acacia senegal*[4] you will also see many of the worldwide uses of the gum that is tapped from this tree: food flavoring and emulsifiers, pharmaceuticals, and industrial products such as inks, pigments, polishes, to name a few.

I found Senegal to be a fun travel destination. In fact, I always found the people of francophone West Africa pleasant and polite, especially when compared to Nigeria, a country I thought I would never have to return to. But no such luck. Jean-Marc and I arrived there on August 23rd to continue our mission. My muscles grew tight as we landed and I prepared for a fight to clear my equipment. Surprisingly, we easily glided through immigration and customs in the new Lagos airport, due to the recently installed military government's "War Against Indiscipline," as spelled out in posters we saw all around us. A soldier almost turned us back on the way out of the airport, but I pointed to one of the posters and to the sign held by the driver from the International Institute of Tropical Agriculture (IITA), who had come to meet us.

We had to obtain journalist accreditation cards from the Ministry of Information and that caused a delay. We experienced a further hold up when we were told to wait for most of a week for a "minder" from the ministry to accompany us wherever we went. He would tell us what we could and couldn't film, and we had to pay for his accommodation and food. As it turned out, Mr. Lawal had been a government cameraman for 30 years, and appeared to be a little worn out. Fortunately, he gave us little direction and he was a pleasant man who protected us against any soldier who had not internalized the messages of the "War Against Indiscipline," and thus he facilitated rather than hindered our progress.

In southern Nigeria near Ibadan, we concentrated on alley cropping: the planting of trees or shrubs to create alleys, within which agricultural crops are grown. When rows of trees and crops are planted in a crosswise pattern on hillsides, they also prevent soil erosion. Some of the best filming of this innovation was arranged by the International Livestock Centre for Africa (ILCA), which was doing on-farm research north of Ibadan near Oyo, using *Leucaena leucocephala* and *Gliricidia sepium*—two fast-growing leguminous trees native to Central America. The trees were intercropped with food crops such as cowpeas. Having already produced a whole film on that lowly legume, in 1979 (see Chapter 11), I had some knowledge of such systems. As with acacia, these trees pump nitrogen from the air into the soil through nodules on their roots, thereby eliminating or reducing the need for chemical fertilizers.

All of this work is called agroforestry, widely defined as land use systems, in which trees and shrubs are grown adjacent to crops and pasture grass, often integrating livestock, birds, bees, and fish ponds on the same land, in such a way that the economic and ecological interaction between all components is positive. Such systems helped to reduce the slash and burn cultivation practiced in Nigeria and by more than 200 million people in the tropical world, at the time. These ancient slash and burn methods can only be sustained if the land is left fallow for a few years between crops.

We also filmed small-scale feed lots, where farmers fed the rich leaves from leucaena and gliricidia trees to sheep and goats, which we found in abundance in Oyo market because Mohammed's birthday was fast approaching. In Nigeria, all Muslims who have the means should sacrifice a ram for the occasion. This is an African ceremonial cleansing ritual, which predates Islam. The sacrifice is said to make amends for evil acts and reverses the negative consequences of sin, or curses put on innocent people by others.

Nigerian goats feeding on gliricidia leaves –Photo by Neill McKee/IDRC

I can't say my last trip to Nigeria went off without a hitch. I had grown weary of the delays, endless hassles, bouncing around on rough rural roads, lifting heavy equipment and repairing, recharging, and cleaning it at night. But it was great to travel with Jean-Marc, who took things in stride, although he sometimes seemed to feel guilty, as if it was his fault when things went wrong. We drank beer together every evening to erase our pain and frustration, and recharge our own batteries for another day. Because of this, and possibly the "War Against Indiscipline," plus the cool hand of Mr. Lawal, I had forgotten many of the negative details, until Jean-Marc reminded me of them, when I was drafting this chapter. I believe I had long-ago decided to think more positively about Nigeria, a country which has produced so many creative people such as the writers Chinua Achebe and Wole Soyinka, who explained so beautifully in their books what it means for a huge and diverse population to emerge out of colonialism.

It wasn't until September 1985 that I had time to film more multipurpose tree projects, this time in Nepal with a professional soundman, Basu Dev Bista. I met him in the lobby of my hotel, the Annapurna in Kathmandu, where I learned a bomb had gone off in June, killing seven people and wounding many more. The hotel was owned by the Nepalese royal family and the perpetrators belonged to a banned political group. We were joined by Pradeep Dixit, our project coordinator, plus Raj Bhandari and Madhav Kari from the Forestry Institute of Nepal. They told me there was little or no terrorist activity where we were headed, fortunately.

On September 25th, we drove south to the "Middle Hills" in the direction of India, where most of the local forestry research was taking place. The weather looked ominous for filming—a continual monsoon rain—as we traveled on washed-out roads, driving around frequent landslides, and peered over guardrails down steep cliffs. I had just flown in from Canada and jetlag caught up with me, so despite all these barriers and dangers, I somehow slept through much of the trip.

That night the monsoon ended—I had been told it would likely last another week. A blessing from Nepal's Hindu gods? I rolled my camera, filming erosion problems, deforestation, and overpopulation in the foothills and then the plains of Nepal—an area they call the *terai*. In Nepal, it was also fast-growing leguminous trees that made the difference: the famous leucaena, as well as *Dalbergia latifolia*, commonly known as Indian Rosewood.

On the plains, I shot sequences of long lines of woodcutters carrying firewood on their heads, and people strengthening paddy bunds by planting trees. I found the *terai* to be a fascinating area. It contains a mixture of people: various tribal groups from the hills who had migrated to take up rice cultivation, and also Biharis from India who considered the Nepal-India border nonexistent. I filmed farmers who had traveled up to 186 miles (300 km) to the Forestry Institute's nursery to put down money for seedlings to be picked up the next year. Even so, the people here were about the poorest I had ever seen in South Asia.

In one area, while walking along a paddy bund, camera slung over my shoulder, I passed a sad man carrying his dead son over his shoulder, followed by another man with a hoe. Pradeep Dixit explained they couldn't afford the firewood needed for cremation. It was one of the few times in my filming career that my necessary objectivity on the poverty of the situation overwhelmed me. My legs weakened and I had to hand my camera to an assistant in our team. I found some peace in the shade of one of the project's leguminous trees and breathed deeply before walking on.

Nepal researchers with terai farmers —Photos by Neill McKee/IDRC

On September 28th, some of my Nepalese hosts and I rode motorcycles to a vague but ultimately rewarding destination. We forded streams and traveled over muddy roads through periodic showers. Then we headed into the mountains around Pokhara to view the famous Annapurna Mountain Range, visible under a full moon as we reached our destination. I rated the day as "five-star," but the hotel we stayed in was definitely a "half-star" establishment.

The next day, a Sunday, it rained and I was glad to recuperate, get my thoughts in order, and clean my equipment. By Monday morning the rain had ceased and, at 6:00 am, I stationed myself on the hotel roof, waiting for the clouds to clear, so I could take a shot of the famous peak called "Machapuchare" or "fishtail mountain." A crowd of skeptical Nepalese gathered to inform me I was wasting my time, but I ordered some tea and stayed in place. An hour later, the sun burned away the clouds and I rolled my camera on the mountain vista. It became the opening shot of the film.

View of Machapuchare (fishtail mountain), at dawn
—Photo from Alamy[5]

My final trip for this film was to Costa Rica, in February 1986. A former colleague from my first Latin American trips, Jaime Rojas, met me at the airport in San José. He had left IDRC to join the Tropical Agriculture Research and Training Center, known by its Spanish acronym, CATIE—a spectacular campus set in a picturesque valley. Derek Webb arrived from IDRC's Bogota office to discuss the overall structure of the film and our draft script. We decided to cut out a number of possible sequences and focus on the leguminous tree—a good decision, for the Central American rainforest is the original home of many leguminous trees used in agroforestry systems, worldwide. We also reviewed plans for the animation sketched out by my artist, Bill Clarke, to illustrate the way leguminous trees act as a nitrogen pump—pulling nitrogen from the air into nodules on their roots, which provide natural fertilizer for the soil, as well as furnishing nitrogen rich pods and leaves, which also fertilize the soil when they fall, or protein-rich food for domestic animals.

For the next few days, we filmed agroforestry systems on the research station: erythrina trees intercropped with maize, coffee, and beans, providing shade and fertilizer; and various methods of pasture/fodder enrichment. They called these systems "protein banks" for raising beef and milking cattle.

We also filmed the system of planting "living fences" on farms. This seemed rather miraculous to me. I took sequences of workers cutting large branches from erythrina trees and simply planting them in the ground to make new fence poles beside older dead wooden ones. The new poles would develop deep roots and grow for many years, outlasting traditional fences.

Harvesting fodder from living fences in Costa Rica
—Photo by Neill McKee/IDRC

When the new living fence poles grow to a respectable height, they are pruned, and their leaves and pods are used as rich animal fodder, while the larger stakes are planted as new fence poles or as stalks for climbing plants such as beans, to grow on. I wondered how I could take interesting film footage on fences, but I "beefed-up" the sequence, so to speak, by introducing how CATIE had taught cowboys to feed their fences to their cattle.

When I finished our 20-minute film later that year, we titled it *Trees of Plenty*[6] an apt name, for the leguminous tree is a marvelous invention of nature, which brings us so many benefits. If only we humans could learn we were put on this Earth to enrich it rather than exploit it, making it and our lives poorer. IDRC helped to start the International Centre for Research in Agroforestry (ICRAF), now known as "World Agroforestry" after merging with the Center for International Forestry Research. *Trees of Plenty* was used for many years to popularize agroforestry techniques, which have spread throughout the tropical world. They are a major strategy against climate change and the environmental degradation we all face today.

I never entered *Trees of Plenty* in any contest because my attention was turning elsewhere. By this time in my career, I had traveled hundreds of thousands of miles over 15 years in shooting films for IDRC and CUSO, and had taken over 30,000 still photos. Besides the fact that hauling heavy filming equipment around the world had taken its toll on my back, I was feeling a midlife crisis coming on. I had asked IDRC if I could be given a leave of absence to join an NGO working in multimedia in Bangladesh, or to do a master's degree in Communication somewhere. They offered me the latter, fully funded. I believe the President of IDRC, Ivan Head, recognized how I had helped to put the organization on the map, at a relatively low cost, through my films.

On the way back to Ottawa from Costa Rica, I stopped in Tallahassee, Florida, to investigate doing a master's degree at Florida State University. I landed mid-day on a Sunday at Tallahassee airport, where I was met by two professors—John Mayo of the Department of Communication, and George Papagiannis of the College of Education. They had both served in the U.S. Peace Corps and knew all about IDRC. They told me at Florida State they would be able to tailor a practical course of study to satisfy my needs, and I could complete it in a year, if I worked really hard. I had applied to a couple of Canadian universities that told me it would take two years to complete a degree, and they required completion of a number of courses, which seemed too theoretical and superfluous for application in international development work.

As I flew out of Tallahassee that day, I had a warm feeling about this meeting. I was impressed that these two professors had taken time on a Sunday to meet me at the airport to persuade me to come to their university. I certainly would apply as soon as I got home. But before beginning my studies, I had two more forestry films to make.

19. Adventures in the Forests of China and Southeast Asia

In March 1986, I traveled to China and Southeast Asia to film bamboo and rattan for IDRC's Asia-based forestry expert, Cherla Sastry. I brought along Denis Sing, my new audio-visual assistant. He had one French-Canadian and one Chinese parent, and he was keen to visit Asia. I trained him on sound recording and taking still photos while, as usual, I focused on cinematography.

I had been to Beijing before on a scouting trip, in 1984, to discuss the film I was to shoot, but also arranging to make Chinese versions of my films and setting up film distribution. I knew the first order of business was an obligatory many-course, mid-day banquet held in our honor by the President of the Chinese Academy of Forestry. I had figured out that, for most government bureaucrats, visits by foreigners provided a way of having a good meal and lots of alcoholic drinks, all for free. At our luncheon, there were so many pauses for *"gan bei"*—bottoms-up toasts—with horrible Chinese plum wine, that we were incapacitated for the rest of the day. Before we left Beijing, according to custom, we had to reciprocate by holding another mid-day banquet for our hosts.

Wherever we went, we were accompanied by Miss Li Ching, our interpreter, and Mr. Li Peng from the Academy's Photography Division, who must have taken 500 photos of us during our visit. Westerners were still a novelty in China, and IDRC's brand of cooperation well suited the Chinese government—providing support to Chinese scientists and exchange of ideas with international scientific networks.

Next, we flew 800 miles (1,287 km) south to Hangzhou, a city that surrounds the beautiful West Lake—an object of art and poetry in China for centuries. Hangzhou is the home of the Subtropical Forestry Research Institute—the national center for research on bamboo. We were met at the airport by local staff, who thankfully required no banquet. Although it was a Sunday, they wanted to begin filming right away because it was the first sunny day after many days of rain. Traveling into the mountainous countryside, I felt inspired. Here are some opening lines of our final film, which reflect that feeling:

> In the mountains of Asia, bamboo forests stretch as far as the eye can see. Rising from the mist, like tall sentinels, these bamboos symbolize abundance in the daily life of Asia, and harmony in its many cultures. Bamboo's long history is a blend of religion and anecdote, of magic, and practical use. Its graceful shape has inspired generations of artists and calligraphers. Its flexibility and strength, even its growing patterns, are celebrated by poet and sage, farmer and engineer. Bamboo has been called the poor man's timber because in many areas of the Third World, people live with it from birth until death.

In fact, I was so inspired that when I returned to Ottawa I asked Beth, who had studied Chinese calligraphy and art in Malaysia, to match one of my closeups of a bamboo branch waving in a gentle breeze with a shot of her doing ink strokes of bamboo leaves on paper. In the plantations we visited, I

Beth McKee's hand at work, painting bamboo —Image from the film

was fascinated to see and film tall stalks of Moso Bamboo, rising 75 feet (23 meters). Bamboo is a member of the grass family (*Poaceae*), along with other flowering plants—cereals, wild grasses, and those we grow for lawns and pastures.

Measuring the growth of monopodial bamboo
—Photo by Denis Sing/IDRC

We learned that perhaps because of its seeming abundance, bamboo is often harvested without proper attention to conservation, with the consequence that bamboo forests, which seemed so limitless to me, were actually in danger of disappearing. This was the reason ongoing research was so important. During the next week, we filmed and photographed: collecting different species and growing them in gardens to ensure their survival; measuring photosynthesis, and the strength of stalks, known as "culms," through stress tests in labs; monitoring and controlling fungi and insect attacks; experiments on fertilizing the roots, and measuring plant growth.

Through making this film, I learned there are about 2,000 species of bamboo native to every region of the world, except Europe. Bamboo can be found in climates whose temperatures range from minus 40°F to plus 104°F (−40°C to +40°C) and from sea level up to 13,123 feet (4,000 meters). This sturdy plant comes in a variety of sizes, shapes, and colors. Besides its wide distribution, bamboo holds another amazing property—the flowering of a single species takes place simultaneously all around the world, and most species flower only once every 60 to 120 years—and then most of the plants die. It takes years for a species to reestablish itself.

I hired Bill Clarke to animate the two types of bamboo distinguished by their underground root systems (rhizomes). The monopodial variety (running bamboo) has single culms rising out of buds on rhizomes, which extend up to 300 feet (91.4 meters) in length. This type flourishes in cooler climates. In contrast, sympodial bamboo has short fat rhizomes, which generate buds directly on them, growing out of the ground in clumps. This type does well in the tropics.

ADVENTURES IN THE FORESTS OF CHINA AND SOUTHEAST ASIA

Due to these large and complex root structures, bamboo grows rapidly and reaches maturity in a matter of months. I set up my camera to capture periodic shots of a bamboo shoot growing 47 inches (120 cm) in 24 hours. I could actually hear it crackling as I filmed it growing.

Equally amazing to me was the number of uses of bamboo in China. As a kid growing up in Canada, I had only known bamboo fishing poles, which we bought at our local hardware store. But in China and later in Thailand, where sympodial bamboo flourishes, we filmed a multitude of products made from it: baskets, paper, toothpicks, charcoal, furniture, fishnet frames, tools, fencing, water pipes, musical instruments, scaffolding, and low-rise housing. We also filmed workers harvesting bamboo shoots, employees working in a shoot canning factory, and a family dining on bamboo shoots cooked in a delicious sauce, using bamboo chopsticks, while seated at a bamboo table. Humans have found at least 1,500 uses for this stately plant. Bamboo truly provides a way of life.

We titled the film *Bamboo: The Miracle Grass*.[1] I believe it was one of my most artistic creations and it was interesting to travel in China while it was a relatively new thing to do. In 1986, the country was still emerging from the strict communist era and the people I met were keen to interact with westerners, especially those who offered a connection to the larger world.

Today, partly due to the research network IDRC helped to establish around the world, bamboo remains much in use, and is coming back into fashion with the creation of bamboo furniture, floors, and even clothing. Unfortunately, like any plant that becomes popular and money-making, humans have a tendency to practice monocropping, thus

Bamboo farm tools in China —Photo by Neill McKee/IDRC

decreasing biodiversity and increasing the likelihood of disease and insect attacks. Bamboo will remain a major renewable natural resource if it is carefully managed. Then and only then can it continue to inspire artists and calligraphers for at least another 5,000 years.

On April 12th, Denis and I flew South to Guangzhou in Guangdong Province (the place the British named "Canton"), where we were met by representatives of China's Institute of Tropical Forestry. The next day, we took a China Airways flight to Haikou on Hainan Island, a tropical part of China to the east of north Vietnam. We didn't see much of Haikou because, on arrival, we piled into a Chinese-made, four-wheel drive vehicle, along with local researchers. We drove for seven hours on muddy roads over mountains to film rattan research.

Rattan, which most of us know as cane, is actually not a tree, but a spiny vine that grows up trees in tropical rain forests. Rattan actually belongs to the subfamily *Calamoideae*, of the palm family *Arecaceae*. It's a parasite of sorts, but in spite of that label, most of us love the products made from it: wickerwork furniture, baskets, walking canes, cords, woven mats, and other handicrafts; tools, hammocks, toys, child carriages, sports equipment, musical instruments; and even medicines for snake bite, rheumatism, and asthma.

We did our filming in one day—a difficult assignment since the rattan vine is practically hidden in a mass of foliage in tropical rain forests. This film, I realized, was going to be a real challenge to make.

The next day we drove back over the same muddy mountain roads to Haikou, to catch a ferry to the mainland, where a car was waiting to take us to a small town near Goazhou. It took, in all, 17-hours to travel 435 miles (700 km) that day. The next morning, we had to be up bright and early to be driven to an experimental rattan nursery and plantation—also not exciting for a cinematographer, but at least I got some shots of Chinese researchers at work.

Rattan vine in tropical forest —Photo by Neill McKee/IDRC

We had a brief break in the late afternoon so I could rest my very sore back. The jostling on rough roads had become tortuous for me. Early the next day we were driven back to

Child carrier made of rattan and bamboo –Photo by Denis Sing/IDRC

Guangzhou, an 11-hour trip. We spent most of our time in south China on poor or congested roads. But at least we avoided more drunken mid-day banquets. In Guangzhou, we filmed rattan research sequences at the Institute and the operations of a factory, which employed 4,000 people making rattan furniture and other products—finally, something more interesting for the camera.

There were no flights available the next day, so Denis and I took a pleasant four-hour ride on a hovercraft to Hong Kong, to catch a flight to Bangkok, Thailand, to film sympodial bamboo research and utilization. Next, we flew to Singapore for a visit to IDRC's Regional Office. There we met with Cherla Sastry to discuss our achievements, so far. We also touched base with Chin Saik Yoon, our new Communications Division representative for Southeast Asia and East Asia. Besides managing publications and film distribution, he had started some multimedia communication projects, which interested me. Chin came from Penang, Malaysia, and we had great rapport since I had spent four years of my early career in his country.

On April 21st, Denis and I flew to Kuala Lumpur, Malaysia, to film rattan research activities of the Forestry Research Institute: tissue culture in the lab, nursery activities, and the computerized Rattan Information Centre established for the network of people working on rattan. Then we headed into the nearby countryside, where I finally got some decent shots of this spiny vine growing up tall trees, searching for sunlight. We also filmed sequences of rattan species identification in the jungle, intercropping rattan with rubber trees, and cane processing, as well as furniture making. Rattan cane is a marvelous material which, with the application of a little heat, can be easily bent into many shapes. Our stop in West Malaysia was worthwhile and I was grateful we experienced no more long trips on bumpy roads.

ADVENTURES IN THE FORESTS OF CHINA AND SOUTHEAST ASIA

During February and March of 1987, I made another trip by myself through Asia to negotiate the possible language versioning and distribution of the films I had produced, as well as those made by IDRC's partner institutions. By this time, our division was also supporting the communication components of research projects such as a health education study in China. I really looked forward to more of this kind of work instead of only making films. Besides China, I visited Hong Kong, Singapore, Malaysia, the Philippines, and India.

One of the main purposes of my trip was to film rattan plantations of the Sabah Forestry Development Authority. On March 12th, I flew from Singapore to the city of Sandakan on the east coast of Sabah, and by evening of the same day I found myself in a boat on the Kinabatangan River, heading into the deep jungles of Borneo. We didn't reach the station at Batu Putih until 9 pm. If there were crocodiles in the water, I couldn't see them. I was accompanied by forestry officer, Norbert Augustine Bolong, a member of the Murut tribe—people who have navigated this river for thousands of years—so I had no fear.

At Batu Putih, I filmed and photographed nursery and transplanting operations, as well as the world's most advanced rattan plantation, where the vines were ready for harvest. At last, I could take clear shots of the difficult job of yanking these ornery thorny vines from their homes on giant tropical hardwoods. I took some travel shots from our boat along the river, but a flood in January had killed off a good deal of the vines.

On my final day at Batu Putih, a helicopter I had hired arrived, and I spent two hours taking aerial shots before flying back to Sandakan. The pilot was experienced and

Rattan nursery and plantation at Batu Putih, Sabah, Malaysia
—Photos by Neill McKee/IDRC

took us low over the forest so I could get good shots of the canopy, even if I couldn't see any rattan. Much more visible, however, was the fact that most of the tropical rain forest in this part of Borneo had been logged to make room for vast oil palm plantations for the production of palm oil. In some areas I could only see barren earth and burnt tree trunks. I wondered if rattan plantations could ever compete with the money being made from the processing and sale of palm oil. Rattan vines need trees to cling to, and they take up to 10 years to grow to full maturity.

To me, the future of rattan seemed less hopeful than that of bamboo. But, as I was writing this chapter, I searched online and found interesting publications by the International Network for Bamboo and Rattan (INBAR), which IDRC helped to establish. Experiments continue at the Forestry Research Institute of Malaysia on the interplanting of rattan in tree plantations.[2] This may become a viable income generation system for smallholders. Another INBAR publication[3] pointed out how rattan was making a comeback in fashion around the world, as humans gradually become educated about climate change and sour on exploitation of forests, as well as ecologically damaging cash crops such as oil palm.

From Sandakan I flew to Kota Kinabalu, where I packed my filming equipment and exposed film and shipped it all back to Ottawa, before continuing on my travels through Asia. That was the last time I used this well-worn equipment. It was fitting that I shot both my first film in Borneo, in 1969–70, and my last sequence there. I never finished the rattan film. I had given the task to a man named Clayton Bailey, a Canadian filmmaker I'd met in Nepal. He had already joined IDRC to replace me while I was doing my master's in Tallahassee, Florida. More filming was required of Philippines and Indonesia projects, and the production wasn't released until 1989. Clayton titled it *Rattan: The Hidden Resource*.[4] By my own experience with this camouflaged vine, it was a true title.

Uprooting and Retooling in Tallahassee, Florida

In early August 1987, we rented out our house in Ottawa and I took my family to Tallahassee, the capital of Florida, where I would begin earning a Master of Science degree in Communication, at Florida State University (FSU). On a scorching day, as I drove our old station wagon across the border at Detroit, the muffler fell off on a potholed freeway. Welcome to America! I managed to get off the highway for repairs in a somewhat questionable neighborhood. Beth, who no longer identified herself as an American, was okay with the Florida adventure if it was only for a year—and she had an idea for a calligraphy project she would do there. At the time, Derek was almost 12 and Ruth was 10. So far, they had only known Ottawa, camping vacations, and visits to their grandparents, aunts, uncles, and cousins living in Canada and parts of the U.S., such as Minnesota, Iowa, and New Mexico. Of course, I promised visits to Disney World in Orlando. But I was secretly glad it was a four-hour drive from Tallahassee. My colleagues at IDRC kidded me about taking off for a year's vacation on the beaches of Florida, but Tallahassee is located in the panhandle of the state, where I would be swimming with alligators in cypress swamps.

After more breakdowns along the way, we decided to buy a new car when we arrived in Tallahassee. We could afford one because I remained on salary at IDRC and was also given some extra funds to pay for my tuition. I had

A Florida cypress swamp —Photo by Neill McKee

been given a sabbatical, of sorts, although the organization had no such policy. It sure was no vacation, for I only had 11 months to fulfill the requirements for my master's degree. Dr. John Mayo in the Department of Communication became my principal advisor. I dove right in, taking his course on the diffusion of innovations, which included readings on such processes in developing countries. When John was a U.S. Peace Corps volunteer in Colombia, he worked in educational television. This was right up my alley. The class included debates on the effectiveness of using communication to change behavior and social norms in the U.S., Latin America, Africa, and Asia. I wrote papers on whether communication theory and models created by Western scholars were relevant when applied to developing countries.

I took my courses with other Master's students and some working for Ph.D.s in both the Department of Communication and the College of Education. In the latter, I also met many students from developing countries and took a Ph.D.-level course with them in the sociology of education. Our class was taught by Dr. George Papagiannis, who had been a Peace Corps teacher in Thailand. He had many entertaining stories to tell about his experiences, and he shared his critical thoughts on America's education system. He and John challenged me to take a course taught by their colleague, Dr. Steve Klees, on evaluation methods, emphasizing cost-benefit and cost-effectiveness analysis. I wrote a paper that clearly distinguished the two. For cost-benefit analysis one must turn benefits into monetary terms. I made up a Papua New Guinea communication intervention, in which I substituted pigs for dollars, because native New Guineans had used pigs as the unit of exchange for centuries. Professor Klees gave me an A+ for that effort.

I also took courses in communication research, including entering data on punch cards, processing them, and analyzing the output. I bluffed a bit, saying I had taken all the statistics I needed in my undergraduate days, and they somehow excused me from that prerequisite, probably due to my senior student status. That decision proved to be a challenge when I was faced with understanding regression analysis, but I persevered.

I enjoyed qualitative research, which involved methods such as in-depth interviews and participant observation. Besides reading and discussing interesting articles, I spent hours observing what was going on in a local television station newsroom. The subject was topical because the movie *Broadcast News* had been released that year. It's about a young television news producer, played by Holly Hunter, who battles with a far less seasoned rival, played by William Hurt, over telling the truth versus providing entertainment in the news. As I sat in editorial meetings and witnessed interactions between reporters, I could see the tension over this issue playing out before me.

I was an odd sight on campus among trendy young undergraduates because I carried my own chair and desk outfit to classes. On the way to Florida, at my father's manufacturing plant, I had designed and welded together a metal collapsible chair, based on a Scandinavian design. It involved kneeling and sitting on upholstered pads, while keeping my back straight, and I included a pop-up desk. I had been using a non-portable version of the chair at my office desk for relief from daily back pain.

At the time, FSU had no regular courses in filmmaking, but during my second semester, I was asked to teach an undergraduate course in the basics of cinematography and editing—for monetary compensation, of course. I found the American system quite flexible in their hiring practices. There was no course curriculum, so I had to create one out of the blue, and also decide on the required textbook. About 15 students joined the class, expecting big things. But FSU had no video equipment, so we had to use old Super-8 cameras and basic editing equipment. That suited me. I had never switched to video because professional equipment was still too cumbersome and delicate in the 1980s. It could break down easily, especially in the climates and rough terrain of developing countries.

The class project involved shooting and editing films. The resulting creations could be silent, but most students chose to roughly synchronize images to their favorite pop music, mimicking MTV. In the 1980s, many North American youth had moved to watching hours of fast-moving images, timed to the latest youth music. When I told them about the kinds of films I had made, their eyes glazed over. But I did succeed in teaching them the basics of filmmaking.

At home in Tallahassee –Photo by Neill McKee

We had rented a small bungalow in a northern suburb of Tallahassee. Beth used the dining nook beside our kitchen for her studio, while our bedroom became my office during the day. She met other calligraphers in the community and taught a class for five of them. She created a series of 36 pieces on the poetry by Joan Finnigan, an Ottawa Valley poet and friend, which she intended to display at a show she would hold when we returned home. Almost every evening during supper, she'd ask us to critique her work. My favorite piece from that period was her calligraphic creation of a long narrative poem on the meaning of home. I think it captured Beth's longing for a permanent place. When I read it, a few lines stood out to me, some traditional and some realistic or truthful:

> *Home is the place where when you go back there you don't have to knock*
> *Home is a place where when they know somebody is coming by night they always put a light in the window*
> *Home is the place where two people lay down steadiness underneath the unsteadiness*
> *Home is a place where when you come home from school nobody is there*
> *Home is the place you think is forever, and find it isn't*
> *Home is love's long-standing relationship to wind*

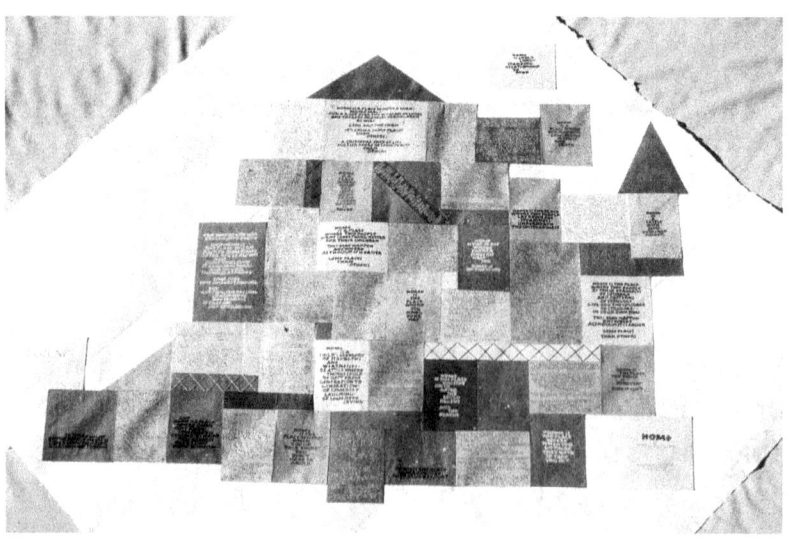

Home, by Joan Finnigan, calligraphed and illustrated by Elizabeth McKee

UPROOTING AND RETOOLING IN TALLAHASSEE, FLORIDA

The children were picked up by buses to be taken to their respective schools—Ruth to a nearby elementary school and Derek into the city to a middle school. They made many friends and came to love their schools, taking all classes in English, for a change, instead of the French immersion stream, in Ottawa. They entered school contests and joined clubs. Beth reverted by taking the kids to a Lutheran church, which had a strong youth program with a drama group and camping trips. So, the move to Florida was good for them.

When at home, I only emerged for meals with the family and to watch the odd movie. I worked on a small Tandy computer with a basic printer, kept up on all academic readings, and completed the communication and education papers required. We did take a few breaks to see wildlife in nearby swamps, watch alligator wrestling, eat shrimp on the Gulf Coast, and wander around the usual sites: Busch Gardens and Epcot Center, as well as Disney World, of course.

I even had time for two joyful reunions with Peter Ragan, my Peace Corps buddy during my first two years in Borneo. Peter had lent me and then sold me my first 16mm movie camera—the one which I used at the start of my career. Peter and his wife Arlene and son Daniel were living in Daytona Beach, where he taught English as a second language at Embry-Riddle Aeronautical University. He and I had created the North Borneo Frodo Society years ago (see Chapter 2) and we touted our first reunion in Tallahassee as a general meeting of the society. I placed a sign concerning the meeting on the roadside in front of our house—something that probably made the neighbors wonder about us. Our second meeting was more traditional—building sandcastles and sailing on the Atlantic coastal waters.

The world's largest pizza –Photo by Neill McKee

One of my favorite leisure time stories from our time in Florida is about taking Derek and Ruth to the creation of the world's largest pizza. It was assembled on a circular steel plate, about 40 feet (12 meters) in diameter. The organizers of this event cooked the crust from underneath with moving gas torches, while they relied on the sun to heat the cheese, tomato sauce, dust, and bird shit on top. Proceeds went to the American Red Cross, but I wondered if the five dollars per slice everyone paid actually covered the cost of the uncooked gritty ingredients. We threw our slices away.

To meet all requirements for my master's degree, I had to complete either 12 semester courses or nine semester courses and write a thesis. I chose the latter and, in early January, I held open-ended interviews with communication experts working in international behavior change programs in Washington, D.C. and Baltimore, Maryland. At the time, many of these people were practicing a method they called "social marketing." For instance, with respect to diarrhea management in developing countries, they claimed to be carrying out formative research to determine the 4-Ps of marketing: the right Product (e.g. oral rehydration solution [ORS] and/or food recipes); at the right Price (the cost of ORS packets, food ingredients, cooking fuel, and time of the mother for preparation); the Place or distribution channels for the product; and the Promotion methods (interpersonal communication with health workers, and/or radio and television ads, etc.). In other words, social marketers resorted to using the language of marketing to describe their work in behavior change programs.

My master's thesis was an enquiry on: 1) the effectiveness of such programs in developing countries, to date, through secondary analysis of strategies and evaluation results; 2) whether the language of marketing was a barrier for the acceptance of social marketing by managers and staff in nonprofit organizations; 3) if social marketing was manipulative—a reputation gained from the American-dominated ad industry; and 4) whether these methods could be used beyond individual consumer choice programs in community-based interventions.

After my last class ended in May, I sweated through the interview transcripts and articles I had gathered to come up with a 182-page document for defense in July. I titled it *Social Marketing in International Development: A Critical Review.* I was quite critical about social marketing. It seemed much too American for application in Canadian-sponsored development programs—possibly trying to sell the American view on free enterprise to the world. I called for a much more participatory community-based approach without using the language of marketing, which might easily raise a communication barrier among development professionals.

In early August, I had to defend my thesis before departing for Canada. Besides Drs. Mayo and Papagiannis, Dr. Edward Wotring and Dr. Gary Heald were on my committee—a formidable assemblage of brainpower. I expected some tricky questions but somehow made it through the process. They only required a few changes, which I would complete in Ottawa, in time to submit the final version for graduation in December. One of them asked me if I would come back to do a Ph.D., but it was out of the question. I had to get back to working at IDRC, earning a living for my family. In fact, I couldn't afford the time to attend the December 1988 graduation ceremony or a special luncheon in April 1989, when I was inducted into the Phi Kappa Phi Honor Society.

Flashing forward, I returned to Tallahassee in December 2008. John Mayo put my name up for a *"Omicron Delta Kappa* Grads Made Good Award." I believe I won due to my scholastic record, all the films I had made for IDRC, and my multimedia productions after that, as described in the remaining chapters of this memoir. Someone even made a weird pen and ink drawing of my face from a photo I had sent. The drawing now sits on a wall or in a storage room somewhere at the university. My return coincided with homecoming weekend at FSU, with all the ceremonial hoopla—including a Florida State Seminoles football game and a parade through the streets. I was asked to ride in a red convertible and wave at the crowd—a strange exaggeration of my achievements. But that's evidently the American way.

It's not the Canadian way. In September 1988, when I returned to IDRC, I presented my thesis in a discussion, where my work was criticized by some participants—especially by those from our Social Science Division, who delivered various criticisms of the concept of Social Marketing—all of which I had outlined in my thesis. Probably none of them had read it, but at least their reaction proved my thesis was right.

I didn't return to making films. Instead, our new director in the Communications Division, David Nostbakken, gave me the title of Associate Director for Dissemination. For 15 months I carried on with my new job of supervising a few staff who worked with me to try to figure out new distribution channels and methods for our publications and films, including in video format. By then my films were in various film libraries around the world, including those of the prestigious National Film Board of Canada, but video distribution was gaining momentum.

I also took the lead in hosting, in Ottawa, a global workshop on development communication, attended by, among others, Dr. Everett Rogers, the scholar who wrote the important textbook I had studied at FSU, *Diffusion of Innovations*.[1] I participated in discussions with my colleagues and other organizations in a few projects involving the popularization of research results, the training of science communicators, farm radio extension work, and small studies on the reach and effects of various communication media. In the first half of 1989, I visited about 50 development agencies in Africa and Asia and their headquarters in Europe, Canada, and the U.S., to find out about their projects and dissemination methods.

On a business trip to New York, I visited UNICEF's headquarters near the United Nation's Secretariat in order to learn how they handled publications, films, and videos. However, I was also there to be interviewed for the post of Chief of Programme Communication and Information in Dhaka, Bangladesh. It was a country I knew well, especially through my work on the film *Prescription for Health*, which UNICEF had used widely there and in many other developing countries.

On a day in early August 1989, Beth called to say I had received a telegram at home from UNICEF's Executive Director, James P. Grant. My application had been accepted and they wanted me to join them as soon as possible. I went home early that day to see the telegram with my own eyes and discuss the implications with Beth before we told the children. They had settled back in Ottawa after our Florida sojourn. Derek was about to start Grade 9, and Ruth Grade 7 in new schools. Also, on return from Florida, Beth had told me, once more, she would like to stay in Ottawa for the rest of her life. But she knew I wasn't happy with my new job. I had no budget to practice what I had studied in Tallahassee and her principal passion, calligraphic arts, was portable. I don't think I had to remind her of the original promise she made to me:

UPROOTING AND RETOOLING IN TALLAHASSEE, FLORIDA

> Move where you want to
> I will go with you
> Fight for what you will
> And I'll stay by your side.

Another line in Beth's calligraphic creation of Joan Finnigan's poem had to be gently explained to our children:

> *Home is the place where your father finds his next job, home is on the move.*

PART THREE

MY YEARS AS A MEDIA PRODUCER AND FACILITATOR

Becoming a Multimedia Producer in Bangladesh

I resigned from IDRC at the end of 1989, but Beth and I decided to make the transition gradual. She would remain in Ottawa with Derek and Ruth so they could finish the school year, and she could complete some on-going calligraphy projects, as well as be on hand to show and sell our house. In January 1990, after passing through UNICEF's headquarters in New York for a brief orientation, I arrived in Dhaka, Bangladesh, where I was met by a driver in a white Toyota Land Cruiser with the blue lettering and logo of UNICEF plastered on its sides and back. I recall being driven through streets clogged with trishaws to the home of UNICEF Representative Cole Dodge, an American about my age. He warmly welcomed me to Bangladesh and told me he'd pick me up in the morning at 8:30 am.

After a jet-lagged sleep in my hotel room, the next day, a Saturday, I found myself speeding through Dhaka with Cole and his driver, a U.N. flag flying on the front fender. Representatives of U.N. agencies have diplomatic status, but Cole was not at all pretentious about it. He introduced his driver to me as a valuable colleague. We headed to a Rotary meeting where Cole gave a rousing speech to a large crowd on the importance of the Expanded Program on Immunization (EPI). I was impressed with his delivery and clarity of message. Rotary International was already a partner in EPI, focusing on polio vaccinations, and Cole only had to thank and motivate them to keep up the good work.

On the way back to my hotel, he asked if I could give a talk on immunization to a Rotary youth meeting in a couple of weeks. I agreed, even though I had no clue what to say. Cole handed me some small spiral-bound pocket cards with talking points, figures, and graphs and said, "Just read these over and make up a speech."

"Sure, I can do that," I replied. But I had a lot of homework to do. That's how things went with this job—learning by doing.

The Bangladesh workweek goes from Sunday to Thursday because Friday is the day of prayer in Islam. The next day, a Sunday, I was driven to work at the old sprawling UNICEF office complex in the Dhanmondi neighborhood of Dhaka. It consisted of a set of office buildings, including some converted houses. At the time, there were about 250 UNICEF staff in Dhaka and seven zonal offices—the second largest UNICEF operation in the world (India being the largest). The majority of staff members were Bangladeshi at almost every level, from drivers to senior program officers. I was taken around to meet them and about 35 international staff from just about every part of the world—a mini-U.N., in itself. I found the atmosphere friendly and welcoming.

My own unit, the Program Communication and Information Section (PCIS) consisted of approximately 10 people, at the time. This was the largest team I had ever supervised. All were Bangladeshis except for Charles Rycroft, a man from U.K. who was about to transfer to another country. He and the former chief had focused on EPI communication—then the priority of UNICEF throughout the developing world. Charles and Afsan Chowdhury, the most senior

BECOMING A MULTIMEDIA PRODUCER IN BANGLADESH

Bangladeshi staff member in my section, showed me the wide variety of EPI materials they had produced: posters, TV spots, videos, plus cards and booklets to support interpersonal communication. We went through all the strategies employed and events held with government and NGO partners, to date. My imagination overflowed with possibilities when Cole told me my job would be to strengthen this work and expand into new areas such as water and sanitation; maternal and child health, including breastfeeding and nutrition; and universal primary education, focusing on girls' enrollment and retention in school.

I soon moved from the hotel to a comfortable guest house in Gulshan, a more modern part of Dhaka with a few restaurants, which I could reach by hiring a trishaw with driver. I ordered a secondhand Toyota van, but it would take a couple of months to arrive. Most evenings, I poured over documents from the office, learning the background on all the work that lay ahead. Local television was mostly in Bangla language and boring. Sometimes I would chat with other guests, but not over a beer. Dhaka was a dry town. You could only get alcoholic drinks at a few large international hotels or from special stores selling foreign goods. Only foreigners and Bangladeshis with "medical needs" for alcohol could acquire a passbook for shopping there, so quite a few richer Bangladeshis managed to get such "prescriptions" from their doctors.

My family arrived in July in time for school, which would start in August. I had found a brand-new house to rent in Gulshan—a two-story affair with terrazzo stone floors and a flat roof with a laundry room, where we could also hold evening parties. The property had a small lawn and garden, which required caring for. I had hired a domestic servant by the name of Mitro, who wanted to become a cook. He didn't know anything about cooking, but Beth, with some reluctance, said she would teach him. She had heard about professional Bangladeshi cooks and was looking forward to stepping away from the kitchen. But, at least Mitro could read and write, so she read out each recipe in English, and he wrote them down in Bangla on small index cards. He also did the house cleaning and most of the shopping. Mitro stayed in a room by the kitchen and we agreed he could bring in his sister Lilly, his brother-in-law Shuntu, and their baby girl Poppi. The family stayed in a small room beside the open garage and Shuntu became the gardener, gate-keeper, carpenter, and general handyman—an invaluable and cheery fellow.

Our extended Dhaka family –Photo by Neill McKee

This was how most middle and upper-class households were run in Bangladesh and we didn't buck the system.

Clothes washing and dishwashing had to be done by hand. I had promised Beth she would be relieved of a lot of housework by agreeing to come to Bangladesh, so she would have lots of time to devote to her artwork.

Derek and Ruth soon found themselves in American International School, Dhaka, which had students and teachers from almost everywhere. Ruth was not happy leaving her close circle of friends in Ottawa, but I believe Derek was relieved. He had been listening to hard metal, and to avoid being treated like a nerd he had refused to enter the gifted stream in high school. But in Dhaka, he quickly teamed up with a Sri Lankan friend in his class, Ananda, who saw one B+ on Derek's first report card and told him there was no excuse for it. From that time on, he only got As. Peer pressure in Canada had driven him in the opposite direction. So, pulling him out of Canadian teen culture had been a good move. I had spent most of my own high school years rebelling, and didn't want him to follow my pattern.

Ruth adjusted to her new situation too. The school had a drama club, and trips, including one to Nepal—many perks she and Derek would not have experienced in Canada. They could also catch a trishaw ride to their friends' homes. Ruth was further cheered by our agreeing she could have a dog in Bangladesh. She chose a small black-and-white terrier an American family had found in a Manila slum. They were moving again and wanted to give the dog away. His name was Tuxedo, or "Tux" for short, because he had white markings on its chest, which looked like he was ready to go to a formal dinner.

By December, we had just settled down to life in Bangladesh when the President, Hussain Muhammad Ershad, was overthrown in a popular uprising. I write "popular" but in Bangladesh many politicians rent crowds for a small fee per person for demonstrations. General Ershad had seized power in a bloodless coup in 1982, and declared himself President in 1983. Khaleda Zia, widow of former president, Ziaur Rahman, who was assassinated in 1981, took over. She put Ershad under house arrest in a place we could see from our roof top. For a few days, we had to stay at home because the demonstrations could be volatile. But eventually the country settled down. In its short history since 1971, two of Bangladesh's presidents had been assassinated and there had been other changes in the country's leadership. Ershad's downfall was par for the course.

Things had just become peaceful again when the Gulf War began, in January 1991. That war was far away but many Bangladeshis revered Saddam Hussein, President of Iraq. He was seen as a strong Muslim leader and Iraq employed many Bangladeshi laborers. We were forced to stay at home for two weeks after a mob stopped a van of another U.N. agency, politely asked everyone to get out, then promptly poured petrol on it, setting it on fire. In their eyes, the U.N. and the U.S. were one and the same.

No sooner had that crisis died down, when a tropical cyclone formed in the Bay of Bengal in late April, making landfall in Chittagong District with winds of 155 mph (250 km/h). It was one of the most powerful cyclones ever recorded in the Bay, creating a 20 foot (6.1 meter) storm surge along the coast, which caused an estimated 140,000 deaths and U.S. $1.7 billion in damage. But Bangladeshis were used to such disasters. UNICEF and other U.N. agencies, the government, hundreds of NGOs, and the private sector fired into action. The very next day the roads south were clogged with trucks carrying fresh water, food, and fuel, as

BECOMING A MULTIMEDIA PRODUCER IN BANGLADESH

well as medical supplies and building materials. Short-term assistance morphed into longer-term strategies such as the building of raised cyclone shelters in coastal villages, which could also serve as schools and community centers in normal times. When the country was born out of the brutal conflict with Pakistan in 1971, U.S. Secretary of State Henry Kissinger described Bangladesh as a "basket case." But the action we witnessed after the cyclone proved he was wrong.

I did not work in emergency relief. My work was concentrated in UNICEF's ongoing programs. I had become a multimedia producer and manager, rather than a lone filmmaker. Gradually, my section became involved in almost all program areas: developing advocacy materials, logos, posters, TV and radio spots, videos, and interpersonal communication guides. We also helped to form program partnerships. I brought onboard new staff members, two British women: Pamela Reitemeier, as my deputy and head of program communication, and Clare Blenkinsop, in charge of information and press relations. I was also given the green light to hire new Bangladeshi staff for each program area. They were placed in my section rather than in program sections such as health, water and sanitation, and education, etc., because I had articulated a new vision for the role of communication. We moved our section to a middle building, surrounded by the program sections, and we welcomed all other staff members to visit or pass through.

I studied all the pieces of the successful EPI program, which achieved near universal childhood immunization by the end of 1990, and I was determined to find out how the parts worked together. I had rejected the idea of social marketing in my master's thesis, and was intrigued by what UNICEF called "social mobilization." But to me, New York's definition was too grandiose—it comprised practically all of the activities of UNICEF and didn't give clarity on who was to do what. Gradually, I redefined the terms:

> **Social mobilization** is the process of bringing together all feasible and practical inter-sectoral social allies to raise people's awareness of and demand for a particular programme, to assist in the delivery of resource and services, and to strengthen community participation for sustainability and self-reliance.

Furthermore, I analyzed all the **Advocacy** activities, which helped to bring so many donors and partners on board to deliver the program, and I differentiated them from those which were targeted at the end user—the parents and older members of families, as well as community leaders, who were key in decisions on children's and women's healthcare. Then, UNICEF called this Programme Communication, later widely known as **Behavior Change Communication**.

To articulate the relationship between these three key concepts, I developed a diagrammatic representation for this strategic approach to communication, which we adapted for almost all UNICEF programs. (See the following diagram that illustrates the general relationships between the key concepts and their functions.)

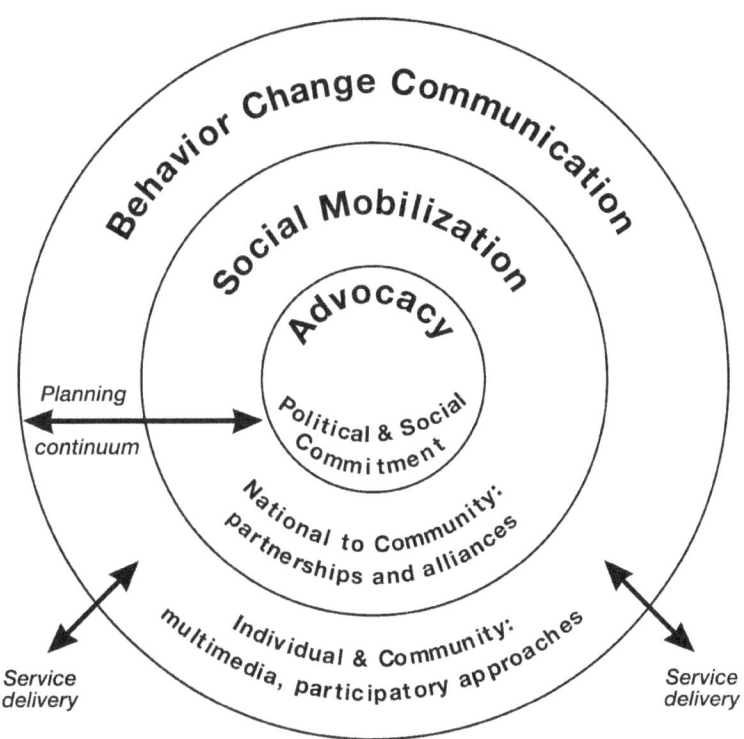

Communication for Development Model

In my spare time, I reworked my master's thesis, adding my experiences with UNICEF in Bangladesh, and wrote a book to be published by my former colleague, Chin Saik Yoon, who had left IDRC and started a publishing company in Malaysia, specializing in books on communication. He named his company Southbound Publications and we titled my book *Social Mobilization and Social Marketing in Developing Communities: Lessons for Communicators* (1992).[1] Cole encouraged me throughout this process and he asked James Grant to endorse my book. Cole saw the value of having publications under your belt. He motivated and paved the way for many staff members' successes.

Creating targeted communication activities and materials required careful research such as focus group discussions, to ensure they were going to bring about sustained behaviour and social change. I knew all this from my recent studies, and I was determined to get it right. For instance, we carried out a communication study on how people were persuaded to get their children vaccinated and found in both rural and urban areas, health and family planning field workers were the main influencers, although mass media had a stronger effect in urban centers. Furthermore, we found some field workers were giving out inaccurate information and required more training on EPI facts, as well as proper interpersonal communication methods.

I continued to give the occasional speech at events, representing UNICEF. During my first year in Dhaka, I attended many meetings, which only consisted of speeches. They were repetitive and tedious presentations by a special guest, honorable guests, and many regular functionaries from the government or NGOs. At one Ministry of Health meeting, time was running out because everyone wanted to say everything about the same subject, usually repeating the points made by earlier speakers. The chairman was having a hard time getting people to stick to their allotted time. The last speaker was no different. But instead of cutting his speech short, he sped up his verbatim reading to the point it was getting comical, causing the audience to laugh. The man remained oblivious to what was going on because he hunched his head down on his many pages, eyes glued on the lines he was speeding through. It was great entertainment, but I'm sure no one could recall a thing he said.

That's when I vowed to try a different form of group meeting. I contacted Hermann (Timmi) Tillmann and Maria

Angelica (Maruja) Salas, my old friends from Huancayo, Peru, whom I filmed 1984 (see Chapter 17). They had moved to Germany and, in 1989, they invited me to attend an interesting seminar on agriculture communication, in the Black Forest. It was then that I was first exposed to the method of having participants in group events write their contributions on color-coded cards, with only one idea per card, and pinning them in patterns for discussion and rearrangement on moveable boards. I invited Timmi and Maruja to Bangladesh as consultants, and we ran workshops to train facilitators of group events. Eventually, we created a manual, calling the method "VIPP," which stands for *Visualisation in Participatory Programmes* (1993).[2]

The methods of VIPP democratized group planning meetings and training events, making them fun, rather than tedious affairs, where the most vocal or senior personalities occupy the majority of discussion time. For instance, at one workshop on improving the national strategy for breast-feeding, the head of the government's institute on maternal and child health, Dr. Talukdar, and the Chief of UNICEF's Health Section, Philip O'Brien, locked horns on some technical issue, stopping progress. I was facilitating and I asked them to go for a walk and talk about their families or something else. While they were gone, the group came up with a visual representation of their problem and a possible solution. When they returned, they took a look at the VIPP cards on a pin board, and after a brief discussion, both agreed the ideas represented there solved their disagreement. This was a clear demonstration of the utility of VIPP.

We trained many UNICEF and NGO staff to be facilitators or to simply appreciate the effectiveness of VIPP events, in which the circularity of discussions was much reduced and

MY UNIVERSITY OF THE WORLD

Timmi Tillmann and Maruja Salas training facilitators
—Photos by Neill McKee

outcomes broadly shared. The use of VIPP methods contributed a good deal to our success in launching so many communication programs during those years. Eventually, Timmi, Maruja, and I trained the Training Division of UNICEF, New York, on VIPP techniques, and the methodology spread to many other UNICEF offices, to other U.N. agencies, and NGOs around the world.

VIPP methods originate from the Latin American empowerment philosophy started by educators such as Paulo Freire in Brazil, and post-World War II German educators and development planners, who were searching for new means of democratization, while avoiding chaos in society. It has rules and ordered methods for wider participation of groups of people in decision making, planning, and training. Such educators estimated that, on average, non-handicapped people learn in the following manner: one percent through taste, two percent through touch, three percent through smell, 11 percent through hearing, and 83 percent through sight, hence the focus on the ordered visual methods in VIPP, rather than predominant oral methods. I especially was attracted to Dr. Hartmut Albrecht of the University of Hohenheim, Germany, who restated the old Dutch saying, as follows:

> Said is not heard,
> Heard is not yet understood,
> Understood is not yet approved,
> Approved is not yet applied.

In Bangladesh, I had seen an extreme version of the oral tradition in conducting meetings, planning sessions, and lecture-loaded training courses. The visual, so important to me as a filmmaker, was usually missing. VIPP became a good counterforce to the predominant oral tradition used in many group events.

Our VIPP methodology had immediate impact; however, my most successful communication initiative in Bangladesh began shortly after I joined UNICEF. In February 1990, I received an invitation from UNICEF-New York to attend a conference in Prague, Czechoslovakia, on the use of animated films in development work. Cole told me I should go, in spite of my increasing workload. He was well aware of the animation sequences in my IDRC film, *Prescription for Health*. In fact, the use of the film by UNICEF in many countries was one of the main reasons he had chosen me for the communication position.

In early March 1990, I flew from Dhaka through New Delhi to Prague. It was only four months after the fall of the Berlin Wall. I recall the city had the air of a second Prague Spring. The first had taken place when the country rose up against the Soviet Union in 1968—a short-lived revolt. But even through communist times, Czechoslovakia had its own UNICEF Committee, which raised money for UNICEF's programs around the world, as most developed countries do, including the U.S. and Canada.

There were two reasons for holding this conference in Prague. First, the UNICEF National Committee there had some local currency to spend, and it had more value in the country than elsewhere. Secondly, despite the effects of

BECOMING A MULTIMEDIA PRODUCER IN BANGLADESH

the Iron Curtain, Czechoslovakia had remained a center for artistic animated film production, and it was now ready to show the rest of the world it was open for business.

I recall walking in a park near our hotel that spring to view many-colored perennial flowers bursting out of the ground. The Cold War was over, but it wasn't the case inside the hotel. There were about 200 of us being served by the unsmiling Czechoslovakian staff, who wheeled in large carts to our tables and slammed down plates of lukewarm food in front of us—few choices, take it or leave it. Perhaps some had never served so many black and brown faces before—communication staff members and others from many developing countries. Or maybe they didn't really believe the communist era was over. The older waiters and waitresses had seen this movie before.

On the first day of the conference, James P. Grant, who had been the Executive Director of UNICEF since 1980, gave a rousing speech about the importance of information and communication in UNICEF's work. He was the main driver of the Convention on the Rights of the Child (CRC), which had been adopted by the U.N. General Assembly on November 20, 1989 and would come into effect on September 2, 1990. That convention and the 1981 Convention on the Elimination of all forms of Discrimination Against Women (CEDAW), guide all of UNICEF's work. Grant's words on the importance of communication were music to my ears.

Also present was Bill Hanna of Hanna Barbera Productions, California, creators of *Tom and Jerry, Huckleberry Hound*, *Yogi Bear*, and *The Flintstones*. What did Hanna have to do with international development programs? Well, James Grant had an entrepreneurial streak—attempting to get the private sector to support our work. In the reception that followed, Mr. Grant was talking to Bill Hanna, when I was introduced to them by a New York staff member. Mr. Grant turned to me abruptly and said, "McKee, I want you to come up with an idea to work together with Hanna Barbera."

I recall saying something like, "Sure, I can do that." I think Cole had actually tipped off Mr. Grant I would be there and had mentioned my previous successful work in animated film. I remember feeling I might be stepping on the toes of some of the New York staff, but hey, I had been challenged by the big boss.

I thought a lot about what I could do and slept fitfully that night, fighting jet lag. But as I woke up the next morning, an image of a cartoon-style South Asian girl flooded my brain. The South Asian Association for Regional Cooperation (SAARC), an intergovernmental organization and geopolitical union of countries in South Asia, had declared 1990 to be "the Year of the Girl Child." It was an attempt to change traditional gender discrimination against girls, in terms of their equal rights to education, nutrition, health care; prevention of early marriage, exploitation in domestic labor, and sexual exploitation through trafficking—a huge task. Later, SAARC declared the 1990s to be the Decade of the Girl Child in the region.

As the conference in Prague continued, I began to talk about my "brainwave," but only got positive feedback from a few South Asian female staff members. When I returned to Dhaka, I advocated with my colleagues, wrote to UNICEF-New York and other South Asian UNICEF offices about the concept, and developed a funding proposal. Cole suggested I stick with making some TV spots, but I wanted to create stories. I knew stories, rather than messages, would be repeated and could get people talking about the situation of girls in their families and communities. They had the ability to change attitudes, and maybe practices. But I recognized animated films were expensive to produce. (At the time, thousands of images still had to be drawn and colored by hand. It wasn't until the mid-1990s that computer-based animation became good enough to use.)

I also knew creating the characters and stories would only be cost-effective if they were suitable for use throughout much of the South Asian region. It was difficult to sell this idea to some countries because UNICEF was then, and remains today, a largely country-based organization, programmatically, and usually doesn't operate regional projects.

In any case, I was too busy with all the other communication priorities to spend much time on my cartoon girl project. Once again, Cole came up with the answer. One evening in a garden party at his house, he introduced me to a tall British woman who had recently arrived with her husband. Rachel Carnegie had experience in creating communication materials for and about children in a U.K.-based NGO called Child to Child. Her arrival out of the blue seemed like magic to me. I hired her as a consultant and she soon became the main creative force and coordinator, co-managing with me. The magic continued when money from the Government of Norway began to flow in, and other donors also jumped on board.

Rachel Carnegie with her daughter, and a staff member, Mr. Saha
—Staff photos

Rachel found Ram Mohan, an animated film expert in Mumbai, India, and we brought him onto the team. I introduced Rachel to Mira Aghi of New Delhi, a former IDRC colleague, who became the research director for Meena. Mira had completed her Ph.D. in the U.S. and brought with her an experience of working with Children's Television Network (CTW) on its now-famous TV program *Sesame Street*. The other person who became a main "mover and shaker" was Nuzhat Shahzadi, a smart and experienced Bangladeshi communicator with two master's degrees—one in English literature and one in Public Health. She had joined my section to work on other programs, but soon became a perfect Bangladeshi counterpart for Rachel. We all worked together with Morten Giersing, the Regional Communication Officer, in Nepal, as well as UNICEF staff from Bangladesh, India, Nepal, Pakistan, and Sri Lanka. We held many participatory

PCIS staff, front row at table L to R: Mira Mitra, Afsan Chowdhury, Nuzhat Shahzadi, with some support staff in back –Staff photos

regional workshops, using VIPP to exchange experiences, research results, and make most decisions.

We audience-tested character designs of young girls by various regional artists, and Ram Mohan's won the most marks, although we incorporated some elements from others in the final design. At the same time, we tested many names for the main character and "Meena"—a common name for girls from Muslim, Hindu, and Buddhist families—came out on top. In addition, we researched various background designs and eliminated features identified with particular regions and religions—no mosques, temples, or churches. We also audience-tested the drawings and names of supporting characters, including Meena's younger brother, who came to be called "Raju." We did not want to alienate boys in the storylines, for boys also had to change their minds about the capabilities of their sisters, female friends, and classmates.

In addition, we tested various animals to act as an alter ego of Meena—a character who could add humor to the stories, while getting away with mischief, which adults might frown upon if seen as the actions of a girl. Audience research revealed a parrot we called "Mithu" was the most popular, and fit well into the reality we were trying to create, for parrots can talk, or at least mimic human speech.

Using storyboards, the team carried out in-depth interviews on the first story about fulfilling Meena's wish to go to school. For each of the first few episodes, the formative research process involved approximately 200 focus groups and 50 in-depth interviews throughout the region, with girls, boys, parents, grandparents, community members, and decision makers. We scaled down the research process thereafter, but in total, over 10,000 children and an equal number of adults were consulted in the process of creating the first five Meena stories.

It was interesting that the majority of respondents saw Meena as a real girl like their sister, daughter, granddaughter, or like girls in their communities, not a cartoon figure. Many said most films shown in cinemas, such as those produced by Bollywood, were fictional and didn't address their own realities. But Meena and the other characters were people from their own village.

We created a girl who was a role model for other girls, not a strident advocate for their rights, but one with emotional intelligence and the essential life skills to facilitate change: problem solving, critical and creative thinking, good communication skills, self-awareness, and empathy. Meena operated within the cultural framework in which she lived, realizing that change takes time.

Meena logo

Meena's extended family

Ram Mohan first worked with Hanna Barbera's FIL Cartoons in Manila, Philippines, which offered a reduced rate to UNICEF for the first few episodes. In December 1992, we launched the first episode of Meena on girls' access to education, which we titled *Count Your Chickens*.[3] It was a great hit in Bangladesh and throughout the region. I was only managing the process, but certainly using what I had learned about communication programming at FSU in Tallahassee. I remember feeling that moving to UNICEF was definitely the right move for me.

Comic book cover, episode 1

Meena stories were broadcast on television in Bangladesh and in many other South Asian and Southeast Asian countries. In all, they were dubbed into 17 Asian languages. The British Broadcasting Corporation (BBC) produced two Meena radio series in Bangla and in three other South Asian languages, which were also broadcast throughout the region. In some countries, girls listening and discussion groups were formed. This approach further popularized Meena among hard-to-reach, under-privileged communities.

For almost every story, we also created a simple comic book. In addition, we made other materials such as stickers and metal plates to fasten on trishaws. Some video distribution companies began to copy the cartoons on video cassettes. There was no way of stopping such piracy and, besides, it was a sign of Meena's popularity. We found one firm that was recycling plastic waste, melting it down to make video cassettes, and selling Meena cartoons at a low cost. They provided entertainment-education to the rural poor and urban slum dwellers, who had little access to television.

In Bangladesh, Meena was integrated into the work of many partner organizations; for example, thousands of nonformal primary schools and village micro-loan chapters run by Bangladesh Rural Advancement Committee (BRAC); the programs of other NGOs, including folk theater, puppet shows, competitions, and celebrations; the Department of Mass Communication's mobile cinemas and outreach work in almost all districts; and even the Department of Education's primary schools in the country. Similar dissemination work was carried out in other countries in the region.

Meena became a popular tool for UNICEF's worldwide advocacy, fundraising, and education initiatives. In December 1995, Meena was identified by *Newsweek* magazine as "one of the actors to emerge on the world's stage in 1996." Meena was appointed as the official "ambassador" of the 1998 International Children's Day of Broadcasting—an event reaching more than 2,000 broadcasters, globally. By 2001, the pilot episode had been dubbed into and broadcast in 30 diverse languages.

Eventually, 31 regional episodes were produced (see: www.neillmckeevideos.com/meena)[4]—most by Ram Mohan in his Mumbai studio. The main episodes deal with addressing many issues of gender disparity:

- challenging the dominant parental norm of son preference;
- girls' rights to quality education, both access and retention;
- girls' and women's right to quality health care;
- girls' equal right to a balanced and adequate diet;
- equal distribution of household chores between girls and boys;
- prevention of teasing and bullying of girls, and children with disabilities;
- girls' rights to recreation and sports;
- delaying marriage until at least age 18 or until completion of education;
- rejecting harmful dowry practice in marriages;
- preventing domestic child labor and sex trafficking; and
- girls' and women's peace and security in conflict situations.

Other stories addressed UNICEF's mainstream programs, for instance: prenatal and newborn care; early childhood development practices; breastfeeding and additional complementary feeding; preventing childhood accidents and injuries; management of diarrhea and use of oral rehydration; as well as safe water delivery, sanitation, and hygiene;

psychosocial support in natural disasters; preventing the stigma and discrimination against people with HIV/AIDS, and giving accurate information on how it is transmitted.

I want to clarify, however, that much of this progress took place after I left South Asia. At the end of 1993, I departed Bangladesh to take up the post of UNICEF's Regional Programme Communication Officer, based in Nairobi, Kenya. But the "dream team" I had set up carried on this great work.

When I left Bangladesh, I had no idea many Meena episodes would continue to be created and used 25 years after our initiative was launched, and that Meena would become part of the culture of South Asia. My waking dream in Prague became real.

22. Creating Our Own Kenyan Village

Beth, Ruth, and I left Dhaka for Nairobi, right after Christmas of 1993, with our little dog Tux. We had lined up jobs for Mitro and Shuntu, plus a school for Poppi. Derek flew back to Boston, for he had left home six months earlier. He had done very well in high school and was offered places at universities in Canada and the U.S. He chose Harvard, and his Sri Lankan friend, Ananda, went to Cambridge. At first, we wondered about the monetary side of Derek's choice, but we could afford it because the U.N. paid for about two-thirds of the overall costs (through part of a mandatory 30 percent deduction from international U.N. staff salaries, in place of our home countries' income taxes). Such an expensive university as Harvard wouldn't have been an option for Derek if we had stayed in Canada. Just the same, we told him he had to earn his own pocket money, and he took a job of cleaning the washrooms in his campus residence.

On arrival in Nairobi, we found it cool and crisp—quite a pleasant change from overcrowded and muggy Dhaka. Nairobi lies at 5,880 feet (1,792 meters) above sea level and becomes chilly at night—even more so in the slightly higher suburb of Gigiri, a large expatriate village about six miles (9.6 km) from Nairobi's city center. It's the home of the United Nations Environmental Programme (UNEP) and where many other U.N. agencies are housed, including UNICEF's Eastern and Southern Africa Regional Office (ESARO). Walking around the fenced-in UNEP complex in the evening, with its many trees, flowers, and birds, was like experiencing Heaven on Earth—not a hardship post at all.

I had visited earlier to get the lay of the land and rent a brand-new house, not far from the U.N. gates, but on arrival we found it far from finished. At first, we stayed with our Irish friends, Philip and Anne O'Brien, who had also left Bangladesh. Our landlord, Mr. Okora, a Kenyan businessman of the Luo tribe, had run out of money to complete our house. So, we made a deal with him to pay the workers directly in cash, rather than pay him rent for six months. I had to begin travels for my work, so Beth ended up carrying a bundle of Kenyan shillings over to the house to pay them every Friday afternoon.

Our unfinished house and garage –Photo by Neill McKee

After many weeks of delay, we finally moved into our nearly finished house. Beth found a gardener by the name of Aggrey, who came from the Luyha tribe, to look after our fenced-in property, and to open and close the gate during the day. I had ordered a secondhand white Toyota station wagon and I painted a wide blue stripe all along its sides and back, because there were a lot of hijackings of more expensive expats' cars, especially in Gigiri. I thought no one would want to steal this inexpensive and unattractive car, which could easily be identified. Our house was far from any shopping center, Ruth's international school, and the homes of the friends she quickly made. So, we shared James, a driver from the central-Kenya Kikuyu tribe, with the O'Briens. He drove Beth sometimes, made pick-ups and deliveries, and worked some evenings on weekends to take Ruth to her friends' homes and meeting places.

At last, we were safe in our new home, which had a good-sized lawn for Tux to run around on. We adopted a young female mongrel from a litter the O'Brien's dog had delivered. This mutt grew to be three times larger than Tux. We asked Ruth what she wanted to call this new addition and she came up with "Laertes," a character in William Shakespeare's play *Hamlet*, but if we didn't like that, how about "Shovel," "Fork," or "Doorknob?" The latter name seemed to fit well with the state of our roughly finished house, so the dog was dubbed "Doorknob."

Beth wanted a real cook and a housekeeper, not someone whom she would have to train, like Mitro in Bangladesh. She hoped to concentrate on her artwork, which was becoming a business. Since our station wagon, and a second car I bought to get around town, were of low value, our large garage wasn't really needed. Beth had the workers install glass windows on its doors so it could serve as a bright marbling studio. She had been practicing the ancient art of marbling, which dates back at least 1,000 years in East Asia and the Middle East. Marbling has been used in the West since the 17th century for making inside book covers, among other decorations. Beth gradually built up her business and at one time had five young Kenyans working for her, creating beautiful colored patterns on paper and cloth: note cards, photo albums, vests, blouses, skirts, ties and hats; and selling these products at craft sales. Beth said she wanted to earn extra money to help pay for our part of the cost of Derek's education at Harvard.

Beth's demonstrating her products -Photo by Neill McKee

Beth's marvelous marbling business –Photo by Neill McKee

Finding and training such artisans was the fun part for Beth; cooks and housekeepers were another matter. She went through a number of them who couldn't cook or couldn't get along with other people. First, she hired Julius, a Kikuyu man who showed up at our gate with an English paperback novel under his arm—a good sign, Beth thought, but it was probably a prop. She also hired a housekeeper who pronounced her name, "Agi-nes." She claimed to be a widow and had been recommended by O'Brien's cook, Levi, a Luo preacher whose outdoor church Agines attended. Agines and Julius worked together harmoniously for a while, but one day Julius found that someone had put a gray powder above the door to his room in the servants' quarters—a form of witchcraft to make him ill, so he believed. He blamed Agines, who denied doing it, of course, and they got into a long argument. Julius also told Beth that Agines was not a widow, as she claimed. Her husband was a cook in another house nearby, so Agines had become real agony. Beth tried to negotiate peace between them, but finally gave up and let them both go.

Next, Beth hired two young ladies, graduates from a housekeeping school. Beatrice, the housekeeper, was a Swahili from the coast and Jacinta, the cook, possibly from the Kisii tribe. They were relatively well-educated, so they didn't believe in witchcraft. But after a year of harmony, Jacinta announced she would have to quit because she was getting married. She'd been made pregnant by a truck driver. Shortly after that, Beatrice said she was getting married too and left her job.

Jacinta, hard at work –Photo by Neill McKee

By this time, Ruth had departed for university in the U.S. and there was just the two of us to feed. But Beth was busy with running her marbling business. So, she hired a housekeeper, another Beatrice, who already had all the children she was going to have. She also hired Esther, a highly recommended older woman cook employed by a Canadian friend who was leaving. But much to Beth's dismay, Esther only knew limited menus, so Beth decided to let her go and train Beatrice No. 2 as a cook. She also agreed to continue to do the housework for extra pay.

The two solid employees were James, the driver, and Aggrey, the gardener. They stayed with us throughout, and I can imagine their conversations about the comings and goings of all the other staff. They were both from Bantu tribes, but their languages were not mutually intelligible and their customs different.

Aggrey didn't sleep in our compound at night. He stayed with his wife and family elsewhere. But one day he showed up to say she had given birth to twins and he needed the equivalent of U.S. $2,000 in Kenyan shillings to get them out of the hospital. Apparently, he and his pregnant wife had waited in line at the regular government hospital, but she was in much pain and was bleeding. It looked like she might die, along with the twins, so he rushed her to Gertrude Children's Hospital, explaining his boss worked for the U.N. and he would pay. He had not asked us about paying the bill, but there was no time to waste.

It should be noted here that in many African cultures, the birth of twins is a bad omen—a curse on the family. I'm not sure if Aggrey believed in this superstitious, but maybe he thought he had to overcome this bad luck, one way or another. Due to his presence of mind and critical thinking, his wife and the babies had lived. We decided saving those children was more important than our money. But later, Aggrey's wife went a little crazy in the city, looking after the twins and their other children, and she ran away, heading back to her family home in western Kenya. Aggrey had to take the twins to her and put her on his father's farm with their babies.

Near the end of our stay in Kenya, Aggrey's father fell sick, so Aggrey brought him to Nairobi for medical treatment. He died soon afterward, and Aggrey couldn't afford to hire the special transport to take his body from Nairobi to their farm near Kakamega, an all-day trip to western Kenya. He politely asked for money to transport the casket, but instead Beth offered our small station wagon to be driven by James, who agreed but didn't know what he was getting himself into. He ended up carting the casket around Nairobi all day to different ceremonies, wailing sessions, and meals. It wasn't until dusk that they departed on the long journey. Unfortunately, the simple wooden box was a little too long for our station wagon and the back door had to be kept ajar, causing exhaust fumes to enter.

James later reported, "It was a terrible journey. I could hardly keep awake and felt sick. We arrived at sunrise and there was a lot more wailing, crying, and praying. After a while, I begged Aggrey to let me leave. He agreed. He said he had to stay for some time to make sure his mother would be okay. But before I left, Aggrey's mother brought me a live chicken, bound at the feet. She told me to release it after I left the area."

James continued, "I asked her why and she said, 'To release the evil spirits from the car.' I laughed at her stupid superstition, but took the chicken as she asked."

Beth asked James, "Did you bring it back to Nairobi to cook?"

"No way. I released it!"

I think he understood why we laughed at his reply.

James our driver and Aggrey with family —Photos by Neill McKee

Today, Beth admits during those years she was suffering from migraine headaches and menopause. She also thought she was finally mourning her mother's death, which happened when she was only seven. In addition, we also speculated her ailments were possibly caused by "empty-nest syndrome," after Ruth left in the summer of 1995. Added to that, her religious beliefs had evolved. In Bangladesh, she had found an ecumenical church run jointly by a Methodist pastor, an Anglican priest, and a Catholic priest, which I occasionally attended. But on our first Easter Sunday in Nairobi, we attended All Saints' Anglican Cathedral, seat of the Archbishop of the Province of Kenya. We were used to Anglican services from our former church in Ottawa, but the Archbishop's sermon was on the evils of HIV/AIDS, satanic devil worshipping, and *matatus* (fancy minibuses). We couldn't figure out what he was talking about. We stayed for the first 45 minutes of his illogical ramblings, and then walked out down the center aisle, in full view of the elite African and white congregation. We never returned.

It wasn't until later, when we asked an educated Kenyan, that we understood the Archbishop was making a partly political speech. President Moi belonged to the suspicious Masonic Movement, who worshipped the devil, so it was rumored. Our Kenyan friend suggested that possibly the Archbishop, a Kikuyu, viewed Moi, a Kalenjin, as a devil worshipper. He suggested it could also be due to the recent conflict in the country. In 1992, an estimated 5,000 people had been killed and another 75,000 displaced in the Rift Valley during tribal clashes over land ownership, primarily between the Kikuyu and Kalenjin communities there.

At least the Kenyan village we had created was more peaceful than that.

23. Travels and Creations in Eastern and Southern Africa

How did we end up in Nairobi? Well, Cole Dodge, the UNICEF Representative in Bangladesh, had left Dhaka over a year before me. He became UNICEF's Regional Director for Eastern and Southern Africa, and asked me if I wanted to apply for the communication post in Nairobi. In January 1994, I was tasked with providing program communication expertise to 22 UNICEF offices in the region from Eritrea and Ethiopia, in the north, to South Africa and around the horn of Africa to Namibia and Angola.

Our regional office was almost a mirror image of a typical country office in terms of staff make-up—a mixture of local national and international staff. The big difference was that the international program staff, like myself, had no program budget. We had our salaries and small travel budgets, and were considered to be advisors to the country offices. There was no requirement for country offices to request our assistance, so we had to sell our services, much like consultants.

I focussed my efforts on strengthening the communication strategies in UNICEF's country programs such as immunization, water and sanitation, maternal and child health, and retention in education. The enrollment of children in school was better than in South Asia, but the retention of girls, especially, remained a big problem due to family poverty, workload at home, sexual harassment, and early pregnancy and marriage. In addition, the growing problem we were facing was HIV/AIDS. HIV infection rates were steadily rising in the region, and increasing numbers of sexually active adults were dying of AIDS. HIV could also be passed to babies through breastfeeding. But, at the time, there were no affordable and fully approved anti-retroviral drugs to interrupt transmission from the nursing mother to her child, or for treating people living with AIDS, although trials had begun in Africa. Furthermore, our region was stricken with the more virulent HIV-1 rather than HIV-2, a milder form of the virus predominant in West Africa.

I was honored to be named as the HIV/AIDS program focal point in the region, which meant I had to organize regional trainings and planning meetings on what UNICEF's strategies should be to prevent infections and mitigate the impact on women and children. Because there were no medical answers on prevention, it was natural that staff carrying out activities in communication for social and behavior change should take the lead. I worked closely with the UNICEF Representative in Uganda, Kathleen Cravero, an American who became the convenor of our HIV/AIDS Program Network in the region. Uganda was one of the countries being hit hardest by HIV/AIDS.

Our Deputy Regional Director, Zerfi Bendow from Ethiopia, was focal point for the Women in Development Network, which focused on helping to strengthen UNICEF programs in addressing gender disparity. I was lucky to work with these women. We saw eye-to-eye on the fact that the disempowerment of girls and women was a major factor inhibiting social development and accelerating the spread of HIV/AIDS in our region.

Besides gender disparity, there were tribal and ethnic divisions in most African countries, just like Kenya, which impeded development. The genocide of Tutsis by Hutus in Rwanda, in early 1994, made that obvious to us and the world. Cole had seen how the VIPP methodology had worked in Bangladesh, and along with a Junior Professional Officer from the Netherlands, Caroline Den Dulk, and my Kenyan Program Assistant, Eunice Wambugu, I began to train VIPP facilitators. Throughout the region, we saw the need to democratize group events in order to allow ideas and opinions of people with differences in gender, ethnicity, and age, to be shared and built into program objectives, strategies, and activities. I didn't believe in flying into a country, consulting with only a few key stakeholders, and then writing a communication strategy on HIV/AIDS or any other program. I knew that by doing this there would be little or no ownership by the people who had to implement the plan, and therefore little chance of success. So, the VIPP methodology became my *modus operandi* in the region.

During my time in ESARO, I trained hundreds of facilitators and facilitated many program planning sessions. I also brought in my VIPP co-creators, Timmi Tillmann and Maruja Salas, to train facilitators. In addition, they helped Esther Wyss, an American facilitator working with UNICEF-Zambia, to build a home for VIPP in that country. Together with UNICEF's Training Section in New York, we also held a global VIPP consultation on the Island of Mauritius in the Indian Ocean, and developed a *VIPP Games and Exercises Manual* (1998)[1] for participatory group events. From the beginning of our experience with VIPP, we had found that including entertaining activities and exercises, which are related to the theme of the events, increases participation, creativity of thought, group cohesion, and consensus building.

VIPP facilitator trainee —Photo by Timmi Tillmann

In mid-1994, I was invited to present the work I had started in South Asia on Meena to UNICEF's Regional Women in Development Network. Kathleen Cravero attended, and she invited the newly elected Vice President of Uganda, Speciosa Naigaga Wandira Kazibwe—the first woman in Africa to hold such a position. At the end of my PowerPoint presentation and the showing of an episode of Meena, there was much applause, and the Vice President made an important public statement, "You must make an African Meena."

So, I had my marching orders. I started right away, writing a proposal and consulting UNICEF communication officers in the region. With support from the fundraising section in New York, once more, I was able to raise money from the Government of Norway. It also was wonderful to gain so much backing in the region, especially from women representatives and their staff. For instance, Catherine Mbengue, a Cameroonian woman who was the UNICEF Representative in Malawi, joined our group, and soon we had 10 countries involved: Eritrea, Ethiopia, Kenya, Uganda, Tanzania, Malawi, Zimbabwe, Zambia, Namibia, and South Africa.

Once again, I was able to assemble a solid team. Besides Caroline Den Dulk, Justus Olielo, a Kenyan man, won the competition for a national officer position. We brought in a writer by the name of Richard Mabala. He had first gone to Tanzania as a British VSO volunteer and remained there, taking on an African surname. He was fully fluent in Swahili and had become a Tanzanian citizen.

During the development of the first episode, we identified African artists, writers, researchers, and UNICEF country office focal points from the 10 countries involved as testing sites. I hired Dr. Mira Aghi from New Delhi, principal researcher for Meena, to come to Africa to train researchers, using the same qualitative research methods we used for Meena. I also contracted Ram Mohan from Mumbai, the artist who had created Meena, to train African artists for the project.

In the early research we undertook, the name "Sara," common in both Christian and Muslim communities, came up on top for the girl we created. Besides the name, we tested different character designs to arrive at the one for Sara, as well as for supporting characters and backgrounds.

Richard Mabala wrote the first story, which was tested widely in the region. We held the first regional synthesis workshop in Machakos, Kenya, where we finalized the characters, backgrounds, and storyline. Besides Ram Mohan and Mira Aghi, I invited Rachel Carnegie, who had returned to the

Many versions of Sara were tested to arrive at the final design

Various background scenes were tested to design Sara's village

U.K., and Nuzhat Shahzadi, then leading the Meena project in Bangladesh. It was a creative and entertaining event, which further solidified our regional group.

The first episode, *The Special Gift*[2] on Sara's retention in school, was produced in video and comic book formats, and became a real hit. It's an entertaining story on how Sara manages to convince her overbearing conservative and somewhat comical uncle to allow her to go on to secondary school to fulfill her dreams, instead of quitting school at the end of primary grades to help with chores at home. At the Machakos workshop, we used VIPP methods and also acted out parts of the story. Richard was excellent at playing the part of the uncle he'd created.

Richard Mabala playing Sara's uncle –Photo by Neill McKee

We wanted to address the themes of sexual abuse and HIV/AIDS. A couple of storylines were written by the team, but none of them were both entertaining and educational—too many direct messages, which might "turn off" young people.

Finally, before she left for university, I asked my daughter, Ruth, if she would take a crack at it, although I couldn't pay her because that would break UNICEF rules against nepotism. In Dhaka, she had written and produced a play, and in Grade 12 in Nairobi, she had a teacher of playwriting all to herself. She had written another play and staged it at the city's French Cultural Center, Alliance française.

The story Ruth crafted involved our heroine, Sara, saving her friend, Amina, from sexual abuse by truck drivers—a frequent happening along busy highways in Africa. Adolescent girls walking home from school might take a joyride for excitement and adventure, and end up being raped. Long distance truck drivers, who traveled from town-to-town and had unprotected sex with sex workers, were major spreaders of HIV and other sexually transmitted diseases.

Cover of the comic book version

I was happy my adolescent daughter, not quite 18 at the time, could contribute to our initiative. Ruth demonstrated good life skills, like Sara—creative problem solving, critical thinking, self-awareness, and excellent communication skills. Beth, especially, had taught such skills early on to both Ruth and Derek. When they were growing up in Canada, Beth received a monthly "baby bonus" for each child from the federal government, and she opened bank accounts for them to buy their own clothes. They were seldom told what to do, but were taught to think about the consequences of their actions and make decisions themselves.

Our Sara team came to the conclusion that adolescent girls in Eastern and Southern Africa, and possibly many other parts of the world, usually lacked such skills due to gender inequity from birth, and therefore the Sara stories should model such skills, in culturally acceptable ways. Attempting to build psychosocial life skills in young people became an important aspect of our work.

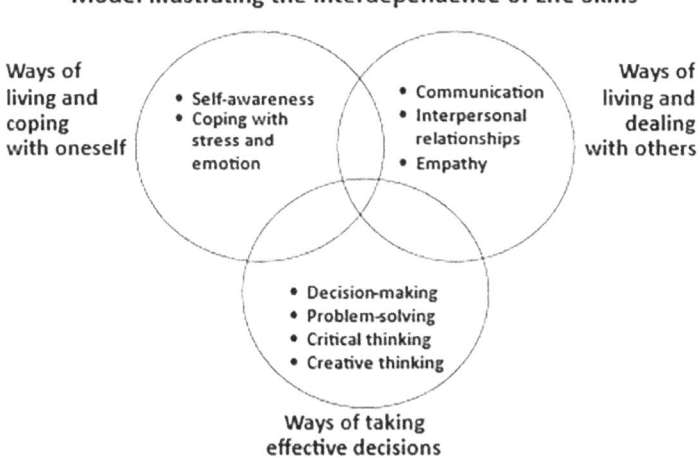

Model illustrating the interdependence of life skills

By early 1996, work on Sara had become too demanding and I needed a regional coordinator who could manage the production of the second episode and create many more stories. The person had to have excellent program communication experience, facilitation skills, cultural sensitivity, a background in gender equity programing, and the ability to carefully manage the money coming from donors. UNICEF advertised internationally and Nuzhat Shahzadi won the competition, hands down. Besides the qualities mentioned above, by then she had demonstrated a flare for guiding educational and entertaining storyline creation and dissemination strategies in her work on Meena.

Nuzhat first had to manage the production of *Sara Saves Her Friend*[3] in Cape Town, South Africa. A company there won the competitive bid for producing the film, but it was a difficult task for them because the small firm, owned and operated by white South Africans, had bitten off more than it could chew, even with their new computer animation setup. With Nuzhat's guidance on her many trips to Cape Town, they finally succeeded. But thereafter, we reverted to less troublesome production in Mumbai by Ram Mohan, who had acquired a computerized animation program.

Ram continued to build the skills of African artists in this work. We flew them to Mumbai to work with him—a cultural interchange, of sorts. One time when they were there during the Hindu festival of *Holi*, people on the street threw colored powder at them and splashed them with water. They ran back to the studio to complain, "Ram, the people here don't like Africans. Look at us, they spoiled our clothes."

Ram chuckled in his usual low-keyed manner and said, "No, they just want to include you in their celebrations of our

Hindu god Krishna. The red color on you stands for love and fertility, while the green stands for new beginnings. Welcome to India!"

Richard Mabala wrote the third episode and Justus Olielo wrote the fourth, with input from Nuzhat, myself, and the regional team, as well as Rachel Carnegie and our lead researcher, Mira Aghi, following the same research methods and workshop process we used for the first and second episodes. The third episode titled *Choices*[4] was on avoiding adolescent sexual activity, and the fourth, *The Trap*,[5] concerned strategizing to catch a "sugar daddy," who offered to help Sara with her school fees in exchange for sex. With guidance from Ram, the African artists produced comic book versions of all the Sara stories. Nuzhat led the writing and design of facilitators' guides to be included in each comic book for discussions in schools and youth group settings.

Sara comic book covers

We wanted to tackle female circumcision—the cutting of the clitoris in childhood or adolescence to reduce sexual drive before marriage, and other forms of female genital mutilation, which continued to be practiced by some ethnic groups. Also, the gruesome tradition of sewing up the vagina until just before marriage was still being carried out in some rural communities. This often led to frequent infections and life-long pain. Older women in the community usually specialized in such traditional practices, using unhygienic instruments. These customs mainly continued in East Africa, so we focused our storyline research and development efforts in Eritrea, Ethiopia, Kenya, Uganda and Tanzania.

Sara comic book on FGM

TRAVELS AND CREATIONS IN EASTERN AND SOUTHERN AFRICA

In the end, Nuzhat led the team in the creation of a dramatic story on this culturally sensitive topic. We titled it *Daughter of a Lioness*[6] and in it, Sara, the potential victim, acts as a community facilitator of change, rather than a direct advocate against such practices. There was a place for advocacy with policy makers, including both men and women at higher levels, but we knew that confronting people directly at the community level would meet with much resistance and drive these unhealthy and cruel practices underground.

It may sound like all I did was work in Africa, but that was not the case. In December of 1996, when Derek and Ruth were home for Christmas break, we hired guides to help us climb Mount Kenya (17,000 feet or 5,182 meters elevation), a four-day hike through a majestic landscape—sleeping, cooking, and eating in rustic cold cabins. We told our children to bring a pair of hiking boots and a pair of running shoes. By the time we arrived at the launching camp for the summit, my old back had had it, and Derek's cheap leather African guard boots gave him terrible blisters. We had warned him about them, but it was his decision and his blisters. Fortunately, he had his running shoes, whereas Ruth didn't. Ruth only had old sneakers, which had fallen apart, so she borrowed Beth's hiking boots to carry on towards the summit, only to be halted by altitude sickness. So, none of us made it to the top of the mountain.

After Ruth returned and rested, we climbed higher over a ridge, camped overnight in tents on a plateau, and the next morning began the slow decent on the other side of the mountain through an area called Chogoria. It was like walking on a strange planet covered with plants we had never seen before.

Descending Mount Kenya on the eastern side
—Photo by Neill McKee

We also boated and fished on Lake Victoria and Lake Naivasha, and walked among the pink flamingos on the shore of Lake Bogoria. We saved some sightseeing for our many visitors from Canada and the U.S. Lamu Island, on the Indian Ocean, was then an almost untouched Arab-African hideaway with only one car. There, we saw remnants of a thousand-year-old interface between two very different cultures, and a donkey sanctuary dedicated to their survival for at least a thousand more years.

My parents took advantage of our location to stay with us for five weeks during December 1995 and January 1996, when Derek and Ruth were also with us part of the time. We all went on a safari through the Serengeti Plains of Tanzania to see elephants, rhinos, giraffes, kudus, impalas, ostriches, and thousands of zebras and wildebeests. By then, we were not big meat eaters, but my dad was a life-long hunter and loved his meat, so before we took my parents to the airport to fly back to Canada, we stopped at a restaurant called "The Carnivore," where Dad devoured samples of antelope, wildebeest, ostrich, crocodile, and possibly other African beasts. We wondered if he would die on the plane over the Sahara. That dinner was something I had to write home to my siblings about.

In between such visits and my official travel, I also did some professional writing while in Africa. My experience with Sara and HIV/AIDS communication led me to take the lead in creating another book. I co-edited and co-authored this one with the program division in UNICEF, New

York, and some of the Meena-Sara team. We integrated the models I had come up with in my first book, published while I was in Bangladesh, but added a section on the need for psychosocial life skills and an enabling environment for sustained social and behavior change. My former IDRC colleague, Chin Saik Yoon, wrote the introductory chapter and his company, Southbound, published the book in partnership with UNICEF, New York. I consider the publication of *Involving People, Evolving Behaviour* (2000)[7] as another major milestone in my career as a communication professional.

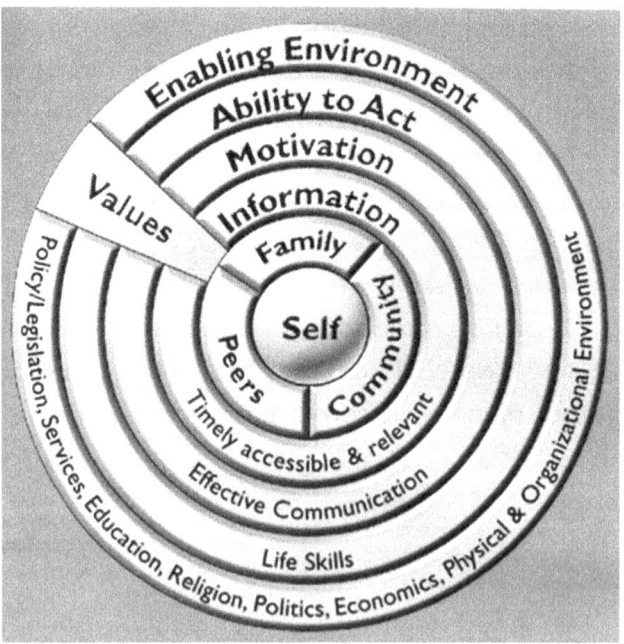

Social and behavior change model

By 1998, I had weathered two changes in leadership in the Regional Office. James Grant died in 1995 and the new Executive Director of UNICEF, Carol Bellamy, started making changes. There had been a major blow up in UNICEF-Kenya operations, involving mismanagement of funds, and the representative, who would never allow our regional office to oversee his operations, was fired, along with many senior staff. UNICEF financial staff and U.N. auditors had caught up with them. Although our regional office was well-run and had nothing to do with this mess, Cole Dodge knew the writing was on the wall. The new Executive Director would want to shake things up. To avoid being transferred, Cole engineered a side step to the United Nations Environment Programme.

The new regional directors who became my bosses, first Shahida Azfar, a graceful and experienced woman from Pakistan, and later Urban Jonsson, a nutrition and human rights expert from Sweden, had different management styles, but I remained the regional HIV/AIDS program focal point and Nuzhat continued to lead the Sara Communication Initiative. By 1999, I had turned the whole process over to her. Shahida knew about Meena's success in South Asia, and Urban could relate to Sara and Meena because of his memories of *Pippi Longstocking*, an empowered, nine-year-old, Swedish girl cartoon figure, popularized in books since the 1940s, and made into movies, spreading to many other countries.

Also, an important factor in the continuation of the Sara Communication Initiative was that it continued to gain much donor support. In addition to the Government of Norway, UNICEF Committees in the U.S., Canada, the U.K., the Netherlands, and Germany, as well as UNAIDS (the overall coordinator of HIV/AIDS programs in the U.N. system), gave us funds for Sara productions and dissemination in various languages in the region, and many country offices were using their own program funds in utilizing Sara materials (see: www.neillmckeevideos.com/sara).[8]

This was all good, but by January 1999, I had been in the same position for five years, and it was time to move on. The U.N. system penalizes international staff, in terms of some benefits, if they stay in one position beyond that period. I toyed with the idea of applying to become a UNICEF country representative, but decided I wanted to remain in communication. There was no senior communication position for me in New York, nor did I want to work there, so far from the field, sitting in endless meetings discussing and developing program guidance for country offices. I had been successful in Dhaka and Nairobi due to supportive supervisors, and the freedom to dream up new initiatives and raise money to create and implement them. So, I accepted a senior position in UNICEF, Uganda, a country just to the west of Kenya. Beth and I had first travelled there on our "honeymoon" filming trip in 1972 (see Chapter 6), when Idi Amin was in power, and I had visited the country many times on assignments while in Nairobi.

In mid-1999, Beth laid off Beatrice No. 2 on amicable terms. She gave her marbling business and equipment to another expat woman, and all her employees found jobs. Beth's enterprise lost money, but she had put her heart into training a group of Kenyans to make beautiful items—an employment creation operation, of sorts. Meanwhile, James found a driver's job with the U.N. and we gave Aggrey enough money to buy land of his own near his mother's farm, hoping he could live again with his wife and the twins we had inadvertently saved.

In August of 1999, we packed and shipped our things and a UNICEF driver took us and our two dogs, Tux and Doorknob, to Kampala, Uganda, to begin another adventure.

A Brief Sojourn in Uganda

Kampala is a thriving jiving city that rocks with a mixture of African music and cultures. In general, I found Ugandans to be happier than Kenyans, at least on the surface. Since independence, they had been through civil and tribal wars, as well as much social-economic turmoil. It's a wonder they still sang and danced. Political stability had come, at least for the moment, but not without growing authoritarianism on the part of President Yoweri Museveni.

We rented a small one-story bungalow in a hilly suburb called Ntinda. Beth had given up marbling to return to calligraphic arts and began to do some freelance graphic design. She took over the garage and the master bedroom for her studio. Large master bedrooms always seemed nonsensical to us, for all you did there is make love and sleep. An important part of our house was the small room where we had an electrician by the name of Paul install an inverter, which would switch to batteries, giving us minimal power on a few lights and the refrigerator when the electric grid failed, which frequently happened.

Probably the most important feature was the front wall—a concrete structure with threatening shards of broken glass embedded on top, but only a low steel fence at the back, which any half-hearted thief could scale. We were given a uniformed night guard service, supplied by the government in an agreement with the U.N. Due to the decades of unrest since independence, these men were armed with semi-automatic rifles. But the one who was usually posted at our house had the habit of taking a break at a small shop across the street, or to talk to other guards, leaving his rifle inside the unlocked gate. We couldn't fire him since he was not employed by us, and we figured complaining about a man who walked around our house with such a gun wouldn't be so wise. Actually, he posed the greatest danger in our peaceful neighborhood.

I took the post of Chief of Basic Education, Child Care, and Adolescent Development (BECCAD) with the understanding my focus would be on helping to develop the components of a new country program addressing the HIV/AIDS epidemic. I continued training people in the use of VIPP and used it in program design. Ugandans proved to be very receptive. Kathleen Cravero had left by then, and the new Representative was Michel Sidibe, a man from Mali, West Africa.

Meetings and office work aren't that interesting to recall and write about, and I found a lot of the work too bureaucratic, compared to my previous duties in UNICEF. This was partly due to a structured computerized management system dreamed up by computer nerds in New York, who would have had me strapped to my desk if I hadn't handed over a lot of the steps to my program assistant. I only signed the hard copies. Another negative feature I quickly noticed was the management style in the office mimicked that of UNICEF in New York—top down. I had read Peter Senge's *The Fifth Discipline: The Art & Practice of The Learning Organization*[1] and Daniel Goleman's *Emotional Intelligence*.[2] It seemed to me UNICEF was trending in the opposite direction from the approaches outlined in these reputable books.

A BRIEF SOJOURN IN UGANDA

My usually cheerful and collaborative Ugandan staff made up for that feature of the office, in part. They were from practically all the ethnic groups of Uganda and I was able to discuss the country's culture and politics with them openly, but one at a time. Another positive feature was UNICEF-Uganda had become a leader in the dissemination and use of Sara materials. Some Ugandan staff worked with Nuzhat Shahzadi to complete three more Sara comic books on priority themes: protecting adolescent girls in emergencies and in domestic labour situations, and reducing stigma and discrimination against people living with or affected by HIV/AIDS. My section was supporting such people through local NGOs, but I didn't realize how important it was until I visited the humble home of a grandmother taking care of her 25 grandchildren. All of her children and their spouses were buried in shallow graves beside her house.

Nuzhat and I continued to work on the future of Sara while I was in Uganda. We knew that because UNICEF programs are usually country-based, interest in Sara could eventually peter out if there was no strong regional champion. Therefore, while I was still in Nairobi, we had begun to search for a home for Sara in the private sector, at least in terms of fulfilling orders for print materials and videos from UNICEF offices, governments, and NGOs. While I was in Uganda, along with our regional procurement officer, Einar Syvertsen, we finalized a partnership between UNICEF and Maskew Miller Longman, an educational publisher in Cape Town, South Africa. They sold and distributed the videos and comic books, but also developed and published new materials for teachers and students, marketing them through educational outlets and bookstores in Africa.

In retrospect, this private sector partnership was a good move, for Nuzhat left Nairobi in 2001 to become Meena Regional Coordinator in Kathmandu, Nepal. Without her enthusiasm and skills, the regional office never was able to complete videos of the last three episodes or produce any new stories. But the deal with Masker Miller Longman continued for over a decade, and Sara stories were spread far and wide in Africa. To this day, I continue to get enquiries from NGOs wanting to know the background on Sara's development and how to acquire and use the materials.

On the social side of life in the country, I found Ugandans to be shy about offering invitations to their humble homes. But our electrician Paul, of the Buganda tribe, invited us to his wedding, an all-day affair with men dressed in white gowns and women in traditional garb called *gomesi*—floor-length, brightly colored dresses with puffed-up, Victorian-style shoulders. In the early 1900s, British colonials succeeded in discouraging Ugandan women from covering themselves with what they considered to be crude cloth, made from the inner bark of the Matuba tree (*Ficus natalensis*). Beth had a *gomesi* made for the wedding and was taught how to wear it properly. The grace and beauty of these Bugandan women helped to keep me awake in the heat of the day, while the steps of the ceremony went on and on. As honored guests, there was no way we could leave until the end.

When we moved to Uganda, I had purchased a secondhand Mitsubishi Pajero and Beth painted Sara on the

A BRIEF SOJOURN IN UGANDA

Ugandan women in *gomesis* –Photo by Neill McKee

Beth being dressed properly in a in *gomesi* –Photo by Neill McKee

spare tire cover at the back. There were fewer vehicle hijackings in Uganda, so we felt safe enough to travel with friends to remote places on rough roads to have picnics, and watch sunsets beside Lake Victoria, while drinking a little wine.

The author with his Mitsubishi Pajero —Photo by Beth McKee

We also did some wider travels in Africa. By this time, our son, Derek, had finished his B.A. at Harvard in Anthropology and Visual Arts, where he had also completed a senior project titled *Darshan in the Age of Mechanical Reproduction*, a photographic study of Hindu Temples in the United States and Canada. After that, he headed to Zambia for a year, working with Street Kids International, a Canadian NGO. He helped with the organization's mission of providing health services, employment, shelter, and human rights education to homeless boys and young men.

A BRIEF SOJOURN IN UGANDA

Derek with colleagues and Beth in Zambia —Photo by Neill McKee

In September 1999, we visited him there, to see how he was doing and to meet his colleagues, as well as to take an overnight boat trip on Lake Kariba, a large body of water created by the damming of the Zambezi River. Following a glorious sunset, we spent the night in sleeping bags on the open deck.

We were glad to see Derek following in our footsteps, seeking international work and adventure, as well as doing visual arts. During our visit, we came to understand a little of his experiences in Lusaka. This was the city where we married in 1972 (see Chapter 6), but by all appearances it had gone downhill since then. Like Uganda, Zambia had become one of the African countries most afflicted by HIV/AIDS. When we entered the same office building where we signed our marriage license, we spotted a dilapidated sign

MY UNIVERSITY OF THE WORLD

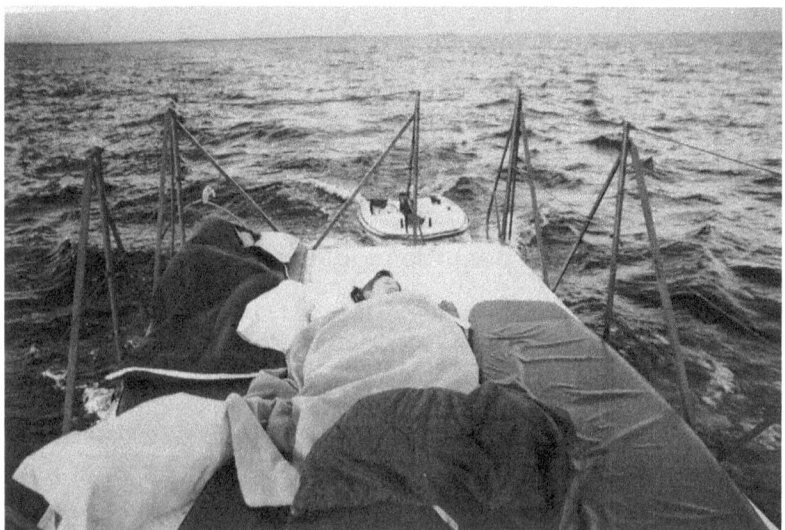

Sunset and slumber on Lake Kariba —Photos by Neill McKee

inside a cracked glass case, which read, "Registration of Births, Marriages, and Deaths—Room 1." We stepped into the designated room only to meet a smiling man in a worn gray suit, who told us he worked for the Ministry of Agriculture.

A BRIEF SOJOURN IN UGANDA

This was just as mixed-up as our marriage vows 27 years earlier, when the official asked me, "Will you, Nelly McKee, take this woman to be your husband?"

Derek finished his work in Zambia and joined us in Uganda for a few weeks in December 1999, along with Ruth and my nephew Kent, who was serving two years as a volunteer teacher in Malawi. Our small house was packed tight, but we enjoyed their company and they loved the nightlife of Kampala. After they left, Beth and I took a New Year's 2000 break in South Africa, flying to Cape Town and renting a camper vehicle. I left my computer and work behind to just relish the summer weather on the Cape of Good Hope, driving around to different vineyards to sample good food and wine, then sleeping it off inside our vehicle, before moving on to a different campsite almost every evening.

We discussed our future, for Beth knew I wasn't exactly thrilled with my new position. Should I look for a different job in Canada or the U.S. closer to our children? While we were living in Nairobi, Beth had helped Ruth get a U.S. permanent residence card, a so-called "green card," so she could work off campus for pocket money, while studying at New York University. By then, she was serious about settling down in the U.S. to pursue a playwriting career. Beth had also started the same process of getting a green card for Derek, but on August 7, 1998, that ended. She had been heading into Nairobi city center with our driver, James, when they were caught in a traffic jam. Al-Qaeda had blown up the American Embassy, and with it, Derek's papers. He decided "that was that"—a sign the green card was not meant to be. From Uganda, he headed home to Canada via the Middle East, to find gainful and meaningful employment, and probably pursue graduate studies someday.

MY UNIVERSITY OF THE WORLD

On New Year's Eve 1999, we toasted the New Millennium before midnight and fell asleep in our camper, not caring whether computers and digital clocks would synchronize with Year 2000 in the morning. We figured a more positive future would soon materialize. After all, we were on the Cape of Good Hope.

Back in Uganda, in May 2000, I went on a field trip to the undulating hills of Rukungiri District, where I experienced a much different and shocking side to the New Millennium. I was curious about an incident that had happened in the Kanungu Sub-County just a few weeks before, and my contact man from the District Health Department (DHD) guided my UNICEF driver and Land Cruiser on a winding dirt road to the former location of a cult, which recently had made headlines around the world. I can't recall what attracted me to go to this place. Perhaps I thought it would hold some answers to the nature of religion in Africa.

As we approached the headquarters of the Movement for the Restoration of the Ten Commandments of God, the setting appeared idyllic, except for the entrance lane which, because of its steep angle, seemed to forewarn us of impending danger by nearly tipping our vehicle over into the valley. Young boys were busy making mud bricks in the adjacent field and a pair of crested cranes could be seen guarding a piece of pasture far below. Inviting flowers covered the hills above us as we crossed a well-worn log bridge over a small brook. As we came closer, it became apparent to me that most of the flowers were Amaranthus, bowing their poisonous bloodred heads in the gentle breeze—another ominous sign?

In front of the tin-roof buildings lay a large earthen parking lot, as if the builders of the establishment had anticipated many visitors. But no one greeted us, not even a policeman or a guard. Our driver, looking a little frightened, said he would stay to guard our vehicle. As my DHD guide and I descend a path into the property, we passed by a rusty old wheelbarrow. The contents had been burned but I could see the remnants of what appeared to be scripture in a Ugandan language, a cross, a chalice, and other religious paraphernalia.

At first sight, the buildings looked normal—a mixture of small and large structures placed in no particular order. But a newer building with a concrete foundation rose taller than the rest. It stood to the right of the downward path and was evidently unfinished, with empty louver holders in the windows. My guide, who had visited just after the event, said, "It was called 'The Ark,' the ship that was supposed to take all the people living here to heaven when the world ended."

A brief walk around the building revealed another story. A gaping hole in the concrete foundation discharged a foul smell. Below lay uncounted decaying bodies of people who had not risen up at the appointed time.

I felt evil hanging in the sunlit air as we continued our investigation, but for some reason I persisted, trying to understand why and how it had happened. Through a wide passage between two buildings, we descended to a school assembly ground. We walked past educational lessons on the walls, including the drawing of a human skeleton, and remnants of learning materials scattered amid haphazardly placed empty benches. I closed my eyes and seemed to hear the echo of pupils' voices. But they were not happy sounds. They were wails of malnourished and ill-treated children who had not been allowed medicine when they were sick, so my guide told me. On one school bench sat a partially broken clay statue of the holy family. On a blackboard beside remnants of lessons, a sympathetic message had been scribbled in broken English after the disaster: "Poor children to going to heaven but gone to hell."

My guide warned me not to step on an oily substance on the floor. It appeared to be petroleum jelly, but he explained it contained a chemical that made flesh burn rapidly when ignited. Inside were other partially used bottles of this jelly, spilling from the window sills onto the floor.

We descend further. The lower side of the assembly grounds was bordered by a beautiful flower garden, which was a welcome relief from the scene above. But on drawing nearer, I saw it was a graveyard for the cult members who died before the horror. Neat piles of rocks could be seen amid the flowers, appearing to shelter the inhabitants of this ground from what took place on that day.

Below the graveyard stood empty dormitories where cult members, separated by age and sex, once slept on woven mats in the mosquito infested air. Beside these lay a newly cleared ground where, I was told, the church once stood, evidently a long hall, which lay below the failed Ark. It was here that 778 people, mainly women and children, began their prayers that morning of March 17th, the windows and doors tightly shut as the ceremony continued. No one remained alive to say exactly what happened or how the fire began. The heat from the tin roof above probably built up gradually and began to blend with the fire below; then panic set in. My guide told me a pile of charred bodies was found at the remains of the door, indicating they had tried to escape when they didn't ascend into heaven. Screams echoed through the valley below. Curious villagers, alerted by the sounds and the smoke, arrived too late to save anyone. At last, they discovered what this strange place was all about. The inmates had been barred from almost all contact with the surrounding population.

We walked down to the edge of the cleared space and climbed freshly formed mounds of earth. The scenery below looked like a Scottish summer landscape painting. Only the sheep were missing on the rolling hills. But this escape was fleeting. My guide informed me the mounds we stood on were hiding human remains. He pointed out a wreath recently laid by the President of Uganda.

We started back, ascending the hill and passing the broken wheelbarrow once more. As we reached the top, my guide pointed to a house on the other side of the valley, where an old man once lived. Unlike other local inhabitants, he had joined the cult. That morning he was also invited to partake in the special prayer so no one would remain to speak to the world about the practices of this twisted form of religious opium, which had gripped the minds and taken the lives of so many innocent people.

Looking down from the car park toward the lane, I could picture the story my guide was telling me. I visualized cult leader, Joseph Kibweteere, stealing away in his car in the early morning, after giving orders to his heavily addicted officers. The Congo border is near this place and he could have easily escaped detection in that country, where a civil war was raging. But others believed he had perished with his flock. No one knew for sure.

As we drove over the bridge and negotiated the precarious angle again, merging onto the main road, I looked back at the deserted buildings. I was numbed by what I had seen and the fact that what had happened here seemed to be almost forgotten, certainly unattended—anyone could wander through. I tried to return my thoughts to my work—the inspection of friendly health services for the young people of Rukungiri, and the communication strategies we were putting in place to protect them from HIV/AIDS. But as we drove off, I felt numb and sat in silence. I had entered and quickly exited the heart of darkness.

In the months that followed, the evil I witnessed on my field trip to Rukungiri District frequently haunted me, and those images remain vivid in my memory, even today. Perhaps my going there was some kind of message I sent to myself. I soon decided seven years in Africa was enough, for now. Working in UNICEF for 11 years had mostly been a creative and fulfilling experience, but it was time to search for the next step in my career. I resigned from UNICEF and Beth and I packed our things. In early December 2000, we found a good home for our dogs, Tux and Doorknob, to live out the rest of their lives together, and we left Uganda.

Finding Myself in America

25.

In late December 2000, Beth and I drove around Chesapeake Bay, Maryland, looking for a house to buy. I wanted riverfront property and that was difficult to find in a good condition at an affordable price. Then we entered a narrow winding road in the sprawling town of Pasadena, situated on the Magothy River. There it was, a newly completed two-story house, located on a hill overlooking the water. It came with a floating dock—a perfect place for me to recreate the boating and fishing adventures of my boyhood in Ontario. The Magothy is about 10 miles (16 km) long and empties into the Bay, a 200-mile (320 km) body of brackish water, which joins with the Atlantic Ocean. I'd found my dream home.

Early morning view from our new house on the Magothy River –Photo by Neill McKee

As we drove out, I noticed a man with a black face on the road. By the U.S.'s Federal Fair Housing Act, real estate agents can't volunteer information regarding the racial, religious, or ethnic composition of any neighborhood, but we eventually found out most of our neighbors would be African American. Of course, that didn't matter to us. We'd just left a Ugandan suburb where we seldom saw white faces, so we made an offer and closed the deal. But were we imposing on an historic black neighborhood, driving up prices in the process? In a few days, we decided that, regardless, it was a good choice.

As it turned out, there were a few white families living there, one located just down the hill from us. On our next visit, we knocked on the door and Mike Christianson popped his head out of an upstairs window to come down and tell us a bit of the history of the place, and that we'd be welcomed. Mike was a lawyer working for U.S. Congressman Elijah Cummings, then leader of the Black Caucus in the House of Representatives. Mike told us during the years of segregation, the area had been donated by a Quaker woman to educated black families from Baltimore for summer residences. Most of the present residents were children and grandchildren of the original owners. Mike had rented his house before buying, in order to prove to them he and his wife Jean would be good neighbors, and he had helped the neighborhood association on legal matters. Jean was a social worker at Johns Hopkins University (JHU) in Baltimore, and they were both peace-loving Quakers, so we felt we were in good company and had found a perfect spot for the next chapter of our lives.

I, too, was working for JHU by then. A good friend, Edson Whitney, who had been in Dhaka, Bangladesh, while we

FINDING MYSELF IN AMERICA

were there, encouraged me to apply to the Center for Communication Programs (CCP) at JHU's School of Public Health, where he had become the head of Asian programs. I had accepted the offer of working as a Senior Program Officer in Edson's section, but when I arrived, the Executive Director, Phyllis Piotrow, said I would be their Senior Advisor for HIV/AIDS Communication. How could I turn that down? I soon learned this was the American way of doing things—flexibility was the word, and salaries were negotiable. There were no rigid grades and steps, as in the U.N. system. Everyone was a free agent and could bargain, based on his on her credentials, experience, and salary history.

JHU is a large private institution founded by the philanthropist Johns Hopkins (1795-1873). His parents named him after his great-grandmother, Margaret Johns, leading to confusion, mispronunciation, and misspelling of the university named after him. His parents were Quakers who owned a tobacco plantation, but they were persuaded by an abolitionist to set their slaves free when Johns was 17, forcing him to quit school and work in the fields. He soon left home to get a better education, and he became a successful self-made businessman. He remained a life-long bachelor, and in his will he left millions "to create a university that was dedicated to advanced learning and scientific research, and to establish a hospital that would administer the finest patient care, train superior physicians and seek new knowledge for the advancement of medicine."[1]

Hopkins succeeded in this goal, but when I first visited JHU's grand hospital complex where the School of Public Health is located, I was shocked to find it to be surrounded by an African American slum—boarded-up and dilapidated rowhouses, graffiti on the walls, with drug pushers and addicts walking the streets. Absent were the cafés and restaurants of a normal university community. I had given up working for an organization dedicated to fulfilling the social and economic rights of children and women, to come to a country famous for its laws on political and civil rights, but where most social and economic rights, such as health care, are not recognized. To this day, the U.S. has not ratified the U.N. Convention of the Rights of the Child nor the Convention on the Elimination of All Forms of Discrimination against Women, as well as most other U.N. conventions. Some Americans say this is rightful "exceptionalism," as the longest-lasting continuous democracy in the world. In spite of helping to create the U.N., and hosting it in New York, most international conventions clash with the U.S. Constitution and both federal and states' legal codes. In fact, I found many of my new colleagues didn't have much respect for the U.N., and with some, it was hard to discuss the value of my previous work in UNICEF.

Fortunately for me, JHU is one of the largest employers in Maryland, and has many branches in numerous locations. CCP is located next to Baltimore's modern inner harbor with its cafés, restaurants, an aquarium, shopping centers, upscale apartment buildings, plus a baseball and a football stadium. Beginning in 1958, the inner harbor was transformed from rotting docks and rat-infested warehouses into an attractive entertainment and tourist destination. I enjoyed walking around the harbor to Federal Hill, a defensive stronghold during the War of 1812, where replica cannons still stand on guard, as if they remain ready to fire on invading British ships. The neighborhood below the hill burned in the race riots of 1968, but has since become gentrified. The harbor is also home to the Visionary Art Museum, which proudly displays the creations of American mental patients, drug addicts, alcoholics, misfits, and kooky non-conformists. I had come to work in a city with a great sense of humor.

I also loved the sense of humor of most of my new American colleagues—program officers, researchers, computer geeks, and support staff—largely white Americans, but with a sprinkling of African, Asian, and Latino Americans. Until I joined CCP, my main experiences with Americans had been with my volunteer friends in the Peace Corps, those I had met during my year in Tallahassee and in UNICEF, and, of course, my wife and her family. In Baltimore, I found debate and rapid-fire discussion to be the *modus operandi* more than in UNICEF or Canada. I'd read many departments of communication in the U.S. had evolved from schools of rhetoric—the art of persuasive speaking or writing. It also seemed to me CCP was more involved in mass media social marketing campaigns for individual behavior change, rather than the more participatory forms of communication programs I had helped to formulate in UNICEF, which attempted to tackle social change. But CCP did do a good deal of work in strengthening the interpersonal communication of health personnel, peer education, and had a library full of some of the best examples of communication materials.

I came to learn there was a reason behind the more campaign-style approach to communication programs at CCP, for most of its work was funded by the United States Agency for International Development (USAID) in five-year global contracts, and quick and visible strategies and actions were expected by the donor. CCP's main experience was in promoting family planning in developing countries. It had recently won its fifth contract, which CCP named Health

Communication Partnership (HCP). It had broader objectives, and the organization needed strengthening in HIV/AIDS communication—which is probably why I was hired.

HCP included other partner organizations such as the Washington, D.C.-based Academy for Educational Development, Save the Children USA, and the International HIV/AIDS Alliance, U.K. I worked with John Howson, a British man who had recently arrived from London to be part of the HCP team. Together, we tried to figure out the ebb and flow of the American office culture we were experiencing, driven by the no-nonsense Executive Director, Phyllis, and her deputies—a lively environment of fast talk and quick decisions. The third tier, Edson, Asia director; Susan Krenn, Africa director; and Walter Saba, director for Latin America, were more soft-spoken and attuned to listening in their approaches to management.

Edson and his wife, Barbara, a professional facilitator, had been trained in VIPP facilitation methods in Bangladesh. We decided it would be best to bring in Timmi Tillmann and Maruja Salas to train a group of CCP personnel in VIPP. Barbara and I co-facilitated to help make the workshop more practical and focused on CCP applications. We soon had some CCP staff members using VIPP to make collegial decisions on programs in Baltimore and overseas, rather than one person doing drafts and then sitting around a table in discussions dominated by whoever was most senior or most eloquent in speech.

But even the most talkative in our office fell silent on the morning of September 11, 2001, when Al-Qaeda hijackers drove jets into the twin towers in New York and the Pentagon in Virginia. Some CCP staff gathered in the conference room to watch TV. I recall I didn't join them immediately, and then only took a brief look before returning to my office. I tried to call Beth but she didn't answer, so I called Ruth in New York, to be sure she and her boyfriend, Brian, were safe. But I remained in a kind of denial when Phyllis told everyone they could go home to be with their families. I stayed in the office until all was eerily silent.

Finally, I walked across the harbor, where the police were setting up barricades, and took the Light Rail, packed with stunned people, back to Glen Burney, where Beth picked me up. We talked a little about the country we had chosen to live in, and what might happen in the future. This was the second time Al-Qaeda had struck near where we lived. Would it be safe for me to travel with an American organization? Did we make the right decision in moving here?

When we reached home, for a short time I looked at the still-evolving horror on television, and then went down to our dock to sit and watch a Great Blue Heron fishing in a cove across the river, and two osprey diving for fish in deeper water. They were swift and accurate, just like the hijackers who had outsmarted America's overbuilt and uncoordinated intelligence agencies.

By the time Al-Qaeda struck the U.S., I had already begun making business trips to Africa and Asia. In fact, I was surprised to find myself going back to Africa, a continent I had had enough of for a while. My work involved working with local CCP staff, helping to formulate HIV/AIDS communication strategies with government officers and members of local NGOs. I organized workshops, in which I used VIPP methods, whenever possible, and worked with younger CCP Baltimore staff to train them on the consultative processes I used to ensure wide ownership in objectives, strategies, and planned actions. What had changed?

Thankfully, most of my time during 2001-2003 was concentrated in Asia. I returned to India many times, working in Mumbai, and this experience made up for the negative impression I had gained on my first visit to the city in 1971, when it was still called Bombay. It was there that I was sent around in circles by the bureaucracy, while trying to send a package of exposed film footage back to Canada (see Chapter 1). By this time, India had become a booming market economy with modern hotels, restaurants, and internet cafés. I enlisted the services of Shana Yansen, a smart young CCP staff member, and we engaged with other USAID contractors, the government, and NGO partners, to develop a comprehensive plan for the prevention, control, and mitigation of the effects of the HIV/AIDS epidemic in the State of Maharashtra. Edson Whitney joined us for the VIPP workshop where all the partners came up with the objective, strategies, and activities.

India is a land of variety and the virus's transmission routes were also many and varied: commercial sex workers with their regular male customers—businessmen, white collar workers, tradesmen, rickshaw pullers, and truck drivers. Young girls were being trafficked to Mumbai from parts of India and Nepal to be sold into the sex industry. Injecting Drug Users (IDUs) were contracting HIV through use of dirty needles. Long-distance truck drivers were having sex with their male helpers, as young as 12, when they couldn't afford female sex workers. Then they'd return to their homes to have sex with their wives, some of whom were infecting their infants with the virus through breastfeeding. At the time, antiretroviral drugs to interrupt transmission were still not widely available or affordable.

We faced complicated overlaps between IDUs and Men who have Sex with Men (MSM). This was before the era of LGBTQIA: lesbian, gay, bisexual, transgender, queer or questioning, intersex, or asexual, but the diagrammatic representation I was given by one of our partner organizations, the Humsafar Trust, demonstrated a complexity of human sexual relations I had never seen before. There were *hijra*, or eunuchs, who, at one time had played social or ceremonial functions in the courts of maharajas and rich households. During the 20th century, they evolved to become mobile musicians for social events, such as marriages. We were told that "straight" men continued to seek out their sexual services because they were more skilled than most women, but feminine in manner and dress. Neither the *hijra* nor the men, in this example, considered themselves to be MSM. Some men identified themselves to be bisexual, including transsexuals, but others claimed they were only "behaviorally bisexual" and never used the bisexual label. A large number of otherwise "straight" males were available for sex: film industry extras, and young men and boys working in hotels, gyms, bars, and massage parlors. Those people who identified themselves as gay were a small minority of MSM, and gay identity was divided between *kothi* and *panthi*—those who were "receptive" and those who were "active" in penetrative anal sex.

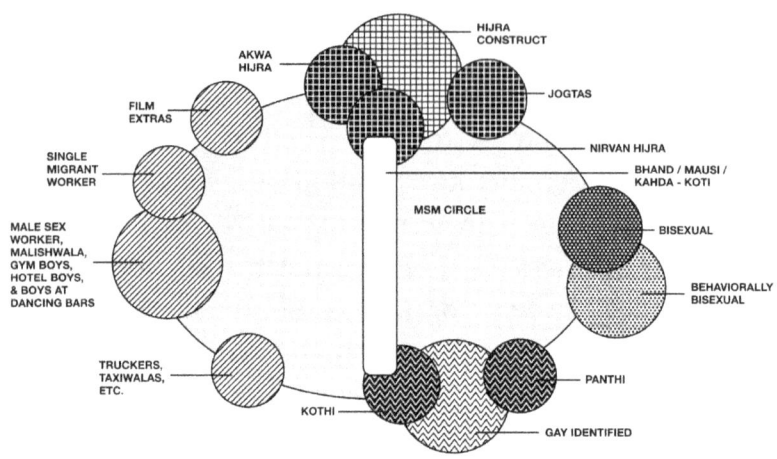

MSM Identities in India, Source: Humsafar Trust

Much stigma and discrimination remained in Indian society against MSM and we generated plans for dealing with this and for controlling the spread of HIV: research on the target audiences and the messages needed, advocacy with decision makers on the real facts about Indian men's behavior, strengthening interpersonal communication and counseling by health professionals, messages on the use of condoms or non-penetrative sex, peer education, and setting up hotlines for distressed people to call. All of this had to be linked to clinical services and drop-in centers.

During this period, I also returned to filmmaking. Another organization, Pathfinder in Boston, working on a USAID project, Focus on Youth Adults, asked CCP if we could help produce a video for educating young adolescents on sexuality in Bangladesh. When Edson asked me to take the lead, of course I jumped at the chance. I had left Bangladesh at the end of 1993, when the Meena Communication Initiative was just gaining momentum. On return almost a decade later, I was elated to see Meena and her pet parrot Mithu painted on walls, school gates, buildings, and on metal plates on the backs of rickshaws. UNICEF had recently conducted research on Meena's reach and effects, and Meena stories and messages had become widely known and understood—now a part of Bangladeshi culture.

I knew educating adolescents about reproductive health in Bangladesh would be difficult, compared to the issues in fostering the health and development rights of younger children, like Meena and her brother Raju. Bangladesh is a predominantly Muslim country with some conservative elements, but radical Islamists had not gained much ground in the country. In my experience, Bangladeshis are more practical. They accept Saudi Arabian money to build new mosques, and send off their men to work in the Middle East to bring back dollars, but they manage to keep Islamists marginalized in politics. So, we had a chance to make an effective video, which might complement what had already been achieved.

Pathfinder was completing four well-researched and well-designed booklets with the overall title, *Know Yourself* and the following subtitles: 1) Puberty, 2) New Feelings, New Passions, 3) Preventing Risks to Our Future, and 4) Preparing for Marriage. The first two booklets dealt with the fact that, traditionally in Bangladeshi society, learning about body and emotional changes in puberty is difficult. Girls are usually segregated from boys, starting around their first menstruation. Being cut off from the opposite sex is not healthy for future behavior between men and women.

The third booklet focused on the dangers of teenage pregnancy and unprotected sex, which might lead to sexually transmitted infections (STIs), including HIV/AIDS, as well as how HIV could be transmitted by used injection needles. The fourth booklet included information on the legal age of marriage in Bangladesh—18 for girls and 21 for boys—but also how this law was often broken by parents for monetary gain through the custom of dowry payments to girls' parents by boys' parents—the opposite of the Hindu custom in India. Information was included on the fact dowry in Bangladesh is a social tradition, not a religious rule, and it is a harmful practice for it lowers the value and status of girls and women. The booklet also included information on female and male reproductive systems, conception, and contraception. Through the long-term efforts of the government and NGOs, with funding from USAID and other donors, most family planning methods were widely available and used in Bangladesh, by then. The booklet also dealt with sexual impotency, infertility, miscarriages, pregnancy, nutrition and care during pregnancy, plus postnatal care of mothers and children.

When I looked through the booklet drafts, I realized they were well-designed but overly detailed. I figured this was much more information than even the average North American adolescent would ever be exposed to or would read. For the next two years, I worked with CCP staff member Caroline Jacobi and staff of the Bangladesh Center for Communication Programs (BCCP), which Edson Whitney had set up during his time in Dhaka. Key to the success of the work was Sanjeeda Islam, Deputy Director of BCCP, a like-minded progressive Bangladeshi woman. We knew it would be difficult, if not impossible, to make only one video to include all the topics in the booklets, so we focused on the first. We came up with the idea of doing a video that involved real adolescents talking to each other about the issues, facilitated by a Bangladeshi who could motivate them to speak out, debate, and act out scenes between themselves and with adults who could play parents, teachers, and health service providers. We also wanted to include short clips of actual interviews with such adults regarding their thoughts on adolescents.

The best person Sanjeeda and I knew to do the job of facilitating the workshops was Nuzhat Shahzadi, who had left the Sara Communication Initiative in Nairobi by then, and was running UNICEF's Meena Communication Initiative from Kathmandu, Nepal. Morten Giersing, who had been the supportive UNICEF Regional Communication Officer when I started Meena, was now the UNICEF Representative in Bangladesh. He was very interested in our adolescent initiative. With his request to UNICEF's Regional Director, Nuzhat was allowed to help us out at no cost to the project, except her airplane tickets and expenses when at work outside Dhaka. She traveled to Bangladesh to run a four-day videotaped workshop with young adolescents.

We also wanted to intersperse sequences from the workshop with entertaining cartoon clips to reinforce points and make audiences remember them. For this I brought on board Ram Mohan, the genius animated film producer from Mumbai, who had created "my daughters" Meena and Sara, and continued to produce Meena episodes, at the time. BCCP hired AV Comm, a video production company I had engaged during my time as communication chief for UNICEF, Bangladesh (see Chapter 21). AV Comm recorded the workshop and produced the video. Sanjeeda also hired a music production firm to write and compose a theme song, and to find a perfect adolescent girl and a boy to sing it. Soon we had an attractive pair whose musical delivery fit the style then popular among youth in Bangladesh.

ARH video singers –Image from the video

Connecting with all these people was like a coming together of the creative forces I had experienced before in Bangladesh—a "dream team." Bangladesh is like a cake that has a foundation of ancient tribal cultures, some of which had become Buddhist; a center of Hindu dance, song, music, dress, and design; and a thick icing of Islam. This mixture exploded onto the screen after we produced, tested with audiences, and finalized our first ARH *Know Yourself* video, *It's My Puberty*.[2] Pathfinder and USAID loved it. By then, Pathfinder's global project was ending, so CCP's global contract, HCP, kicked in to allow us to produce three more videos following the themes of the booklets. With Nuzhat's help,

FINDING MYSELF IN AMERICA

we also developed facilitators' guides on each theme for use with adolescents in educational workshops, along with the videos and booklets.

In addition, we developed a storyline with a storyboard to address boys' anxiety concerning wet dreams. This was tested with adolescents and adults in various parts of Bangladesh. We found those who could read were easily able to follow the comic book format, if we kept it straightforward. The results were presented, along with the booklets and videos, during a four-day VIPP workshop outside of Dhaka. At the event, the adolescents we invited mixed with adults from all our partners in the Adolescent Reproductive Health Working Group of Bangladesh: people from relevant

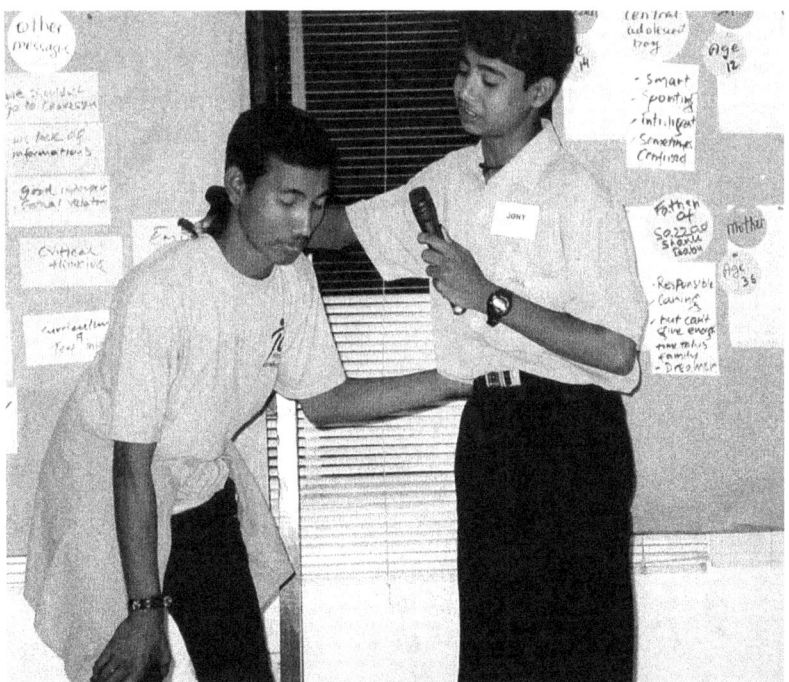

Adolescent Bangladeshi boys give story input −Photo by BCCP staff

government departments, researchers, program officers from NGOs, UNICEF, and UNAIDS, who joined with writers and artists. The Group consisted of more than 30 enthusiastic and committed members who invested many hours to make sure the much-needed ARH communication package was developed, and was based on strong research findings. They gave their input on the first comic book storyline and came up with draft storylines to be researched.

In the end, we produced four comic books, which also included facilitators guides: *Wizard of Nightmares* on wet dreams, *The Circus Girl* on breast development and menstruation, *Flower Boat* on emotional changes and sexual attraction, and *Adventures of the Science Gang*, on dealing with peer pressure. All these parts were packaged as the Adolescent Communication Toolkit (see: www.neill-mckeevideos.com/arh-bangladesh).[3] We decided to produce everything in English, in addition to Bangla, so international partners and donors could appreciate the materials:

ARH Toolkit containing all our materials

By 2003, I was riding high, working for CCP. I was back to my most creative days as a film and multimedia maker. In addition, I was working with Jane Bertrand, a Ph.D. in sociology and expert in international health and sustainable development. Phyllis Piotrow had retired from JHU and Jane became our new Executive Director. We saw eye-to-eye on many things, had the same sense of humor, and along with another staff member, Antje Becker-Benton, we wrote a book on the role of communication in dealing with HIV/AIDS. *Strategic Communication in the HIV/AIDS Epidemic* (2004)[4] was published by Sage Publications, a major academic publisher. It became an important resource for communicators, program designers, and educators. It contains strategies and case studies for addressing almost all people at risk, as well as those who had already contracted the virus.

Writing this book was a calculated move on our part, for the year before President Bush had launched the President's Emergency Plan For AIDS Relief (PEPFAR), the U.S. Government's initiative to address the global HIV/AIDS epidemic. (It continues today, providing US$90 billion, by 2022, in cumulative funding for HIV/AIDS treatment, prevention, and research.) In my humble opinion, that's the best thing George W. Bush ever did. Around the same time, I joined Beth and our Quaker neighbor, Jean, to march in Washington against one of the worst things he did, the invasion of Iraq. He had already committed the U.S. to what turned out to be the unwinnable 20-year war in Afghanistan. Thinking back to those years, I was certainly learning the ups and downs of American foreign policy.

I learned even more about those ups and downs when I returned from India and Bangladesh in early March 2004. Gary Saffitz, one of CCP's deputy directors, asked me to come to his office. He had a pleasant but direct approach to business. With a slight smile on his face, he asked me point blank, "How would you like to go to Russia?"

I replied, "Interesting, but I've never done any work there or in former Soviet countries. What's the assignment?"

"COP—Chief of Party."

Knowing this was a USAID-contractor term for a resident director of a project, I said, "What, me? I don't speak Russian."

"That's not a problem. We've got great bilingual Russian staff there."

"Are you serious?"

"Yes, USAID asked us to replace our COP. The original five-year project, Healthy Russia 2020, which we won in 2003, was all about social mobilization for health in general, but USAID has been ordered by the State Department to focus on HIV/AIDS—the President's priority. We need a COP who knows all about HIV/AIDS, and that's you."

And so, the conversation went on. One of CCP's largest country projects needed help, so would I step up to the plate? Gary asked me to consider it and discuss the move with Beth. I was flattered that my work, so far, had been well-regarded by my American colleagues, but I wondered if Beth would be happy with such a move after so recently settling down in the U.S. Our daughter, Ruth, and her fiancé Brian had moved to San Diego, where she had begun an M.F.A. in playwriting, and our son, Derek, had started a second bachelor's degree in law at McGill University, in Montreal. He didn't think much of our home on the river—not an interesting place to visit because it was far from cafés and city life.

That evening, I surprised Beth with this offer from Gary and she roared with laughter. It took her a while to digest the possibility. Eventually, she saw a few positive angles. Neither of us had seen Russia nor much of Europe, so that was a plus. Also, Beth had been creating a major piece of illustrated calligraphy titled *Assault of Angels*, on a poem of the same title by Michael Roberts (1902-1948), a British teacher and broadcaster. It ends with these lines:

> And a time comes when a man is afraid to grow,
> A time comes when the house is comfortable and narrow.
> A time when the spirit of life contracts.
> Angels are at your door: admit them, now.

We should forgive Roberts for his use of typical male-dominated gender language of his era. The challenge in the poem can now be understood to apply to women too, or to people with any gender identity, for that matter. It's not that Beth needed any challenge. She was creating a nine-page, 70-pound (32 kg), accordion-fold book, which opens to 33 feet (10 meters) in length when all pages are displayed.

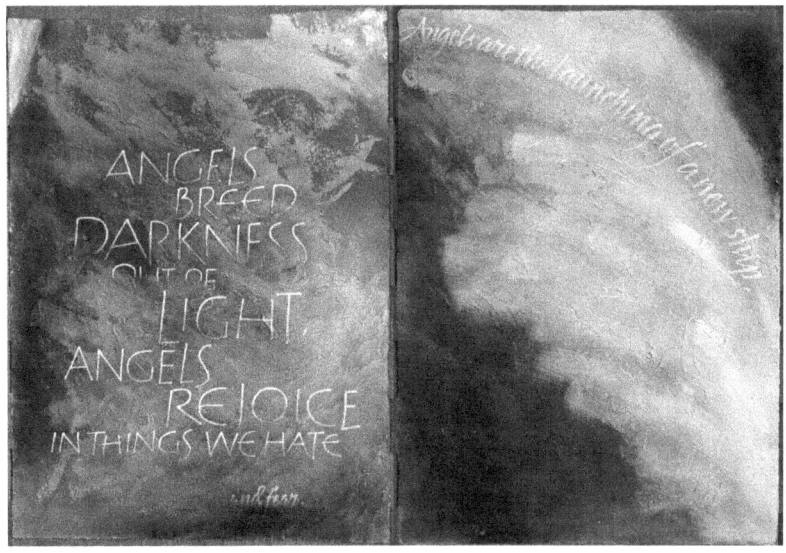

A page from Elizabeth McKee's large book

The problem was the *Assault of Angels* had assaulted her. She thought she had developed an allergy to the bark cloth she brought from Uganda, which she used on the cover and to frame each page. It resulted in a large red rash on the left side of her face, running down her neck to her upper torso. She found a special treatment called Bicom Bioresonance Therapy, in Washington, D.C., which a medical doctor was doing "under the table" because it was only legal for treatment of animals in the U.S., whereas it was widely used in Europe, including Russia, to treat humans. (More on this in the next chapter.)

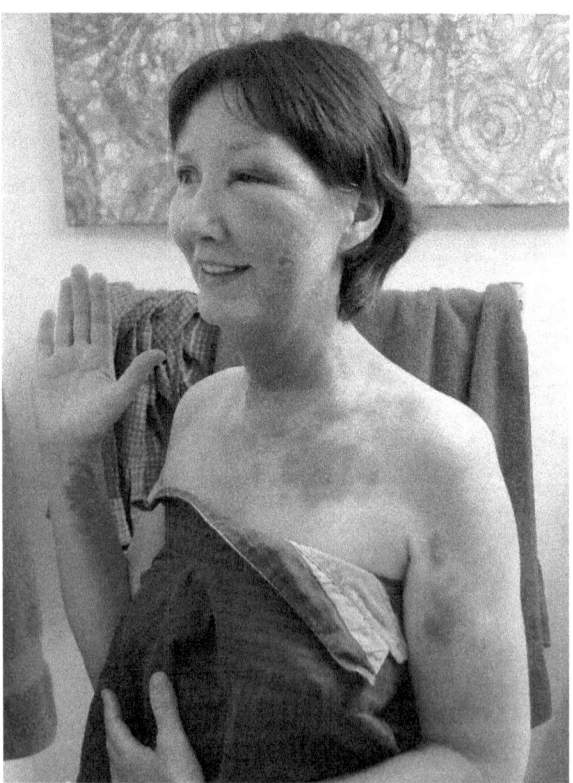

Beth before Bicom treatment –Photo by Neill McKee

We decided to take on this next challenge. I was worried my *Know Yourself* creation in Bangladesh would be left in the lurch. UNICEF had agreed to co-fund and help to popularize it. The UNICEF Representative, my friend Morten Giersing, wasn't happy when I told him I would be going to Russia. But we found a solution. Nuzhat Shahzadi would soon be ending her term as Meena coordinator in Kathmandu, and didn't have another UNICEF post lined up. Morten said he would only go ahead with the deal if CCP would hire Nuzhat to take my place. Nuzhat agreed, but only if she could be hired on an American salary and benefits, and be based in Baltimore.

So, in April 2004, I was off to Moscow. Beth would stay behind to rent out our house, pack, and follow me there in a few months.

26. Russia: Life and Work in Our Last Overseas Posting

I would wake early, have my first cup of coffee and some toast. From the vantage point in my furnished apartment on the 5th floor of Naberezhnaya 3, Tarasa Shevchenko, Moscow, I could now see the first sign of early May sunlight breaking through the gloom of winter. The apartment seemed hollow without Beth and her artistic paraphernalia, not due until a few more weeks. I guessed at one time the same space housed two Russian families, or more. With privatization of such properties starting in the 1990s, restructuring began—tearing down a center wall. The combined larger apartment made a good base for us: a master bedroom, a study for me, and a space for Beth's studio, both of which could be converted to guest bedrooms. It even had a modern open space kitchen, dining and sitting room. I wondered what happened to the families who once lived here. Did they profit or lose with the restructuring of the Russian economy, *Perestroika*—a vague 1980s term for a policy that was originally only intended to bring about modest changes so communism would work more effectively for Soviet citizens.

Many things had not yet changed by 2004. Most days I had to open the apartment windows to let out some of the excess heat pushed up from a large underground hot water radiation system, baking all the apartment buildings in our complex from heat generated by a huge oil-fired factory

Our gloomy apartment building in winter –Photo by Neill McKee

about a mile away. There was little control on the radiators in the apartment. I was told the system would be shut down for a month in the summer for maintenance, during which time we would have no hot water.

I would exit my apartment, avoid the small elevator, which often didn't work, and skip down the stairs instead. It was a short walk from the ugly brown metal exit door to Ulitsa Borodinskiy Bridge, which crossed the Moscow River. From the bridge, I would always see the imposing skyscraper housing the Ministry of Foreign Affairs, one of Stalin's Seven Sisters—a beauty or a beast? That's in the eye of the beholder, I suppose. To me its spires looked sinister and reminded me of the oppression suffered by Soviet citizens throughout that dictator's reign.

Another choice I had was to walk to Kievskaya train station, where I could take the Moscow Metro most of the way to the office. The other thing about the metro is that it was nearly always on time, like a fine-tuned clock. I also loved the artistry and ornateness of Moscow's metro stations, each one different. This compensated for the gloomy faces I would encounter on the old-fashioned utilitarian metro cars—everyone staring straight ahead, without making eye contact. Such indifference—or courtesy?—was sometimes broken by a few well-behaved feral dogs that would go down the steep escalators and enter open metro car doors, then exit at exactly the station of their intended destination—possibly for an expected treat from a street vendor. It must be that each station also had a particular smell we humans couldn't detect. The sight of these canine friends would make some passengers smile.

However, most mornings, I would leave early enough to take a 45-minute fast walk down Arbat Street, a narrow pedestrian-only way to the office. The street had been constructed in the 15th century, but in 1812, Napoleon's army set fire to most of the buildings on it, before ordering a westward retreat, only to be defeated by the Russian winter. The street was restored to become the home of artists, academics, minor nobles, and then high-ranking officials during the Soviet era. Now I found it lined with coffee shops, restaurants, clothing stores, tourist shops, theaters, and gambling parlors.

I usually stopped for a cappuccino at a café in the Tchaikovsky Conservatory, only a block from my office. With warmer weather, I could walk from the office to the café and sit outside to have lunch, read the English language *Moscow Times*, and listen to various students practice their string and wind instruments, causing a pleasant cacophony of classical music to filter out of the Conservatory's open windows, through the leaves and around the statue of the famous composer. From the café or my office, it was only a short walk to Red Square and the Kremlin. It didn't escape me that my new job was located near the center of Russian history and power.

Tchaikovsky Conservatory –Photo by Neill McKee

RUSSIA: LIFE AND WORK IN OUR LAST OVERSEAS POSTING

Johns Hopkins had signed an office lease for a wing of rooms inside a large ugly green building on Gazetny Lane. It belonged to the Institute for the Economy in Transition, a non-profit founded by Yegor Timurovich Gaidar, the economist who had engineered "Shock Therapy" to Russians in the 1990s. For a brief time in 1992, he had also been Prime Minister. But by 2004, he was despised by a good percentage of Russians, as were Mikhail Gorbachev and Boris Yeltsin, former Presidents. The hyperinflation of Gaidar's policies had hit Russians hard in their pocket books and had destroyed the morale of older people, especially. Just before I arrived, Vladimir Putin had won a second term as President, after rigging the election and taking control of most television stations through his oligarchs. At the time, I was reading *The Oligarchs: Wealth and Power in the New Russia* by David E. Hoffman,[1] and slowly coming to understand what made this country tick. The Russian oil and gas industry was booming.

By May, I was deep into reformulating our Healthy Russia 2020 project with my 16 Russian staff members. Over half of them could speak English fairly well. I knew I'd never get my tongue around the complicated cases and genders of Russian nouns and adjectives, or its verb conjugations, in order to work in the language. I was told there are 25 different ways to say "to go" in Russian, depending if it's by foot, by vehicle, one way-one time, multi-directional, multi-temporal, or whether there's other parallel action in the same sentence. I jokingly speculated that perhaps it was necessary because the country is so big. In the olden days during winter, you had to be specific about directions and intentions when you were going places, or you could get lost and would freeze to death before being found.

At most, I learned enough Russian to be able to greet people, ask for directions, and order meals. The project had just over three years to run, so my time to learn the language was limited. My staff were well-educated in a variety of fields such as mathematics, science, social science, medicine, accounting, office management, IT, and they were proud of it. Some of them could speak allegorically, infusing references to Russian literature in sentences. One was a medical doctor by the name of Irina, who had come from the institute guiding the country on maternal and infant care. My counterpart, Yelena, was a young Russian woman with a doctorate in sociology. The only problem was, none of them had worked in HIV/AIDS and they were doubtful about the change in direction of the project, as demanded by the U.S. Government. Yelena had also been appointed as the Executive Director of the Healthy Russia Foundation (HRF), a Russian-registered NGO, which CCP had set up as a parallel organization with the aim of raising additional funds from Russian and possibly European sources, to expand the health communication work we did, and ensure its continuance after the project ended.

For the first few months, I had to get used to working in this new environment. I enjoyed interacting with my lively Russian staff and meeting Russian health counterparts in their offices and at conferences. My most demanding task was dealing with the U.S. Embassy. I had to visit it frequently, which always required being searched and scanned by Russian guards overseen by a U.S. marine holding a semi-automatic rifle. The U.S. Embassy is located in a compound approximately one mile square (1.6 by 1.6 km) with high walls. Many Americans lived within the walls in typical row houses, not unlike those you could find in any suburban

RUSSIA: LIFE AND WORK IN OUR LAST OVERSEAS POSTING

neighborhood in the U.S. They had their own shopping facilities and social clubs, so they didn't have to meet many Russians other than those they worked with, unless they went outside to shop or go sightseeing. To me, this seemed to be an unfortunate set up, left over from the Cold War, and was surely bad for American-Russian relations.

The Russian woman from USAID who had been put in charge of our project, then called our CTO, or Cognizant Technical Officer, made many *ad hoc* demands, in addition to our required monthly report on program progress and expenditures. She continued to call my staff directly and was often impolite or sarcastic with them. Early during my time in Russia, she accompanied me and some of my staff to Ivanovo Region, not far from Moscow, to help us set up our new program there. This required many meetings and visits to health facilities. Then at 4:00 pm there was the necessary get-together with the Governor of the region to consume a huge spread of salads, pickles, breads, cheeses, cold cuts, fruits, and sweets, while participating in the delivery of speeches—each time raising small glasses of vodka in toasts to our cooperation.

After the Ivanovo visit, my staff told me our CTO had been badmouthing me in Russian from the backseat of our car—how could I understand anything about Russia without speaking the language? When I heard this, I thought, *How dumb was she to think her derisions would not be reported to me?*

The next day, I called her American boss at USAID to tell her about our visit and deliver an ultimatum, "Get her off our case or I will resign and leave Russia."

That worked. For the rest of my stay we reported to Sylva Etian, an Armenian American woman with emotional intelligence and a great sense of humor. She supported us and our mission. American embassy staff were given up to a year to learn Russian before coming to the country, and Sylva was practically fluent. She insisted on living outside of the embassy compound so she could improve her Russian and make Russian friends. I respected her for that.

Sylva Etian, on the left, hamming it up with a friend
—Photo by Neill McKee

Meanwhile, Beth had shipped some of our favorite furniture, her vital studio equipment and supplies, and I was finding it a struggle getting these through customs. Anna, my office manager, took me through the process. There were many steps to follow and I had to be present at the notary's office several times to sign papers. In Canada and the U.S., a notary public is only a respected and registered citizen who certifies signatures, but the Russian notary I met was a powerful lawyer and overlord of many lesser lawyers and legal assistants. He sat in a higher chair above them and was demanding and autocratic, instilling a tone of fear throughout the office. His signature was the final one on documents, and it ensured that he had followed Russia's codified law, which is ever-changing with each act of the Duma—the Russian parliament.

Office regulations also demanded strict steps to be followed. If I signed a travel authority for a staff member, I also had to sign an ordinance, which certified I signed the travel authority. I asked too many questions and joked about procedures, and my staff learned to laugh with me about such antiquated systems. Two months after I arrived, I discovered I had been working illegally without a proper work permit. No one had informed me of the type of permit needed. I had to hire a law firm to deal with the large number of legal and bureaucratic steps involved in rectifying this. I even had to fly to London to get the proper visa and re-enter Russia. At times, I felt like a blind man running through a maze. Sometimes I wondered, *Had I put myself in jeopardy by taking this job, caught between the American and Russian systems?*

It was lonely in my apartment at night. Most evenings, I would listen to a "switched-on" Moscow jazz station, cook something basic, and drink a little Moldovan wine, while taking a hot bath in the jacuzzi the landlord had installed when he bought and renovated the place. I wasn't suffering, but was so glad to see Beth when she finally arrived at the end of May. We can't recall, but probably we celebrated by having dinner at the modern hotel, shopping, and dining plaza, just down the bank of Moscow River. It also contained an English language cinema where wine was sold to drink, while eating popcorn during the movie—very civilized. We could also walk across the bridge to a Scandinavian grocery store and shopping complex with just about everything, and more restaurant choices—not a hardship post at all.

Beth could see her life here was going to be very different, compared to her situation in Maryland. She quickly got into visiting Russian markets and trying to converse in Russian. She had started to study the language before she arrived, using the Pimsleur method on CDs borrowed from her library, and had bought a set of CDs for our use in Russia.

The other immediate benefit for Beth in coming to Russia was the continuation of treatment for the rash caused by work on her artist's book, *Assault of Angels*. She had found a German-owned clinic that used the same method she had found in Washington. A Russian doctor by the name of Irina was assigned to Beth's case. (I wondered, *Are they all called Irina?*). This Dr. Irina had good experience in Bicom Bioresonance Therapy.[2,3] The method was founded in Germany in the 1970s, and is used throughout Europe and other countries around the world, including Canada. It regulates the patterns of electrical energy in our bodies with what we eat, inhale, or touch. Electrical energy, in turn, regulates the chemical interactions in our bodies, and I figure American pharmaceutical companies want to keep a monopoly on that, so the technology remains illegal for treatment of humans in the U.S., as briefly mentioned in the previous chapter.

Beth eventually managed to get rid of her rash and her food allergies. She ended up bringing Dr. Irina all her art supplies, and the good doctor found that the glue she was using was the main culprit, not Ugandan bark cloth. She also had food allergies. I, too, had skin irritations after moving to Moscow, and found a cure through the Bicom method.

RUSSIA: LIFE AND WORK IN OUR LAST OVERSEAS POSTING

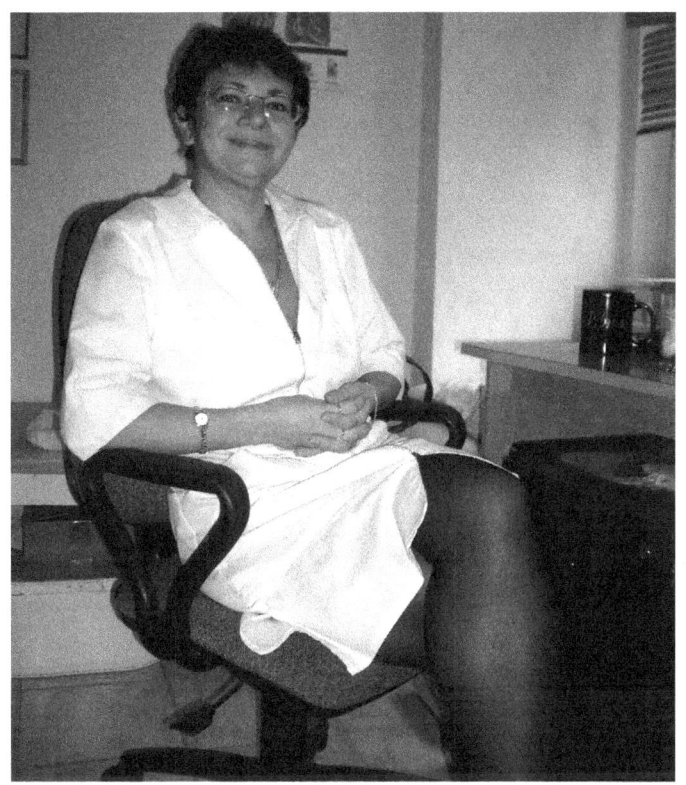

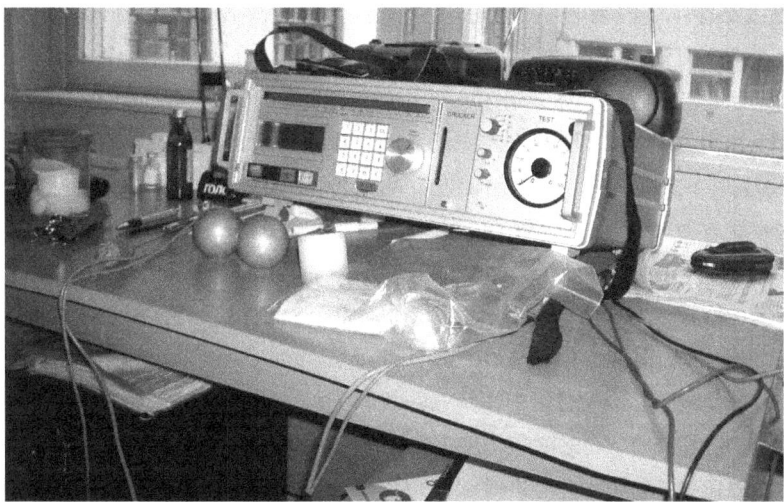

Dr. Irina and her Bioresonance therapy machine –Photos by Neill McKee

Beth after Bicom treatment, at the Bolshoi Theatre
—Photo by Neill McKee

I continued to love my early morning walks down Arbat Street to the office, now listening to Pimsleur Russian language lessons on my CD player. When I reached the café at the Tchaikovsky Conservatory, I would stop to have my usual cappuccino, while transcribing in Cyrillic alphabet, the sentences I had just learned. I had hired a middle-aged teacher, Anastasia, whom I would meet at the café two or three times a week to correct my transcriptions and teach me conversational Russia. Mostly, we talked about what was happening in the country and in the world. Until the mid-1990s, she had a job in a government language institute, which she had assumed was for life. The institute had been abolished due to *Perestroika* and she was bitter about that. Now she had to market herself as a freelancer and search for different clients, like me, to earn a living.

In November 2004, when the democratic Orange Revolution broke out in Ukraine, she scoffed at it, saying, "My father is a Russian speaker from eastern Ukraine. Ukraine is part of Russia."

I said, "But the majority of Ukrainians have a different language and culture. I realize some speak Russian too."

Anastasia insisted, "Ukraine simply means 'borderland' in Russian. They are not a separate people."

I laughed, "Tell that to my Ukrainian-Canadian friends back home." My friends' mother had escaped from Ukraine due to Stalin's starvation of millions of Ukrainians, so I didn't take Anastasia's words too seriously.

I didn't want to get into talking about Stalin. By 2004, many Russians were denying his crimes and bemoaning the death of the Soviet Union. I had finished reading *Russia and the Russians: A History*,[4] by Geoffrey Hosking. I was well aware of the historical union of the Slavs and the Rus Vikings along the Dnieper River, in present day Ukraine, and that, beginning over a thousand years ago, part of the population shifted northeast to Suzdal and then settled along the Moscow River. I knew people, their cultures, and their languages evolve. In fact, it wasn't until writing this book when I read *The Gates of Europe: A History of Ukraine* by Serhii Plokhy[5] that I realized how wrong my Russian teacher was. If we really want to consider historical roots, Russia was really an offshoot of what is present-day Ukraine.

A good deal of our work on HIV/AIDS was carried out by program partners, both U.S. and Russian: an in-school and peer education curriculum for youth; advocacy networks; involving Russian policy makers in economic modeling on the projected long-term cost of HIV/AIDS to Russian society, plus the cost-effectiveness of various interventions; and training of medical professionals on how to counsel patients, as well as people most at risk of contracting HIV. I found the latter work interesting because the typical Russian method of dealing with these people was to lecture them—a blame the victim approach. Counseling was not part of the menu of skills for most medical doctors. We developed a set of videos showing the wrong way and then the right way of interacting with patients, plus manuals on counseling.

We also produced a video drama titled *Nastya's Diary*.[6] It portrays a high school boy who fears he may have contracted HIV and his struggle to get tested. The story includes his relationship with a supportive girlfriend, Nastya, and the stigma and discrimination felt by affected people. I was only the executive producer, approving budgets and making small changes to the shooting script, but when I finally saw the end result, I was surprised with the quality of the acting and the whole production.

My staff and I created a solid program in the five regions USAID wanted us to work in. Besides Ivanovo, we had to travel to St. Petersburg (Leningrad Region), Saratov, Orenburg, and Irkutsk on Lake Baikal in Siberia, bordering Mongolia. Russia is spread over 11 times zones, and Irkutsk, five time zones from Moscow, is as far as I ventured. I enjoyed traveling with my staff and having more time to talk in the evenings at dinner, so I could learn about their hopes and fears for the future.

Nastya with her boyfriend, Nikita –Image from the video

I began to bond with them early in my stay in Russia when Yelena, Dr. Irina and I, together with our IT man, Dmitry, who went by the nickname "Dima," attended an important conference hosted by Russia's Federal AIDS Center. It was held in Suzdal, the historic city mentioned above, about three hours by road northeast of Moscow. Suzdal dates back to around 1000 C.E. and functioned as the capital at a time when Moscow was still a cluster of cowsheds. We were occupied by the proceedings, and I saw little of the city, except for an evening walk with Dima, who had just visited the place on his vacation. He was able to relate some of the history in his limited English. As we walked, the smell of autumn in the air brought back my boyhood memories, for the climate was much like Canada's.

Moscow and St. Petersburg had been transformed into modern cities, but the Suzdal conference center was an old Soviet-style tourist hotel, where the ladies at the reception desk appeared to greet us with a good deal of distain—customers disturbing their otherwise peaceful existence. I had seen this attitude in Prague, in 1990 (see Chapter 21), but it was rather shocking to see it in a Russian tourist town 15 years after the Berlin Wall had fallen. I had lunch in the hotel cafeteria with a Russian colleague, where the ladies were more customer-oriented, giving out huge quantities of food: soup and *blini* (dumplings with meat or cottage cheese). But when I went to pay, the cashier added the cost of all the items on a worn abacus, before transferring the information to the cash register, where the sum was registered legally.

At the conference, a lot of data came together on the growing threat of HIV/AIDS to Russians, if they didn't do more about it. It wasn't just drug addicts and sex workers who were at risk, so my staff became more interested. There were many overlapping risks to subsectors of society such as spouses and children of addicts and sex workers, men who have sex with men, adolescents and young adults, members of uniformed services, internal and external immigrants, and factory workers.

Besides our growing mutual understanding of HIV/AIDS in Russia, I bonded with my staff in another way on this trip. We had taken a long-distance taxi from Moscow to Suzdal. I'd decided we didn't need to waste money on a full-time office car and driver. The center of Moscow was usually jammed with cars on the roads and cars parked in every direction and space possible, including sidewalks, where "car minders" connected to the traffic police, collected "facilitation fees" without issuing receipts.

RUSSIA: LIFE AND WORK IN OUR LAST OVERSEAS POSTING

We had arranged for the same taxi company to pick us up in Suzdal on Friday afternoon, at the end of the conference. While waiting, we received a call from Alex, the driver, telling us his car had some problems but he was on the way. My staff proposed we take a Suzdal taxi to Moscow at the cost of 4,000 rubles (US$ 133.00). The only problem was, the Suzdal taxi driver couldn't provide a proper receipt and Russian accounting systems are strict. So, I proposed we take a taxi to nearby Vladamir, to connect with Alex. Reaching Vladamir, we waited for him. He kept informing us by cell phone that he was very close, then that he was lost. We were in the process of hiring another taxi when Alex finally showed up in his old Opel. So, we transferred our luggage to his car.

A few minutes into heavy traffic, Alex's ancient Opel stalled. It appeared to me to be a fuel pump problem and I told my staff we wouldn't make it to Moscow with this car—best to get a different taxi from Vladimir. Yelena asked Alex if he was sure we could make it and his answer in Russian was *absolutno* (absolutely)—a word that had become common parlance in Russia too, and which I absolutely mistrust to this day, for I believe there are few things that fit such a category in human experience. But my decision-making power had already been put into question for originally choosing to go with Alex, so we continued.

Alex pumped the gas pedal furiously, a technique that went against all my mechanical training in my youth, but he surprisingly got the engine going again. Then, 30 minutes later, the car stalled once more. Alex cursed and jumped out, blocking heavy traffic. In an instant, a car from behind drove around us and backed up in front of the Opel. The driver of that car threw out a rope, which Alex fastened on his front bumper, before jumping behind the steering wheel.

Moving forward, the Opel started immediately, but the tow car kept pulling us, and Alex had to brake and nudge it to the right shoulder, cursing more loudly now, while keeping his foot on the gas to prevent further stalling. Somehow, he managed to rein in our energetic helpers. Suddenly, I saw a man jump out of the pull car to detach the rope, while Alex kept cursing. He pulled our car away without even a glance or a nod of thanks. When did he pay them? I hadn't noticed.

I asked for a quick clarification from my colleagues in the back seat, "So there are lots of guys out there in the traffic with tow ropes, looking to earn a few rubles?"

I received the typical Russian answer, "*Konieshna*"—(of course).

Reaching the open road, I began to gain more confidence in Alex's ability to negotiate the brake and the gas pedal at the same time. I could feel all of Alex's subtle moves to keep the engine alive at stoplights, just as I had done with my old jalopies in my teens. We advanced on Moscow for the next 80 minutes. Alex was so confident he asked for permission to smoke, which I denied him.

On the outskirts of Moscow, we had to drop off Irina to meet a friend, who would take her home more directly, rather than into the center of the clogged city. We reached the designated crossroads (arranged by constant mobile phone chatter, which I am proud to say I more or less understood), passing the occasional head-on collision and great confusion. I offered to keep my foot on the gas while Alex helped Irina transfer her luggage to her friend's car, but he said with absolute confidence that it wouldn't be necessary.

Dima and I visited the bushes behind a nearby bus stop, to relieve ourselves, as was the custom along roads in Russia. Then we explored a somewhat battered stone sculpture in a dark spot a few meters ahead—two large animals, which looked like something between moose and reindeer without antlers, bowing down to the highway, non-majestically.

We returned to the relative warmth of the Opel and speculated about the animals' scientific and common names. Dima proposed different solutions to the puzzle, in Russian, until Yelena, who had not gone to look at the statue and admitted ignorance of all zoology, pronounced with absolute certainty that it was of a mother "Rus-Moose" (a *Samka Losya* in Russian), and its calf. I assured Yelena I would be able to sleep better that night with such knowledge locked in my brain.

I actually thought that maybe the statue had been placed there in memory of some large animals, or lover of large animals, killed in a traffic accident on the spot, but there were none of the usual flowers indicating a place of death. At least we had a few moments of comic relief while Alex was delivering Irina, and having a quick smoke.

While having so much fun, I noticed the engine had stopped. I turned off the ignition to save on the battery. Alex returned and asked a question, which literally means in Russian, "It, by itself?"

Dima confirmed, "Yes, it, by itself," meaning we had not been dumb enough to turn off the engine.

Then Alex lunged into two long tries at starting the car, pumping even more furiously now, almost as if he thought that action in itself would propel us forward to Moscow. Finally, he stopped, cursed, and slammed his glasses on the dash board. I looked to see if they were broken, but apparently they were strong enough to withstand many past tirades like this. There were some quick exchanges between Alex and Dima, and I soon found myself outside, pushing the car up a slight incline. I felt this way of trying to start the heavy Opel would be useless, but decided I had better show some team spirit. Two attempts and we failed. Alex steered the car off the busy highway, leaving the back end sticking out as a challenge to oncoming traffic. This seemed to be the custom when you have a breakdown on Russian roads.

So, what now? Another tow?, I naturally thought. Standing on the road, I stuck my hand out, waving at drivers for help. No success. Dima joined me and stuck his hand out using a different motion. In a minute, a fancy looking car pulled to a stop on the right lane behind us, blocking oncoming trucks and cars. After quick negotiations, I found myself helping to switch our belongings to a "gypsy cab" or unofficial taxi service offered by car owners who just want to make a few rubles—only 400 rubles (U.S. $13.00) to get to the center of Moscow, we were told. Yelena and Dima started to discuss our departure with Alex, who actually wanted us to sign the receipt for his service.

I told them, "No, do not do that!" As we departed, I looked back to see Alex throwing a cherished cigarette to the ground with the loudest of all curses. I think I saw the "Rus-Mooses" turn to look his way as we took off toward Moscow.

And did we take off! Russian drivers are noted for their love of speed and weaving through tight spaces. The traffic on this highway, a main artery to and from Moscow, had vastly outgrown the road itself. In most places there were no barriers or islands between oncoming traffic—just a double white line to separate cars speeding towards each other in the opposite direction. I turned to ask my colleagues, "So there are many drivers out here looking to make a few rubles as illegal taxis?"

They answered in harmony, "*Konieshna*".

It seemed to be an honor in Russia to sit in the front passenger seat, which my staff granted me. I had buckled up immediately, keeping my eyes on the road. Occasionally, I looked down at Victor's dashboard to see his crazy speed and then quickly shifted my eyes to a plastic icon, which must have given him courage and comfort—the Russian Orthodox version of Christ the Savior.

But Victor was victorious. We dropped off Yelena at a place beside the highway so she could find another gypsy cab home, more directly, but it was wisely decided that Dima should stay with me. In only a few fast-moving minutes, we pulled into the road beside my apartment building. I had arrived home from Suzdal six hours after we set off on our journey. At least I lived to tell this tale and to continue my adventures in this fast-moving land.

Also, because of this experience, I felt justified in not buying a car. My pronouncements to many were correct—the chances of injury or death on Russian highways are much greater than from a terrorist attack on a train or the Moscow Metro—absolutely.

27. Our Final Period in Russia and Travels Thereafter

Beth also worked on an international development project during her time in Moscow. She decided to make an artist's book, which included a speech by Stephen Lewis, a Canadian politician, public speaker, broadcaster, diplomat, and former Deputy Director of UNICEF. He was also the U.N. Secretary General's envoy for HIV/AIDS in Africa from 2001 to 2006. His speech titled, "This World is off its Rocker When it Comes to Women," was delivered at the University of Pennsylvania's Summit on Global Health Issues in Women's Health, April 26, 2005. Beth engaged her full calligraphic and artistic skills in creating this work, weaving in Lewis's words with the poem *Bread and Roses* by James Oppenheim, which was popularized in the 1976 protest song by Judy Collins. It begins:

> As we go marching, marching,
> In the beauty of the day
> A million darkened kitchens
> A thousand mill lofts gray
>
> Are touched with all the radiance
> That a sudden sun discloses
> For the people hear us singing
> Bread and roses, bread and roses

Beth also added the words of a fugue by Robyn Sarah—the first two stanzas below:

> Women are on their way
> to the new country. The men watch
> from high office windows
> while the women go.
> They do not get very far
> in a day. You can still see them
> from high office windows.
>
> Women are on their way
> to the new country. They are taking
> it all with them: rugs,
> pianos, children. Or they are leaving
> it all behind them: cats,
> plants, children.
> They do not get very far in a day.

Complicated artwork, I thought. But issues facing women and girls around the world are complex, especially in relation to HIV/AIDS, which I had come to know a thing or two about. In 2005, the world's attention was needed on women and girls like never before, because they were bearing the brunt of the epidemic. Beth gave her artist's book the clever title *For Immediate Release*. She made five original copies of this multipage accordion-folded book, decorated with colorful cut-outs she made of women and children from every part of the world, marching, marching. It eventually evolved into a project for her when we returned home. She made poster kits for women's groups in the U.S. and Canada to get together and complete by making their own marching women and children, and through this activity, Beth sold the kits to raise funds for the Stephen Lewis Foundation.

Pages of *For Immediate Release* by Elizabeth McKee

In Moscow, Beth joined an international women's group and learned Russian better than I did by interacting with people on the street, and with *babushkas* (old women or grandmothers) and other sellers in markets. She also became an unofficial tour guide for the many friends and relatives who visited us in Russia. She would usher them around Moscow and take them north to St. Petersburg, especially during its almost 24-hour "White Nights" of summer. She tried to make each tour different so she would learn more about Russia. I found meandering through art galleries and museums, just like shopping, painful for my back, and, at any rate, seldom had the time to join these tours.

I occasionally took the train to St. Petersburg, but mostly on business. I enjoyed watching the countryside from train windows—vast forests and fields crossed by rivers and dotted with impoverished villages, unpainted houses, sheds, and barns. Like many visitors, I wondered, *How did this country beat the Americans into space?* Then, I'd observe carefully as the train entered the bleak high-rise landscape of the city, now full of disappointed youth and crime. The transition from Communism still held little promise for many of them.

One time when I did accompany Beth to St. Petersburg with my visiting sister Karen, and brother-in-law Ed, I gained a little experience in dealing with the underworld of St. Petersburg. We were in a hurry, so we stopped at a McDonald's to eat—a surprisingly popular food outlet for Russians by then. The women went to the ladies' washroom and I left Ed in charge of my bag without asking him to guard it, and headed to the men's. While I was gone, a man distracted Ed by speaking to him in Russian and holding a Russian newspaper in front of his face, while another man must have stolen my bag, for when I returned it was missing. It had contained the keys to our apartment, my new digital camera, and my precious Russian notebook with all my transcriptions in Cyrillic.

With my limited Russian, I alerted the manager, who called the police. A policemen arrived on the spot fairly quickly and I tried to describe the problem. I didn't care about the camera, but was worried about the keys because our address was on the bag. Most of all, I bemoaned the fact my precious notebook, which contained hundreds of hours of work, was gone. *Probably the thieves threw it into a garbage bin*, I thought.

In the presence of the manager and the policeman, I phoned our landlord in Moscow, who spoke good English, to warn him about the keys and describe my predicament. He asked me to give my cell phone to the policeman and, after some discussion, I was told to be in the restaurant at 2 pm. I sent off my companions to continue with our planned sightseeing, and hung around. Surprisingly, the policeman did come back on time to lead me to a small police station, where I met his boss and a man they said was an undercover policeman. They had recovered my bag, without the camera, but much to my delight the keys and notebook were inside. I thanked these fellows, and gave each of them 500 rubles (US$ 16.60) for their service, knowing full well I was speaking to one of the thieves and his co-conspirators. I had learned not to leave a bag anywhere with anyone, and that it was easy for the police in Russia to find thieves because they were often part of the same network.

As the months passed, I became quite engaged with Russia and loved to work and celebrate with my staff. Besides the daily interaction with them, occasionally I had to attend meetings with the Board of Governors of our foundation—really just a "non-governmental organization," a term that doesn't translate well into Russian. During the Soviet era, people considered health services to be the responsibility of the government and they remained passive, not taking

Celebrating our success with my Russian staff —Photo by HR staff member

responsibility for their own health. Starting in the 1980s, services became underfunded and began to fall apart, declining rapidly after the Soviet Union collapsed. The HRF was supposed to develop partnerships between government, the private sector, and civil society, to help rebuild and improve the health of Russians—a challenging task.

In 1990, the life expectancy of Russians was only 69 years, but by 2005, it had dropped to 65 years,[1] and male life expectancy was only about 58 years.[2] Excessive alcohol consumption and smoking were probably the main direct causes, but acute psychosocial stress and declining well-being were underlying these behaviors during transition to the market economy. The HRF board wanted us to continue to focus on youth, which I agreed with—probably the only section of the population where there was hope for change. I felt privileged to be interacting with these well-educated, thoughtful people, even if it was mainly through interpretation, for working with a cosmonaut and an Olympic champion, who both spoke English well, was something to write home about.

Healthy Russia Foundation's Board of Governors

Chairperson

Dr. Liubov Posiseeva, Director, Ivanovo Research Institute of Maternity & Childhood

Vice Chairperson

Vladimir Dobrenkov, Head, Sociology Department, Moscow State University

Treasurer

Dmitry Korobkov, President, Union of Social Advertisers

Regular Members

Sergei Krikalev, Cosmonaut, Hero of the Soviet Union and the Russian Federation

Irina Rodnina, Olympic Champion figure skater, President's Council on Physical Fitness & Sports

Victor Kramarenko, Head of External Relations, Procter & Gamble, Russia

Vladimir Pozner, President of Russian Television Academy and TV Journalist

Alexander Tsaregorodsev, Director, Research Institute on Pediatrics & Pediatric Surgery (former Minister of Health)

Igor Yurgens, Vice President, Russian Union of Manufacturers & Entrepreneurs

Alexander Auzan, President, Russian Union of Consumers and President of the International Federation of Consumer Societies

Tatiana Troubinova, Head of Public Interface Department, Administration of the President of the Russian Federation

USAID pushed us to hire a senior Russian figure to become the overall head of the foundation. I can't recall how we found him, but a man by the name of Gerasimov was hired. On paper, he had an excellent resumé: experience in public health issues, strong negotiating skills, good contacts with government officials and political leaders, as well as international donors. On his resumé he also stated he was a "State Adviser, Class 3." I wondered what that meant, *Was he a Federal Security Bureau (FSB) agent?* By the end of the Soviet Union, there were hundreds of thousands of KGB secret police embedded in every department and organization, each sending huge amounts of data back to headquarters, where little of it was analyzed. Did this information gathering continue under Putin's FSB? Probably, but what would they make of our rather innocent objectives and activities?

Gerasimov spent about six months traveling around the city and to Russian regions, holding private talks with government officials and Russian businessmen, trying to drum up funding for our foundation. He couldn't speak English, so I could only talk to him with one of my staff acting as interpreter. In the end, he never raised a *kopek*. I asked him to present what he had found to the Board, and, with help from my staff, he created a long meandering PowerPoint presentation, which ended on a pair of empty work boots with the laces bound together—indicating "my hands are tied." We had timed his presentation to be followed by Yelena's on the dwindling budget of the foundation (separate from the project's money), ending with the fact we needed to make some cuts. There was a brief discussion in Russian, and then I chimed in on cue with the need for *perestroika* (restructuring) and everyone started saying, *"Da, da, perestroika!"* The

Board chair turned to look at Gerasimov and he nodded his head, smiling and agreeing he had to resign. And that was the end of his short career with us. I felt I had really become a Russian bureaucrat, playing the game just right.

Following Gerasimov's failure, and during my last year in Russia, I put more effort into raising money for the HRF. Yelena and I made calls on business leaders, and had some success. But the greatest collaboration we won was a partnership with the American health and pharmaceutical company Johnson & Johnson (J&J) for expanding training of Russian health care providers on HIV/AIDS counseling skills, using the media package we had already created. We set up a team of trainers from the Federal AIDS Center, the World Health Organization, and Moscow State University. I have to admit my connection with an American friend based in J&J's European headquarters in Belgium, made all the difference. That old adage proved true once again: "It's not what you know, but who you know."

Our other visible achievement of my last year in Russia was our production of a dramatic video on a fictional pop star, and his beautiful female vocal lead, returning to the depressed Russian city where he had grown up. The script called for him to interact with disgruntled and rebellious youth, who smoked and drank. Peer pressure was also leading them to get involved in drugs and unprotected sex. The stars were trying to break down stereotypes about rock bands and promote healthy living.

Once again, I could only act as the executive producer, discussing and approving the script and the budget. But when my staff brought the first cut back to me, I was overwhelmed with the quality of the production. The acting was superb and was infused with thematic musical numbers

Images from *Life Themes* video

acted out by the pop star, his attractive female co-star, and their band. The producers also cut a CD of all the musical numbers in the video, to be played on radio stations. This matched well with the in-school and peer education programs we were expanding across Russia. We made a version with English subtitles, giving it the title *Life Themes*,[3] so it could be appreciated by potential donors who might help to expand the work of our foundation. In fact, before I left Russia, our work stretched as far as Vladivostok and the Kamchatka Peninsula in the Far East, the latter being 10 time zones from Moscow.

Our exciting video hit the mark—an entertainment-education approach, which would help to counter the growing destructive youth culture in the country. At the same time, Vladimir Putin's political party, United Russia, had created and rallied a youth wing, called the "Young Guard" in English, which was gaining ground across Russia—a counterforce to western youth culture, advocating for conservative social values and allegiance to the Kremlin. The Orthodox Church, an ultra-conservative body, had also gained much political influence. We were asked by USAID to work with them on HIV/AIDS, but that proved to be almost impossible, for its main approach was to blame the victim. As I wound up my time in Russia, I could see these strong counterforces butting up against each other, with the youth of Russia squashed in the middle.

In April 2007, at the end of my third year in Moscow, I felt I had helped to give new direction to the project and the HRF, and my presence was eating up a large part of our budget. With the help of more junior Baltimore staff, I could oversee developments from afar, and with occasional visits. USAID agreed. I communicated this to Gary Saffitz and Jane Bertrand, CCP's Executive Director, and got a surprising reply through a phone call. Jane wanted to propose my name to USAID, Washington, as the project director for our bid on the next five-year global health and development communication project. I was flattered by this offer and agreed. I knew I'd be working closely with Jane, Gary, and others, who could give me good guidance on dealing with Washington. I recalled how unsure I had been in entering this American work world in 2001, and now they asked me to lead their largest project, which funded many positions in Baltimore and around the world—a huge responsibility.

We shipped most of our things home and Beth left in May to visit family. I rented a small apartment and, in June, headed to Baltimore to defend our bid for the next big project. After our presentation, I felt pretty good. Then I returned to Moscow to wind up my work there.

In July, I said goodbye to all my colleagues and friends in Russia and I flew back to be with Beth in Maryland, where she had reclaimed our house on the Magothy River. Then, we took a long-needed August vacation in Canada. When I returned to work in September, I learned CCP had lost the bid. Jane assured me we had received high marks for my proposed leadership of the project, which made me feel better, but we had lost points on our proposed conceptual framework and other issues. I had had little input on those elements from Moscow. Jane figured that, after 25 years, USAID just wanted a new contractor. The new project went to the Academy for Educational Development (AED), in Washington, D.C.

I only returned to Russia once, to run a staff retreat, using VIPP. During the time I was based in Russia, I co-authored an updated VIPP manual[4] with Timmi Tillmann, Maruja Salas, and Nuzhat Shahzadi—a coproduction of UNICEF, Bangladesh and Southbound Publications—which helps to keep VIPP alive today. Timmi and Maruja have remained continual disseminators of VIPP methods for over 30 years, reinforced by hundreds of trained facilitators around the world.

I had attempted to train my Russian staff and some partner organizations in this participatory methodology, so we "VIPPed" the staff retreat, coming up with their strengths and weaknesses, threats and opportunities, in a visual manner. I saw it as a team-building exercise, but I have to admit VIPP methods are the antithesis of the usual Russian way. At the end of the retreat, they organized a paintball war in a forested area. We divided into two teams and shot the hell out of one another for a couple of hours, a symbolically violent end to my team-building attempts. The experience left a sour taste in my mouth.

A VIPP workshop in Russia, where participatory methods were almost unknown –Photos by Neill McKee

On that trip, I also traveled with Yelena and another staff members to Orenburg, a city to the southeast of Moscow near the border with Kazakhstan, where opium-based drugs were flowing in from Afghanistan—the American war against the Taliban had only increased the growing of poppies to fund their resistance movement.[5] The spread of HIV through dirty needles used by addicts was still growing, and infecting both heterosexual and gay partners. This was happening in just about every part of Russia. There was also a growing link between the traffickers, the police, and some government officials.

We attended a meeting with the Orenburg AIDS Center on our cooperation. The head of the Center was a friendly talkative man, and that made me relax. I had been told that some doctors, who were treating addicts in St. Petersburg, had been murdered, probably by drug traffickers with the backing of the police, and I made reference to this in the meeting. It was a *faux pas* for there was a silent FSB secret policeman in the meeting.

It wasn't until we were flying back to Moscow, the next day, that Yelena told me she had been pulled in and grilled by local FSB officers about who I was and what I was doing in Russia. I apologized to her and felt so dumb. For the rest of the visit, I looked behind me and searched for microphones in my hotel room.

I didn't know the full situation I had stepped into in Russia until I was writing this chapter. Much of the real story was classified until only recently. I learned about it by reading *Not One Inch: America, Russia, and the Making of Post-Cold War Stalemate* by M. E. Sarotte.[6] James Baker, the Secretary of State under George H. W. Bush, had promised Mikhail Gorbachev the North Atlantic Treaty Organization (NATO) would not move "one inch" further east, if the Soviet Union would remove its armed force from East Germany—a promise for which he was chastised as soon as he returned to Washington. The book is a detailed history of subterfuge—a game of ping-pong between the U.S. and Russia over the borders of NATO, throughout the Bush One and Clinton administrations. It factors in Clinton's tell-tale semen stain on Monica Lewinsky's blue dress, and Yeltsin's alcoholism, heart condition and corruption, all leading to Vladimir Putin's rise to power, when he promised not to put Yeltsin in jail.

I also read, *The Man Without a Face: The Unlikely Rise of Vladimir Putin*, by Masha Gessen,[7] an engaging account of Putin's early life as a child and young thug in St. Petersburg, his boring years as a KGB officer in Dresden, East Germany, where he watched with astonishment as the Berlin Wall crumbled and the Soviet Union fell apart. The book details his rise to power through criminality, his destruction of Chechnya, the bombing of Moscow apartment bombings, political murders, and rigged elections. It was chilling to be reading this account in 2022, while writing about my time in Moscow and watching, on TV, the butchering of Ukrainians by Putin's army. My Russian teacher's words came back to me: "My father is a Russian speaker from eastern Ukraine. Ukraine is part of Russia."—"Ukraine simply means 'borderland' in Russian. They are not a separate people."

I wondered what lay in store for my former team members in Moscow and their children. They had aspired to be part of Europe and the West. Would their lives ever get back on track?

In 2007, I also found myself back on the road again, giving advice and developing communication strategies for HIV/AIDS in India and Indonesia. I loved working in the latter country, since its root language is the same as Malaysia's, where I had started my international career. I helped the office undertake participatory processes with government and NGO partners to develop plans, traveling all the way to Jayapura, Papua, on the island of New Guinea.

That same year, I returned to Bangladesh where I found the Adolescent Health Communication Toolkit, which I had put so much effort into during 2001-2003, had not been widely popularized. After a year with CCP in Baltimore, Nuzhat Shahzadi had rejoined UNICEF to work in emergency programs. Also, Sanjeeda Islam, the Deputy Director of BCCP, had left the organization. Neither of these empowered women saw eye-to-eye with the leader of BCCP. Our well-researched materials and strategies were hardly being used. It appeared the toolkit had been treated as a product of a five-year project, and when the funding ended, the push for utilization also ended. Besides, Morten Giersing, the Representative of UNICEF, a proponent of the toolkit, had also left the country.

By the fall of 2008, I wondered what I should do next. I wasn't happy traveling around like a consultant. Also, I was expensive for CCP's budget because the organization no longer held the large global project from USAID, and the overhead it provided. I was asked if I wanted to go to Jordan as director of CCP's USAID-funded project there. But it mostly involved family planning, which I had little knowledge of, nor interest in. I mentioned the offer to Beth, who said, "Are you kidding? I'm not going anywhere." I had dragged her around the world enough for one lifetime.

Then, by surprise, Mark Rasmuson, the head of communication for international health at AED in Washington, contacted me. We had kept in touch over the years. As mentioned above, AED had won the five-year contract with USAID, a project they named Communication for Change—"C-Change" for short—a clever acronym with a pun on a phrase in William Shakespeare's play, *The Tempest*. "Sea change" had come to stand for "a profound or notable transformation." That sounded interesting to me and AED needed more communication expertise. As must be evident by now, I had never been a believer in sticking to an organization if it didn't fulfill me. I always wanted to go where I felt I could have the greatest input and create innovations.

And so, in October 2008, I was off to Washington, D.C., an easy train ride from our home on the Magothy River, or so I thought at the time.

Last Post in Washington, D.C.

For a few months every weekday, I drove our new Toyota Prius for about 20 minutes to the MARC commuter train stop near the Baltimore-Washington International Airport, where I usually waited 10 to 20 minutes for the train, which was often delayed. Usually it was overcrowded, so no place to sit as it rattled over old tracks through woods and small towns towards Washington. It stopped at many stations to pick up more passengers, and sometimes was held up by track repairs, oncoming Amtrak trains, or other confusion I couldn't figure out. I found it hard to read on board because of the animated conversations among regular passengers. I began to play music on earphones, so I could concentrate.

After entering Washington, I'd disembark at Union Station to wait for the often-delayed Metro to Dupont Circle. From Dupont, I walked up Connecticut Avenue to reach AED's office, just south of the famous Washington Hilton, where President Reagan was nearly assassinated on March 30, 1981. The whole commute to work took me up to two hours, and I had to face the same gauntlet of connections and delays going home in the evening. I often thought about the trains in Moscow, which ran like clockwork—mass transport, not mass confusion.

By 2008, AED was almost 50 years old, with 700 employees in Washington and 2,000 more around the world. It managed about U.S. $500 million per year and worked on domestic projects, but the majority of its contracts were issued by USAID for work in developing countries—health, nutrition, education, improving democratic governance, building civil society, and relief in emergencies.

I had been hired as a senior advisor for communication in the international health division. I believe AED knew me most for the books I had written and my work in UNICEF on Meena and Sara, and perhaps my recent work at CCP. I made some presentations on my experience and perspectives, and began discussions with various people on their on-going projects. But I found everyone to be busy and fairly self-assured. It seemed to me that few, besides Mark Rasmuson, who had persuaded me to join the organization, wanted to discuss new ideas.

Since I landed in the U.S., I had been in touch with Don Simpson, the man I collaborated with in 1978, by making films on an IDRC primary education project in Southeast Asia (see Chapter 10). His company and network, Innovation Expedition, had fostered the development of a process he called "Challenge Dialogue," a method of solving complicated issues in government, industry, and international development, which involves many diverse stakeholders. Rather than first organizing large in-person meetings, conferences, or workshops, the method entails holding in-depth discussions with a few key informants and developing a challenge paper on the main issues, with a set of questions to be answered by a wider group through email. The answers are then consolidated and sent back to the whole group with additional questions. Ideally, this takes place two or three times before a "white paper" is produced, which then forms the basis of discussion at a large in-person workshop with as many stakeholders as possible.

LAST POST IN WASHINGTON, D.C.

Don and his colleagues had found that by carrying out this process, they could obtain up to 80 percent agreement on the issues among stakeholders before in-person workshops or meetings were held. I saw the Challenge Dialogue methodology as a natural complement to our VIPP methodology for in-person group meetings. I had tried to introduce Don and his method to CCP in 2003, but it fell flat. Not giving up, I felt that surely it would be an innovation a large organization like AED could employ.

Don and his colleague, Keith Jones, flew from Canada to Washington to plan a Challenge Dialogue on HIV/AIDS with international program stakeholders in the U.S.—a very tall order, I knew, because most of these organizations were competitors for contracts with USAID and other donors, and probably would not want to collaborate at all. These agencies, including AED, Johns Hopkins University, other non-profits and for-profit organizations, were being chided by the press and some people in government as "beltway bandits" because of overhead charged on contracts, high salaries, and their engagement in cut-throat competition. *It was time for collaboration*, I thought. I had joined AED to do something different, to innovate, not just carry out "cookie-cutter" activities. After all, President Obama had just been sworn in, so Washington should be ready for big new ideas.

In 2009, we were in the middle of developing this initiative, which old hands in AED were only lukewarm about, when Mark and our department director, Peggy Parlato, asked me to take over as director of our large communication project, C-Change. USAID was unhappy with the progress made in its first year—and with its leader, a researcher who had previously been accepted by them as project director. I gave it some thought. I had been with AED for about eight months, so, enough time had gone by since CCP had lost the bid for the contract. USAID knew I was now with AED and probably wanted me in the project. So, of course I said yes—what choice did I have?

I soon found myself in charge of a large budget and a team that grew to about 35 people in Washington and over 100 more around the world. This took all the management skills I had ever learned. The deputy director I inherited wanted to leave that post to work remotely from Seattle. I had recruited my former CCP colleague, Antje Becker-Benton, as a senior program officer in C-Change. Antje, born in West Germany, is a kindred soul with the same work ethic and sense of humor as me, and she was promoted to be my deputy.

My new job was demanding. Almost every hour I had to hold meetings with staff to solve problems, make decisions, or attend divisional meetings. The telephone calls and emails from USAID began at about 7:30 am and seldom ended before 4:00 pm, when I'd have time to catch up on some paperwork and answer emails before returning home. We bought a second Prius and I started driving into Washington instead of wasting so much time on the train. But if I left at 5:00 pm, it could take 90 minutes or more to get home on the heavily clogged streets and highways—no different than the Metro and train. So, I'd leave the office around 6:00 pm, reach home about 7:00 pm, and then drive back as early as 6:30 am to avoid the traffic—truly a rat race.

In September 2009, following the subprime mortgage crisis, real estate was cheap, so I bought a bachelor apartment about a block from the office to avoid the daily commute. I drove home on Friday evenings, while staying awake by playing loud music such as the Russian rock songs from the video I had helped create in Moscow, *Life Themes*—bringing back images of the totally different world I had left, not so long ago.

On a cold weekend in December 2009, three feet of snow fell on most of the region. It took me hours to dig out our two Priuses, and I ended up with severe backpain. Ever the experimenter, I tried acupuncture treatment for it, but the acupuncturist added electricity to the needles, vastly increasing my pain. During most of January and February, I had to work from home in an easy chair, computer on my lap, cell phone by my side. Beth acted as my nurse, while I watched many more feet of snow fall on our hill by the frozen riverside. I sought a proper diagnosis and treatment and finally found answers when I went full circle back to

Snowed in on the Magothy River, Maryland —Photo by Neill McKee

Johns Hopkins University's specialty clinics. My long career as a filmmaker in developing countries had finally caught up with me. I thought, *It serves me right for taking on this high-pressure job in my mid-60s, when I should have been thinking of phasing out and getting more exercise.*

When I returned to work in Washington, spring sunshine was gradually melting the enormous dirty snowbanks left on the streets. I did exercises in the mornings and took walks in evenings, slowly building up the strength of my back. As I walked down Connecticut Avenue to Dupont Circle, I found it ironic to read "Taxation Without Representation" on D.C. license plates. This was the very complaint that set off the American Revolution, and here I was, over 230 years later, among people who were disenfranchised.

The city had been designed for George Washington by the French-American engineer, Pierre L'Enfant. They envisaged it as a majestic "diamond on the Potomac River." Author J. D. Dickey, in *Empire of Mud: The Secret History of Washington, D.C.*[1] writes about the first 70 years of the capital's life: a swampy land with pigs and cattle running free, animal carcasses and foul odors, muddy and stinking streets with garbage piled up everywhere, no street lamps so utter darkness at night, no waterworks, open sewers, filthy canals, cockfights, fistfights, mud fights, swindlers, forgers, thieves, corrupt police, murderers, pimps and prostitutes, gamblers and pyramid scheme promoters, a debtors' prison and overcrowded jails, religious strife, slave traders and many slaves. Dickey described it, as "a dysfunctional village with a confusing web of radial baroque avenues overlapping a rectangular grid."

The main problem was that from the time of Washington's founding, federal politicians stayed in separate boarding houses, seldom mixing with local people, those from other political parties, or with civil servants, and they took no responsibility for the squalor surrounding them. They seldom voted for bills and budgets to improve the city. Services eventually improved, especially after the Civil War. Different forms of local government were experimented with, but it was not until 1974 that the federal government approved popular elections of the mayor and city council for four-year terms. However, the citizens of D.C. remain disenfranchised at the federal level, to this day.

In 2010, not much had changed for the descendants of slaves. About 50 percent of D.C.'s 602,000 citizens were black, with about half still living below the poverty line and on Medicaid—limited government-funded health care for the poorest sectors of society. In March, President Obama had managed to get his Patient Protection and Affordable Care Act signed into law, but many Washingtonians could not even afford that program. The Republican Tea Party wing was flexing its muscles, trying to block everything the President and the Democrats tried, while the Great Recession and wars in Iraq and Afghanistan continued.

Despite these dark clouds, I loved living in Washington during the week. I could easily walk to Dupont Circle, which was included in Pierre L'Enfant's original plan. The area had a long and varied history. In the 1970s, it started to take on a bohemian feel; then it became popular with the gay and lesbian community. By the time I bought the apartment there, the area had been gentrified and was full of coffee shops, restaurants, bars, bookstores, and upscale boutiques. Beth planned to drive in and stay some weekends, but only did that once while I worked in Washington. She was too busy with her artistic community, and some of her new artist's book creations were selling for thousands of dollars.

Besides, at least in warmer weather, I preferred to be at our riverside home on weekends, relaxing my back, exercising, and boating, to recharge my batteries for the challenges to come in the following week. I had no clue that an even greater challenge was appearing on the horizon.

In the fall of 2010, a disaster descended on AED. The President of the organization had attempted to resolve financial mismanagement problems in two of the many contracts the organization held with USAID, and he did so without first alerting USAID's Inspector General's Office on the issues. After many months of internal action, he sent a check to USAID for a million dollars, outlining the problems he discovered, and how he had fixed them. He thought his actions would solve the situation, but after months of negotiations, he had to resign, and the Vice Presidents, one by one, eventually followed him out the door. In December, AED was temporarily suspended from receiving payments from USAID and all other federal government departments for "evidence of corporate misconduct, mismanagement, and lack of internal controls." I knew that was not the case with my project, but it didn't matter. We were stuck in the same boat.

On March 3, 2011, after 50 years of operation, AED announced it would sell its assets and be dissolved. Some outside commentators thought it was an over-reaction by USAID, due to the political climate—the Congressional Republicans criticizing every step the Obama administration was making. Why bring down a whole organization that had a good record, except for one project in Pakistan and another in Afghanistan?[2]

Most AED staff were shocked and demoralized. C-Change had enough money in the bank to operate for a few months. On the plus side, I stopped getting all those early morning calls from USAID. But about six months went by before Family Health International (FHI), another NGO registered in Durham, North Carolina, took over the assets of AED. They named the new organization FHI 360 because, in addition to international health, FHI was now taking on all of AED's international work in improving democratic governance, building civil society, and relief in emergencies, as well as many of its domestic contracts in education and health.

AED's main assets were its contracts with the USAID and other federal government agencies, and, of course, its staff, equipment, and furniture. Although FHI and AED were both non-profits, for the next few months I witnessed what I thought of as a corporate takeover in the private sector. There were periodic general meetings with staff, trying to assure us all would be okay—our work would carry on. But rumors floated and people clustered in hallways, talking in hushed tones, or behind closed doors. Some former AED executives had their pass keys confiscated and, with little notice, were marched out the door by security staff, just like you see in the movies and television dramas.

I continued to try to boost the morale of my staff and fight for them, as the two organizational cultures came together, trying to merge job descriptions and salary levels. We lost a few months of progress, but the funds finally started to flow from USAID again, and I resolved to achieve our goals, somehow.

At the same time, like most USAID projects, C-Change was designed to include a wide range of other organizations as operational partners in the U.S. and overseas—the "more the merrier" it seemed to me, for that's what won contracts. But the reality of trying to satisfy those partners with adequate activities and funds to meet expectations, was problematic. A good deal of my time was spent in listening to their complaints and explaining our constraints. It seemed to me once a contract was signed, USAID didn't really care about partners. They just wanted results.

And results we gave them. We implemented programs in about 25 countries in Social and Behavior Change Communication (SBCC) for HIV/AIDS, malaria, and other health issues. By the end of the project, we managed to program U.S. $67 million and were also given associate awards worth U.S. $125 million from USAID to continue work in particular countries. Our final report details many achievements.[3]

C-Change developed a range of evidence-based learning tools to help organizations in mastering the process of implementing SBCC programs. The C-Modules were at the core, while the SBCC Capacity Assessment Tool helped measure participants' SBCC knowledge. Taking training to a higher level, C-Change also partnered with academic institutions to develop the first graduate-level SBCC program in Africa at the University of Witwatersrand, South Africa, and worked with universities in Albania, Guatemala, and Nigeria to improve SBCC education. Other communication tools were also created and widely disseminated.

LAST POST IN WASHINGTON, D.C.

Antje Becker-Benton took the lead in shaping the SBCC framework and key tools, while I steered the whole ship through rough waters. But the C-Change legacy contained much of my own thinking and writing, as articulated in the three communication books and the many articles I had authored and co-authored over the years. I never considered myself to be an academic, but figure I didn't do too badly for a guy without a Ph.D.

By mid-2012, our son, Derek, had completed a doctorate in law at the University of Toronto, and had begun teaching law at the University of Sherbrooke, in Quebec. He never lost his ability in French. In fact, for a year he was the clerk from Quebec for the Chief Justice of the Supreme Court of Canada. When we reflect on his chosen career, we laugh at the way, as a child, he used to set the rules and regulations for all the kids playing with him in our backyard in Ottawa.

Our daughter, Ruth, always preferred to facilitate her childhood friends to play more creatively. By 2012, Ruth had completed an M.F.A. and was making progress with a playwriting career in Los Angeles. In 2004, just after Beth had followed me to Russia, we briefly returned to New York for her marriage to Brian—a gathering of the clan from both families. Brian K. Vaughan became a well-known graphic novelist, movie script writer, and executive producer. Ruth and Brian had also produced two beautiful grandchildren—a boy and a girl. We had begun to take breaks to see them, whenever possible, and Beth would go to Los Angeles to babysit when Ruth and Brian wanted a longer break from parenting.

Also, by 2012, C-Change's term was coming to an end and USAID issued a call for proposals for a new five-year global health and development communication project. Mark Rasmuson took the lead in putting together FHI 360's bid, and he and our new director of global health, asked me if they could include my name as project director. I told them I would think about it over the weekend, and let them know.

It was on a sunny Sunday afternoon when I made my decision. Our house was situated in shallow water near the source of the Magothy River, so I could only have a low-draft pontoon boat. It was great for parties and for going out on Chesapeake Bay to fish or just explore—a refreshing mental break from Washington. That day, the wind and waves were just right, giving my vessel and me some extra thrust, skipping over the waves. I liked to do this with *Santana Abraxas* playing in my earphones, just like I did while rolling across the plains of India on a train in December 1970, as described on the first page of this book.

It was then I decided 45 years in my line of work was enough.

Epilogue

We stayed in our Magothy River home in Maryland for a couple more years. I set up my own consulting company, working on a few projects in the U.S. and Canada with Don Simpson and his colleagues. But my heart wasn't it. I began to dabble in creative writing, taking an evening course at St. John's College in nearby Annapolis. I made frequent trips to my hometown in Canada to visit my aging mother, siblings, relatives, old friends, and also our son in Quebec. It was then I began to formulate stories for my memoirs. My father had passed away in 2007, just after we returned from Russia; and after my mother died in early 2015, Beth and I decided to move to New Mexico, "the land of enchantment" with its multi-ethnic population, and plenty of sun, mountains, deserts, forests, river valleys, and milder temperatures with little snow, except on ski slopes in winter. We also found calligraphic and artist's book societies for Beth to join, organizations interested in international affairs, and a flourishing community of writers.

In August 2015, soon after we arrived in Albuquerque, I joined a writers' group and registered in a master's-level, semester-long workshop in creative writing at the University of New Mexico. That's when my creative writing juices really started to flow. I exchanged critiques with other students and writers I met, and spent many hours drafting and revising the stories I had in my head for so long, but never had time to write. First I completed *Finding Myself in Borneo* and then carried out more travel and research for, *Guns and Gods in My Genes: A 15,000-mile North American Search Through Four Centuries of History, to the Mayflower* (2020).[1] I published the latter book just as the Covid-19 Pandemic struck. Grounded at home and having nothing better to do, I turned my attention to book promotion and writing *Kid on the Go!: Memoir of My Childhood and Youth* (2021),[2] and then continued with this present memoir on my career.

As I was writing, I wanted to determine if my efforts in international communication had made any difference in people's lives. I knew, overall, during the past 70 years there had been much progress. Despite all the problems that remained, global international development efforts had contributed to a vast decrease in extreme poverty, the doubling of world literacy, an almost doubling of life expectancy, access to improved health care, clean water and sanitation, and, if climate change doesn't overtake us, sustainable forestry and agriculture. I guess I played a small part in that success.

I decided to incorporate my conclusions on the initiatives I worked on in the chapters themselves, rather than write a huge summary at the end, which might put readers to sleep. My CUSO films, discussed in Part One, were used across Canada in the 1970s and 1980s to recruit volunteers—either through CUSO-Ottawa's efforts or by CUSO committees on university campuses and learning centers—and helped with overall fundraising and development education efforts. Researching and writing about this part of my career brought me in touch with so many former volunteers—teachers, medical doctors and nurses, engineers, technicians, agriculturalists, foresters, etc. I found many who had committed themselves to fruitful careers in international development or in their own communities and fields of endeavor in Canada.

In Part Two, on my years as a filmmaker with IDRC, I included the results of research projects that paid off—many more than I expected. Others had less success, but that's the nature of research—sometimes it provides a way forward, sometimes it doesn't, but even negative results are positive in a way. They provide direction for future investigations. My job expanded my own knowledge in many fields—health, education, forestry, agriculture, aquaculture and fisheries, water and sanitation, and rural development. I still think of those years with IDRC as my "dream job." I had to digest a good deal of knowledge to produce these films, guided by first-rate colleagues from around the world, some who mentored me. Probably the most salient thing I learned in all this work was the importance of communication and community participation in achieving positive and lasting results.

Part Three, on my years as a multimedia producer and manager with UNICEF in Bangladesh, Eastern and Southern Africa, and with Johns Hopkins University, based in the U.S. and Russia, and finally AED cum FHI 360 in Washington, are more complicated to evaluate. In this work, the interventions were communication strategies in social and behavior change. We carried out formative research, mid-term, and final evaluations, showing positive results. But many factors have to be taken into account, such as the length of time donors commit funds, and whether people who take over after you are willing to put energy into initiatives started by the previous person in charge. Often, they want to leave their own mark—that's human nature.

Most of my films, videos, and multimedia materials were used in developing countries through TV networks, video sales, lending libraries, educational institutions, project meetings and trainings, and outreach efforts such as rural cinema and video shows, or through the educational activities of schools, other government departments, and NGOs. Some of my IDRC films were distributed through Canada's National Film Board and Canadian embassy libraries around the world, and in the 1990s and early 2000s, they were sold in video format by a Canadian distribution company. Some were shown on educational television channels. I decided to set up a website on all the films and media projects I could locate—a digital library: www.neill-mckeevideos.com.[3] In that way, readers could go to that source to learn more, if they so desire.

On the personal side, during my career, I learned a good deal about management and leadership. A good leader needs to inspire but not dictate, listen more than talk, assemble a like-minded team and facilitate that team to achieve agreed-upon objectives, rather than taking the lead in everything. In that regard, my experience in co-creating and using the VIPP methodology in so many countries was paramount in understanding this.

When people ask me, "Which film or media project you created made the most difference in people's lives?" I don't have to think too hard to come up with the answer. Today, I get plenty of feedback on the Sara Communication Initiative, which I started in Africa (see Chapter 23), and the Meena Communication Initiative (see Chapter 21), which I started in South Asia. These come in emails and through comments placed on YouTube from young women and men who were influenced by these stories during their childhood and adolescence in the 1990s and early 2000s. Some are just brief and nostalgic reflections about how they missed their childhood or how these were their favorite TV programs, but many mention the important themes covered, and how the cartoon stories helped shape their lives.

In November 2021, while writing this book, I was surprised when a young Afghani woman from a minority community, who calls herself "Darya" online, reached out to tell me how she saw the Meena films and read Meena comic books as a refugee in Pakistan during her childhood. Meena helped to teach her that she should have all the rights boys have and she had to fight to attain them. She migrated to Afghanistan with her family in 2010, after the Taliban were pushed out by the U.S. and NATO allies. In Kabul, she received a good education up to the secondary level, but her university attendance was interrupted when the Taliban took over again in August 2021, and the family fled to Pakistan once more. Today, I am helping her with her education and am encouraging her budding artistic talents, while she seeks a new home country. Meanwhile, she continues to help needy children in Afghanistan through an online art therapy program she has designed herself.

I am also heartened by the young men who write to me to say these entertaining cartoons and comic books taught them to appreciate girls' rights. As I was finishing the last chapter, one young man from Uganda, Derick, wrote to me to say, "The Sara materials created a huge positive impact in my general view of female children in society. This also affected the way I started to treat them. I learned to appreciate their roles and also protect their rights and recognize their achievements. I have also grown to fully comprehend the struggles of girls and the need to work hand-in-hand to assist in accomplishment of our dreams, regardless of gender differences."

So, in my golden years, I am in touch with some of the people influenced by my creations, and the efforts of the teams I set up. I also remain connected with many of the people who influenced me, and networks of former colleagues I worked with around the globe. I have reinvented myself as a creative nonfiction writer, thankfully still with a clear memory of what I experienced and learned in "My University of the World." What more could a person ask for in one lifetime?

Chapter Notes

Chapter 1
1. Photo from Lilibaba, accessed on December 14, 2022 at: lilibaba.tumblr.com/post/45756224215
2. Photo from *The Wire*, Independent Newspaper, India. Accessed on December 14, 2022 at: thewire.in/culture/mumbai-taxi-fiat-padmini-bombay-kaali-peeli-taxi

Chapter 2
1. Photo from Alamy Stock Images, accessed and purchased at: www.alamy.com
2. North Borneo Frodo Society (NBFS), www.northborneofrodotolkien.org/
3. Tolkien, J. R. R. (1971), *The Lord of the Rings: Part One: The Fellowship of the Rings; Part Two: The Two Towers; Part Three: The Return of the King*, Allen & Unwin, London.
4. McKee, Neill. (2019), *Finding Myself in Borneo: Sojourns in Sabah*, NBFS Creations, LLC, Albuquerque, New Mexico, USA. www.neillmckeeauthor.com/finding-myself-in-borneo
5. *Four Times CUSO* (1971), a film by Neill McKee for CUSO, Ottawa, Canada. (Original film not found.)
6. *Tanga Man* (1971), a film by Neill McKee for CUSO, Ottawa, Canada. Available on YouTube at: www.youtube.com/watch?v=5PW1Z045rX8&t=31s.

Chapter 3
1. Photo from Alamy Stock Images, accessed and purchased at: www.alamy.com

Chapter 4
1. Gibran, Kalil. (1923), *The Prophet*, Alfred A. Knopf, New York.
2. Tillich, Paul. (1963), *The Eternal Now*, Scribners, New York.
3. Bonhoeffer, Dietrich. (1997), *Letters and Papers from Prison*, Touchstone Books, New York.

4. Buber, Martin. (1937), *I and Thou*, Translation by Ronald Gregor Smith, T. & T., Edinburgh.
5. Hesse, Herman. (1971), *Siddhartha*, Bantam Books, New York.
6. *CUSO in Papua New Guinea* (1972), a film by Neill McKee for CUSO, Ottawa, Canada. (Original film not found.)

Chapter 6

1. The World Bank (2020), *Mortality rate, infant (per 1,000 live births), Malawi. Estimates developed by the UN Inter-agency Group for Child Mortality*. Accessed on June 21, 2021 at: data.worldbank.org/indicator/SP.DYN.IMRT.IN?locations=MW
2. United Nations, World Population Prospects (2022), *Malawi Fertility Rate 1950-2022*, Department of Economic and Social Affairs, Population Division. Accessed on December 15, 2022 at: www.macrotrends.net/countries/MWI/malawi/fertility-rate

Chapter 7

1. *CUSO in Ghana* (1972), a film by Neill McKee for CUSO, Ottawa, Canada. Available on YouTube at: www.youtube.com/watch?v=QiMiDdx35KA
2. *CUSO in East and Central Africa* (1972), a film by Neill McKee for CUSO, Ottawa, Canada. Available on YouTube at: www.youtube.com/watch?v=5BYqBBuSVlk&t=83s
3. *CUSO in Forestry...Malaysia* (1971), a film by Neill McKee for CUSO, Ottawa, Canada. Available on YouTube at: www.youtube.com/watch?v=JEPEjF9Z9w4

Chapter 8

1. Dorozynsky, Alexander. (1975), *Doctors and Healers*, International Development Research Centre (IDRC), Ottawa, Canada. Accessed on December 1, 2022 at: idl-bnc-idrc.dspacedirect.org/handle/10625/1745
2. Werner, D., Thuman, C., and Maxwell, J. (1973), *Where There Is No Doctor: A Village Health Care Handbook*, Hesperian Health Guides, , Hesperian Publishing, Berkeley, CA.
3. USAID and Pan American Health Organization (2007), *Health Systems Profile: Panama*, Monitoring and Analyzing Health Systems Change. Accessed on June 20, 2021 at: www.paho.org/hq/dmdocuments/2010/Health_System_Profile-Panama_2008.pdf
4. World Health Organization, *Fact Sheet: Trypanosomiasis, human African (sleeping sickness)*. Accessed on June 20, 2021 at: www.who.int/news-room/fact-sheets/detail/trypanosomiasis-human-african-(sleeping-sickness)

CHAPTER NOTES

5. Gro Intelligence (2015), *Triticale: A Hardy, Tolerant Alternative to Wheat?* Accessed on June 25, 2021 at: gro-intelligence.com/insights/triticale-a-hardy-tolerant-alternative-to-wheat
6. *Stretching the Earth* (1976), a film by Neill McKee for IDRC, Ottawa, Canada. (Original film not found.)

Chapter 9

1. *Common Task* (1977), a film by Neill McKee for IDRC, Ottawa, Canada. (Original film not found.)
2. *Continent in the Making* (1977), a film by Neill McKee for IDRC, Ottawa, Canada. (Original film not found.)
3. *Asia: The Search for Solutions* (1977), a film by Neill McKee for IDRC, Ottawa, Canada. (Original film not found.)
4. *Rural Health Workers* (1977), a film by Neill McKee for IDRC, Ottawa, Canada. Available on YouTube at: www.youtube.com/watch?v=Xun_JiN9iFU&t=1016s
5. *Pâa-noi, The Village Midwife* (1975), edited and produced by Neill McKee for IDRC, Ottawa, Canada. Available on YouTube at: www.youtube.com/watch?v=yXb1c4jIcBU&t=7s
6. *A Message from African Healers* (1979), edited and produced by Neill McKee for IDRC, Ottawa, Canada. Available on YouTube at: www.youtube.com/watch?v=hZGLuZUK99E&t=24s
7. *Thought For Food* (1977), a film by Neill McKee for IDRC, Ottawa, Canada. Available on YouTube at: www.youtube.com/watch?v=r0A9fuTjFrI&t=41s

Chapter 10

1. Mante, R. F. (1981), *Multiple outcomes and perspectives in the evaluation of Project Impact*, IDRC. Accessed on July 21, 2021 at: idrc.dspacedirect.org/handle/10625/18214
2. *Project Impact: The Overview* (1978), a film by Neill McKee for IDRC, Ottawa, Canada. Available on YouTube at: www.youtube.com/watch?v=Aw6zN4T-2Js
3. *Project Impact: The System* (1978), a film by Neill McKee for IDRC, Ottawa, Canada. Available on www.youtube.com/watch?v=KkF2Z-JvcWE&t=65s
4. Simpson, Donald G. (2005), *Under the North Star: Black Communities in Upper Canada before Confederation*, Africa World Press, Trenton, N.J.

Chapter 11

1. *Pods of Protein: The International Cowpea Improvement Program* (1979), a film by Neill McKee for IDRC, Ottawa, Canada. Available on YouTube at: www.youtube.com/watch?v=stgIhndXNLc
2. *When the Harvest is Over* (1978), a film by Neill McKee for IDRC, Ottawa, Canada Available on YouTube at: www.youtube.com/watch?v=ZXLNU32mKvo
3. Rohrbach, D., Mupanda, K., and Seleka. (2000), *Working Paper Series No.6: Commercialization of Sorghum Milling in Botswana: Trends and Prospects*, International Crops Research Institute for the Semi-Arid Tropics (ICRISAT). Accessed on July 23, 2021 at: http://oar.icrisat.org/1093/1/RA_00363.pdf
4. *An End to Pounding* (1980), a film by Neill McKee for IDRC, Ottawa, Canada. Available on YouTube at: www.youtube.com/watch?v=gqT3ByHFQpQ&t=31s

Chapter 12

1. Brief biography of Daniel Quayle. (1994), Accessed on September 13, 2021 at: shellfish.memberclicks.net/assets/docs/in%20memoriam%20daniel%20branch%20qualy%20131.pdf
2. *Oyster Farming in the Tropics* (1979), a film by Neill McKee for IDRC, Ottawa, Canada. Available on YouTube at: www.youtube.com/watch?v=eIfXyN227Gg.
3. Whitstable Oyster Company in Sierra Leone (2019), including UKAID final report. Accessed on September 20,2021 at: www.whitstable.rocks/sierra-leone/
4. *Oyster Farming in Green Island* (2021), a video by OCM Productions, Executive producer, Indi McLymont-Lafayette. Accessed on September 20, 2021 at: www.youtube.com/watch?v=tqmVIsj5-IA
5. The Gleaner, Kingston, Jamaica (January 27, 2021), *Oyster farm takes aim at cash-rich global aquaculture industry*. Accessed on September 13, 2021 at: jamaica-gleaner.com/article/news/20210127/oyster-farm-takes-aim-cash-rich-global-aquaculture-industry
6. *The Power of the Oyster* (2022), Centre for Blue Economy and Innovation, Caribbean Maritime University, Kingston, Jamaica. Accessed on February 11, 2021 at: cbei.blog/oyster/

CHAPTER NOTES

Chapter 13

1. Durrell, Lawrence. (1962), The Alexandria Quartet, Faber and Faber (UK) & Dutton (US).

2. *Making Ends Meet: An account of the Commonwealth Fund for Technical Co-operation (CFTC)* (1979), a film by Neill McKee for the Commonwealth Secretariat on the Commonwealth Fund for Technical Cooperation. Available on YouTube at: www.youtube.com/watch?v=TsxjdbAOq-U&t=125s.

3. Alverston, D.L., Murawski, S,A, and Pope, J.G. (1994), *A global assessment of fisheries bycatch and discards*, Food and Agriculture Organization of the United Nations, Rome. Accessed on September 15, 2021 at: www.fao.org/3/t4890e/T4890E00.htm#TOC

4. Oceana Canada (September 27, 2017), *We waste almost half of what we catch: 5 reasons that's disastrous for the oceans*. Accessed on February 13, 2021 at oceana.ca/en/blog/we-waste-almost-half-what-we-catch-5-reasons-thats-disastrous-oceans/

5. Trade Sea-food Industry Directory, Guyana. Accessed on January 20, 2021 at: www.trade-seafood.com/directory/seafood/country/guyana.htm

6. Trading Economics (2022), *Report on Guyana seafood exports to the USA*. Accessed on July 21, 2021 at: tradingeconomics.com/guyana/exports/united-states/fish-dried-salted-smoked-ed-fish-meal

7. Kaieteur News, Georgetown, Guyana (July 4, 2011), *Guyana's per capita fish consumption highest in CARICOM Countries*. Accessed on February 21, 2023 at: www.kaieteurnewsonline.com/2011/07/04/guyana%E2%80%99s-per-capita-fish-consumption-highest-in-caricom-countries/#:~:text=Guyana's%20per%20capita%20consumption%20of,Leg

8. *Fish By-Catch: Bonus from the Sea* (1980), a film by Neill McKee for IDRC, Ottawa, Canada. Available on YouTube at: www.youtube.com/watch?v=m4S44wGCQa4.

9. Aquaculture Economics Research in Asia Proceedings of a workshop held in Singapore, (2-5 June 1981), p. 35. Accessed on February 18, 2023 at: *idl-bnc-idrc.dspacedirect.org/bitstream/handle/10625/17878/IDL17878.pdf?sequence=1&isAllowed=y*

10. U.S. Soybean Export Council (USSEC) (May 5, 2020). Accessed on November 13, 2022 at: ussec.org/philippine-milk-fish-farm-takes-part-feed-comparative-feeding-demonstration/

11. De Guzman, Mari-Len. (August 21, 2020), *Philippines beefs up milkfish fry production with new five-year program*, Hatchery International. Accessed on February 12, 2022 at: www.hatcheryinternational.com/philippines-beefs-up-milkfish-fry-production-with-new-five-year-program/

12. Yap, Wilfredo G.; Antonio C. Villaluz; Ma. Gracia G. Soriano; and Mary Nia Santos. (2007), *Milkfish Production and Processing Technologies in the Philippines,* World Fish Center, Penang, Malaysia and SEAFDEC, Philippines. Accessed on October 23, 2022 at: pubs.iclarm.net/resource_centre/WF_783.pdf.

13. The Fish Site (June 12, 2021), *Ensuring Year-Round Production of Milkfish in the Philippines*. Accessed on June 22, 2022 at: thefishsite.com/articles/ensuring-year-round-milkfish-production-in-the-philippines-bangus

14. *The Mysterious Milkfish* (1982), a film by Neill McKee for IDRC, Ottawa, Canada. Available on YouTube at: www.youtube.com/watch?v=6TGXiR-o2jk&t=13s.

15. *Choices: The Role of Science and Technology for Development* (1980), a film by Neill McKee for IDRC, Ottawa, Canada. Available on YouTube at: www.youtube.com/watch?v=AYr19PAZjRc&t=130s

Chapter 15

1. *Ancient Irrigation in Sri Lanka: The History* (undated), Accessed on June 21, 2001 at: lakpura.com/pages/ancient-irrigation

2. *Harnessing the Monsoons: Improved Cropping Systems in Asia* (1982), a film by Neill McKee for IDRC, Ottawa, Canada. Available on YouTube at: www.youtube.com/watch?v=SUwaQPZj_A8&t=175s.

3. Satoyama Initiative, Japan (2012), *Sri Lanka: Tank Irrigation Farming in Dry Zones*. Accessed on January 23, 2022 at: satoyama-initiative.org/case_studies/sri-lanka-tank-irrigation-farming-in-dry-zones/

4. United Nations Development Programme (UNDP) (2016), *Ancient water tanks of Sri Lanka to adapt to a changing climate*. Available on YouTube at: www.youtube.com/watch?v=bmfBAvSKB_8.

Chapter 16

1. History of Water Supply and Sanitation. Accessed on December 12, 2021 at: en.wikipedia.org/wiki/History_of_water_supply_and_sanitation

2. *John Snow – The Father of Epidemiology* (2015), A Brief History of Public Health, MPH Modules, Boston University School of Public Health. Accessed on January 23, 2021 at: sphweb.bumc.bu.edu/otlt/mph-modules/ph/publichealthhistory/publichealthhistory6.html

CHAPTER NOTES

3. *Cholera* (undated) National Institutes of Health, Office of NIH History and Stetten Museum. Accessed on January 31, 2021 at: history.nih.gov/display/history/Cholera

4. *Prescription for Health* (1983), a film by Neill McKee for IDRC, Ottawa, Canada. Available on YouTube at: www.youtube.com/watch?v=-eLYajz-Fa4&t=5s.

5. Dr. A.T. Ariyaratne (2022), A brief bio by Now Partners. Accessed on June 20, 2022 at: now.partners/team-member/dr-a-t-ariyaratne/.

6. *A Handle on health* (1985), a film by Neill McKee for IDRC, Ottawa, Canada. Available on YouTube at: www.youtube.com/watch?v=QgPfmYpKExg&t=6s.

7. Black, R. et al. (2019), *Drivers of the reduction in childhood diarrhea mortality 1980-2015 and interventions to eliminate preventable diarrhea deaths by 2030*, Journal of Global Health, December 1, 2019. Accessed on June 1, 2021 at: europepmc.org/article/MED/31673345

Chapter 17

1. Freire, Paulo. (2000), *Pedagogy of the Oppressed* (30th anniversary ed.), Bloomsbury, New York.

2. La Fundación para la Aplicación y Enseñanza de la Ciencia (FUNDAEC), fundaec.org/

3. Centro Andino do Accion Popular (CAAP) www.caapecuador.org/

4. Proyecto Andino de Tecnologías Campesinas (PRATEC) pratec.org/wpress/

5. CPES, the Centro Paraguayo de Estudios Sociológicos (CPES), policy-commons.net/orgs/centro-paraguayo-de-estudios-sociologicos/

6. Grupo de Investiogaciones Agrarias (GIA) www.gia.cl/

7. Who are the Mapuche? People of the Land (undated), by Mapuche Foundation (Folil). Accessed on July 21, 2021 at: www.mapuche.nl/english/mapuche.html#:~:text=Today%20the%20situation%20of%20the%20Mapuches%20in%20Chile,to%20assimilate%20the%20Mapuches%20into%20the%20Chilean%20society

8. *Footholds* (1984), a film by Neill McKee for IDRC, Ottawa, Canada. Available on YouTube at: www.youtube.com/watch?v=v9A9sBnOAwI&t=118s

Chapter 18

1. *Trees of Hope* (1985), a film by Neill McKee for IDRC, Ottawa, Canada. Available on YouTube at: www.youtube.com/watch?v=i-YdUSfcKiQ&t=27s

2. Maclean, Ruth. (August 16, 2017), *The Great African Regreening: Millions of 'magical' new trees bring renewal*. The Guardian, London, U.K. Accessed on January 21, 2021 at: www.theguardian.com/world/2018/aug/16/regreening-niger-how-magical-gaos-transformed-land

3. Sendzimir, J., Reij, C.P., & Magnuszewski, P. (2011), *Rebuilding resilience in the Sahel: Regreening in the Maradi and Zinder regions of Niger*. Ecology and Society 16 (3). Accessed on January 21, 2021 at: pure.iiasa.ac.at/id/eprint/9499/

4. *Gum arabic tree (Acacia senegal)* (2009), on Feedipedia. Accessed on June 23, 2022 at: www.feedipedia.org/node/342

5. Photo from Alamy Stock Images, accessed and purchased at: www.alamy.com

6. *Trees of Plenty* (1986), a film by Neill McKee for IDRC, Ottawa, Canada. Available on YouTube at: www.youtube.com/watch?v=JG08BJYSs6A&t=33s

Chapter 19

1. *Bamboo: The Miracle Grass* (1987), a film by Neill McKee for IDRC, Ottawa, Canada. Available on YouTube at: www.youtube.com/watch?v=48UttgYWG8g&t=34s

2. Forestry Research Institute Malaysia (2001), *Interplanting Rattans in Tree Plantations, Transfer of Technology Model (TOTEM)*, International Network for Bamboo and Rattan (INBAR). Accessed on June 23, 2021 at: cgspace.cgiar.org/bitstream/handle/10568/64377/InterplantingRattan.pdf?sequence=1

3. *Bamboo and Rattan Update (BRU), Vol. 2, Issue 2* (June 2021), International Bamboo and Rattan Network (INBAR). Accessed on January 15, 2022 at: www.inbar.int/wp-content/uploads/2021/07/BRU-V2-I2-2.pdf

4. *Rattan: The Hidden Resource* (1990), a film by Clayton Bailey and Neill McKee for IDRC, Ottawa, Canada. Available on YouTube at: www.youtube.com/watch?v=seKPQMbEGJg&t=30s.

Chapter 20

1. Rogers, Everett M. (1983), *Diffusion of Innovations (3rd Edition)*, The Free Press, Macmillan Publishing, New York.

Chapter 21

1. McKee, Neill. (1992), *Social Mobilization and Social Marketing in Developing Communities: Lessons for Communicators*, Southbound

CHAPTER NOTES

Publications, Penang, Malaysia. Available at: www.southbound.com.my/behaviour/smsm-cn.htm

2. McKee, N.; Tillmann, H.; Salas, M.A. (1993). *VIPP: Visualisation in Participatory Programmes: A manual for facilitators and trainers involved in participatory group events*, UNICEF, Dhaka, Bangladesh. Available at: www.unil.ch/files/live/sites/euteach/files/Takeuchi/PDF%20documents/VIPP_Unicef.pdf

3. *Count Your Chickens* (1992). Episode 1 of the Meena Communication Initiative, UNICEF, Dhaka, Bangladesh. Available on YouTube at: www.youtube.com/watch?v=63yIni3KQtM

4. Neill McKee's Meena Communication Initiative webpage, available at: www.neillmckeevideos.com/meena

Chapter 23

1. McKee, N.; Tillmann, H.; and Salas, M.A. (1998), *Games and Exercises: A Manual for Facilitators and Trainers Involved in Participatory Group Events*, Communication Section, UNICEF-ESARO, Nairobi, Kenya and Organizational Learning and Development Section, Division of Human Resources, UNICEF House Three United Nations Plaza, New York, New York. See file:///C:/Users/Owner/Documents/unicef_games_and_exercises.pdf

2. *The Special Gift* (1995), Episode 1 of the Sara Communication Initiative, UNICEF-ESARO, Nairobi, Kenya. Available on YouTube at: www.youtube.com/watch?v=IpApx_fR_IM

3. *Sara Saves Her Friend* (1996), Episode 2 of the Sara Communication Initiative, UNICEF-ESARO, Nairobi, Kenya. Available on YouTube at: www.youtube.com/watch?v=FGssXRakOgM&t=10s

4. *Choices* (1999), Episode 3 of the Sara Communication Initiative, UNICEF-ESARO, Nairobi, Kenya. Available on YouTube at: https://www.youtube.com/watch?v=fg-F8bUDKnU&t=45s

5. *The Trap* (1999), Episode 4 of the Sara Communication Initiative, UNICEF-ESARO, Nairobi, Kenya. Available on YouTube at: www.youtube.com/watch?v=bA6_CxxVpak

6. *Daughter of a Lioness* (1999), Episode 5 of the Sara Communication Initiative, UNICEF-ESARO, Nairobi, Kenya. Available on YouTube at: www.youtube.com/watch?v=tCJIUPKLJs8

7. McKee, N.; Manoncourt, E. Chin, S.Y., and Carnegie, R. (eds) (2000), *Involving People, Evolving Behaviour*, UNICEF, New York & Southbound, Malaysia, 2000. Available at: www.southbound.com.my/SB_InvolvingPeopleEvolvingBehaviour.htm

8. Neill McKee's Sara Communication Initiative webpage. Available at: www.neillmckeevideos.com/sara

Chapter 24

1. Senge, Peter M. (1990), *The Fifth Discipline: The Art & Practice of The Learning Organization*, Doubleday, New York.
2. Goleman, Daniel (1996), *Emotional Intelligence: Why It Can Matter More Than IQ*, Bloomsbury, London.

Chapter 25

1. *Who Was Johns Hopkins?* Marketing & Communications Office Johns Hopkins Medicine. Accessed on November 11, 2022 at: www.hopkinsmedicine.org/about/history/_docs/who-was-johns-hopkins.pdf.
2. *Know Youself: It's My Puberty* (2002), Episode 1 of the Adolescent Health Communication Program, Center for Communication Programs, Johns Hopkins University, with Bangladesh Center for Communication Programs, Dhaka, Bangladesh. Available at: www.youtube.com/watch?v=ux1BgAS6V3k&t=243s
3. *Adolescent Health Communication Toolkit* (2004), Center for Communication Programs, Johns Hopkins University, with Bangladesh Center for Communication Programs, Dhaka, Bangladesh. Available at: https://www.neillmckeevideos.com/arh-bangladesh
4. McKee, N.; Bertrand, J.T.; and Becker-Benton, A. (2004), *Strategic Communication in the HIV/AIDS Epidemic,* Sage Publications, New Delhi, 2004. Available at: www.amazon.com/Strategic-Communication-HIV-AIDS-Epidemic-dp-0761932089/dp/0761932089/ref=mt_other?_encoding=UTF8&me=&qid=1619730333

Chapter 26

1. Hoffman, David E. (2002), *The Oligarchs: Wealth and Power in the New Russia*, Public Affairs, A Member of Perseus Book Group, New York.
2. Bicom Bioresonance Therapy website, available at: www.regumed.com
3. Development of Bicom Bioresonance Therapy, available at: www.spine-pluschiropractic.com/bioresonance-therapy-history-science-behind-treatment/
4. Hosking, Geoffrey. (2001), *Russia and the Russians: A History,* Belknap Press of Harvard University Press, Cambridge, MA.
5. Plokhy, Serhii. (2015), *The Gates of Europe: A History of Ukraine*, Basic Books, A Member of Perseus Book Group, New York.

CHAPTER NOTES

6. *Nastya's Diary* (2006), a video by Healthy Russia 2020, Center for Communication Programs, Johns Hopkins University. Available on YouTube at: www.youtube.com/watch?v=rBzuSCcMy3M&t=1552s

Chapter 27

1. Statista website (2020), *Life expectancy (from birth) in Russia, from 1845 to 2020.* Accessed on June 21, 2022 at: www.statista.com/statistics/1041395/life-expectancy-russia-al:~l-time/#time/#:~:text=Life%20expectancy%20in%20Russia%20was,to%2072.3%20years%20by%202020.

2. Springer Link website (2021), *Mortality in Russia Since the Fall of the Soviet Union.* Accessed on June 21, 2022 at: link.springer.com/article/10.1057/s41294-021-00169-w

3. *Life Themes* (2007), a video by Healthy Russia 2020, Center for Communication Programs, Johns Hopkins University. Available on YouTube at: www.youtube.com/watch?v=N8p8XBLBlNM&t=815s

4. McKee, N.; Salas, M.A.; Tillmann, H. J.; Shahzadi, N. (2007), *VIPP: Visualisation in Participatory Programmes – How to facilitate and visualize participatory group processes,* UNICEF Bangladesh with Southbound, Malaysia, 2007. www.southbound.com.my/Vipp/Vipp_VisualisationParticipatory.htm

5. Lind, Jo Thori; Karl Ove Moene and Fredrik Willumsen. (December 2014), *Opium For the Masses? Conflict-induced narcotics production in Afghanistan*, pp. 949-966, The Review of Economics and Statistics, MIT Press, Cambridge, MA. Accessed on November 11, 2022 at: www.jstor.org/stable/43554969.

6. Sarote, M.E. (2022), *Not One Inch: America, Russia, and the Making of Post-Cold War Stalemate*, Yale University Press, New Haven, CT.

7. Gessen, Masha. (2012), *The Man Without a Face: The Unlikely Rise of Vladimir Putin*, Riverhead Books, New York.

Chapter 28

1. Dickey, J.D. (2014), *Empire of Mud: The Secret History of Washington, D.C.*, Lyons Press, Essex, CT.

2. Beam, Christopher. (March 31, 2011), *Contract Killer? Why did USAID suspend one of its biggest contractors without any explanation?* Slate: Jolly Digital Infrastructure. Accessed on February 20, 2022 at: slate.com/news-and-politics/2011/03/usaid-aed-suspension-why-did-usaid-suspend-one-of-its-biggest-contractors-without-any-explanation.html

3. *C-Change Final Report* (March 2013), Communication for Change, FHI360, Washington, D.C. and USAID, Washington D.C. Accessed on September 21, 2022 at: pdf.usaid.gov/pdf_docs/pdacx163.pdf

Epilogue

1. McKee, Neill. (2020), *Guns and Gods in My Genes: A 15,000-mile North American Search Through Four Centuries of History, to the Mayflower*, NBFS Creations, LLC, Albuquerque, New Mexico, USA. See at: www.neillmckeeauthor.com/guns-and-gods-in-my-genes
2. McKee, Neill. (2021), *Kid on the Go! Memoir of My Childhood and Youth*, NBFS Creations, LLC, Albuquerque, New Mexico, USA. See at: www.neillmckeeauthor.com/kid-on-the-go
3. Neill McKee's digital media library, available at: www.neillmckeevideos.com

Repeated Acronyms

AED—Academy for Educational Development
AFNS—Agriculture, Food, and Nutrition Sciences
BCCP—Bangladesh Center for Communication Programs
CAAP—Centro Andino do Accíon Popular (Andean Center for Popular Action)
CATIE—Centro Agronómico Tropical de Investigación y Enseñanza (Tropical Agriculture Research and Training Center)
CCP—Center for Communication Programs
C-Change—Communication for Change
CIDA—Canadian International Development Agency
COP—Chief of Party
CPES—Centro Paraguayo de Estudios Sociológicos (Center for Sociological Studies of Paraguay)
CTO—Cognizant Technical Office
CUSO—Canadian University Services Overseas
DHD—District Health Department
EPI—Expanded Program on Immunization
ESARO— Eastern and Southern Africa Regional Office
FHI—Family Health International
FSB—Federal Security Bureau
FSO—Field Staff Officer
FSU—Florida State University
FUNDAEC—La Fundación para la Aplicación y Enseñanza de la Ciencia (Foundation for the Application and Teaching of Science)

GIA—Grupo de Investiogaciones Agrarias (Agriculture Research Group)
HRF—Healthy Russia Foundation
ICDDR,B—International Centre for Research in Diarrheal Diseases, Bangladesh
IDRC—International Development Research Centre
IITA—Institute of Tropical Agriculture
IMPACT—Instructional Management by Parents, Community, and Teachers
INBAR—International Network for Bamboo and Rattan
IRRI—International Rice Research Institute
JHU—Johns Hopkins University
J&J— Johnson & Johnson
MSM—Men who have sex with men
NGO—Non-Governmental Organization
ORS—Oral Rehydration Salts
PDA—Population and Community Development Association
PNG—Papua New Guinea
PVC— Polyvinyl Chloride
RIIC—Rural Industries Innovation Centre
SAARC—South Asian Association for Regional Cooperation
SBBC—Social and Behavior Change Communication
SEAFDEC—Southeast Asian Fisheries Development Center
TM—Transcendental Meditation
UNEP—United Nations Environmental Programme
UNICEF—United Nations Children's Fund
USAID—United States Agency for International Development
UWO—University of Western Ontario
VIPP—Visualisation in Participatory Programmes

About the Author

Neill McKee is a creative nonfiction writer based in Albuquerque, New Mexico. *My University of the World: Adventures of an International Film & Media Maker* is a stand-alone sequel to his first travel memoir, *Finding Myself in Borneo: Sojourns in Sabah*, which has won three awards. McKee holds a bachelor's degree from the University of Calgary and a Master of Science in Communication from Florida State University. He worked internationally for 45 years, becoming an expert in the field of communication for behavior and social change. He directed and produced a number of award-winning documentary films/videos, popular multimedia initiatives, and has written numerous articles and three books in the field of development communication. During his international career, McKee was employed by Canadian University Service Overseas (now Cuso International); the International Development Research Centre (IDRC), Canada; UNICEF

ABOUT THE AUTHOR

in Asia and Africa; Johns Hopkins University, Baltimore, Maryland; the Academy for Educational Development and FHI 360, Washington, D.C. He worked and lived in Malaysia, Bangladesh, Kenya, Uganda, and Russia for a total of 18 years and traveled to over 80 countries on short-term assignments. In 2015, he settled in New Mexico, where he uses his varied experiences, memories, and imagination in creative writing.

www.NeillMcKeeAuthor.com

NeillMcKeeAuthor@gmail.com

www.ingramcontent.com/pod-product-compliance
Lightning Source LLC
Chambersburg PA
CBHW052129070526
44585CB00017B/1757